The Black Homelands of South Africa

Perspectives on Southern Africa

University of California Press
Berkeley 94720

The Black Homelands of South Africa

The Political and Economic Development of
Bophuthatswana and KwaZulu

by

Jeffrey Butler, Robert I. Rotberg,
and John Adams

UNIVERSITY OF CALIFORNIA PRESS
BERKELEY · LOS ANGELES · LONDON

University of California Press
Berkeley and Los Angeles, California

University of California Press, Ltd.
London, England

ISBN 0-520-03231-4
Library of Congress Catalog Card Number: 76-7755
Printed in the United States of America

Contents

Illustrations

Figures

Maps

Tables

Preface

Since 1948 the government of the Republic of South Africa has focused much of its policy-making upon the political as well as the social segregation of the country's various population groups. However much economic life depends upon intimate cooperation and permanent intermingling, the government has limited modern politics, in the form of participation and representative institutions with real power, to whites. The disenfranchised majority has played no overt and recognized part in political life, particularly as regards policy-making at the national level. Partially as a result, the literature on politics in South Africa is almost exclusively an examination of white institutions and history. Studies of the administrative methods by which Africans have been governed are few. There is a more extensive literature on the merits and demerits of segregation and its economic and social consequences, but much of what has been written is selective or polemical.

South Africa's program of separate development, of which the homelands are the major component, is widely detested inside and outside the Republic. Separate development has, however, brought into existence new political and administrative mechanisms, and provided a number of new roles, which were previously unavailable to Africans. Simultaneously, new organizations have been created to promote economic growth. Hence there is a need for a dispassionate examination of the homeland program as it has evolved to bring at least one political entity, the Transkei, to independence.

Of the ten South African homelands, the three largest are the Transkei, Bophuthatswana, and KwaZulu. They include 70 percent of the entire homeland area; the total *de jure* population of these three areas comprises over 60 percent of the African population of South Africa.[1] Of the three only the Transkei has been studied.[2] Unlike the Transkei, Bophuthatswana and KwaZulu are made up of many separate pieces of land, located in the major growth areas of the South African economy—the Transvaal and Natal,

1. The *de jure* population of a homeland is the population allocated to it by ethnic group, whether resident there or not.
2. Gwendolen Carter, Thomas Karis, and Newell M. Stultz, *South Africa's Transkei: The Politics of Domestic Colonialism* (Evanston, 1967).

respectively. There are, however, significant differences between them in geographical environment, ethnic composition of their resident populations, political traditions, and in the personalities, policies, and styles of their leaders. A study of Bophuthatswana and KwaZulu provides a basis for analyzing the impact upon South Africa of the present trend in the development of homeland policy and of the political and economic potential of that policy for the peoples of both the homelands and the Republic.

This book began as a study commissioned by the Office of External Research of the United States Department of State. Under the direction of Robert I. Rotberg, it was completed in late 1973 and discussed in a seminar in the Department of State. The present volume, expanded, revised, and updated, was made possible by grants to the authors from the Ford Foundation. Our major debts of gratitude, therefore, are to the Office of External Research of the Department of State and to the Ford Foundation. All views expressed herein are those of the authors and not necessarily those of the Foundation or the Department.

In South Africa politicians and officials in and out of the homelands gave generously of time and information. Chief Lucas Mangope, chief minister of Bophuthatswana, Chief Gatsha Buthelezi, chief executive councillor of KwaZulu, and Professor Hudson Ntsanwisi, chief minister of Gazankulu, granted interviews both there and in the United States. Many officials of the homeland governments, the Bantu Investment Corporation, the Bureau for Economic Research re Bantu Development (BENBO), and the South African Consulate-General in New York willingly responded to our inquiries. Libraries and staff at the Africa Institute in Pretoria and at the South African Institute of Race Relations in Johannesburg made material and other facilities available. We are especially grateful to W. G. Breytenbach, Norman Bromberger, Mary Holmes, Dudley Horner, Jean LeMay, Gavin Maasdorp, Theo Malan, Tim Muil, Benjamin Pogrund, G. J. Richter, Lawrence Schlemmer, P. J. van der Merwe, David Welsh, and Francis Wilson.

In the United States our debts are equally great. Hugh Campbell, Gwendolen Carter, William Foltz, William Herman, Lambert Heyniger, Edward C. Holmes, Thomas Karis, Edwin Munger, Harvey Summ, and C. Thomas Thorne gave us helpful criticism and advice about one or both of the manuscripts. Joëlle Attinger, Margaret Heffernan, and Alma Harrington Young provided valuable research assistance. Dorothy Hay, Edna Haran, Donna Louise Rogers, Evalyn Seidman, and Nancy J. Simkin typed the book in its many stages with skill and patience.

April 1976   J.B., R.I.R., J.A.

1

Introduction

The government of South Africa has decided unilaterally that its black population consists of a group of "nations," each of which is entitled to a homeland. As a result, the government has designated ten preponderantly rural areas as homelands. Together they constitute less than 13 percent of the total area of the Republic. In them Africans have been accorded some of the rights of citizenship whether or not they were born there or are regularly resident there. Each homeland has been granted a measure of self-government, and further advances — including independence — are promised. Some areas, like the Transkei, have exercised limited autonomy for some years. The newer homelands, like Bophuthatswana and KwaZulu, have been given legislative assemblies and some local power only recently.

Homeland leaders are currently engaged in a complicated dialogue with the South African government over the structure and exercise of power — over defined responsibilities, the expansion of budgets, the acquisition of more arable land, and the consolidation of disparate fragments of territory into contiguous holdings. Still unwilling to despair of peaceful change, they are involved in exploiting the flexibilities that have been introduced into South African politics by recent commitments to internal accelerated political and economic development and to external détente. The existence of the homelands and the recent elaboration of their institutions provide for Africans new and potentially beneficial leverage on the otherwise rigid politics of South Africa.

Apartheid, which entered the lexicon of South African politics with the victory of the National Party in 1948, differs from separate development, its successor in the early 1960s, in its approach to the autonomy of the homelands. At first the change was merely euphemistic, but with time it has been given limited content. Unthinkable in the 1950s, the issue of self-government is now taken seriously by policy makers who acknowledge an obligation to prepare the homelands for independence in a foreseeable future. As recently as 1968 the minister of Bantu administration laid down prerequisites for independence so stringent that they would have required at least a generation to be achieved.[1] Yet, the Transkei, which in 1963

---

1. M. C. Botha in the House of Assembly, 6 April 1968, quoted in Muriel Horrell, *A Survey of Race Relations in South Africa, 1968* (Johannesburg, 1969), 141 (hereafter cited as *Survey of Race Relations*).

became the first homeland, is rapidly marching toward independence in 1976. Bophuthatswana has also asked for independence. If the South African government has *its* way other homelands will follow suit in the near future. (See map 1.1 for the location and sizes of the homelands and table 1.1 for their ethnic composition and stages of self-government.)

Despite the fact that 70 percent of the people of South Africa are blacks representing considerable ethnic diversity (see table 1.2), neither size of population nor cultural identity has been considered a criterion in locating homelands. Most of the homeland territories are direct legacies of the haphazard system of reserving certain lands for African use during the final stages of white settlement in the late nineteenth and early twentieth centuries. In designating these territories as homelands, homogeneous societies have not been consistently sought. Rather, the Republic has relied on tradition, propinquity, practicality, and political expediency. The Pedi and North Ndebele are combined in Lebowa, as are the Tsonga and Shangaan in Gazankulu; the South Ndebele, who are widely dispersed in Bophuthatswana, Lebowa, and elsewhere, have been given a homeland of their own. The

Table 1.1 Ethnic Composition,[a] Size, and Stages of Self-Government of the Homelands

Homeland	People	Land Area (sq. miles)	Date of Establishment of Legislative Assembly	Date of Self-Government
Transkei	Xhosa	14,178	1963	1963
Ciskei	Xhosa	3,547	1971	1972
KwaZulu	Zulu	12,141	1972	1976 (?)[b]
Lebowa	Pedi/N. Ndebele	8,549	1971	1972
Venda	Venda	2,333	1971	1973
Gazankulu	Shangaan/Tsonga	2,576	1971	1973
Bophuthatswana	Tswana	14,494	1971	1972
Basotho Qwa Qwa	S. Sotho	144	1971	1975
Swazi	Swazi	818	— —[c]	— —[c]
S. Ndebele	S. Ndebele	?	— —[d]	— —[d]
		58,813		

SOURCE: Muriel Horrell, *The African Homelands of South Africa* (Johannesburg, 1973) and the annual reports *A Survey of Race Relations in South Africa* (Johannesburg, 1969–1975).

[a]Ethnic composition refers to the ethnic group allocated to the homeland, the *de jure* group, not to the actual composition of the population.

[b]KwaZulu is to hold elections in late 1976 that may be preliminary to a grant of self-government.

[c]Swazi received its territorial authority, the stage before the granting of a legislative assembly, only in December 1975.

[d]A homeland is to be established near Groblersdal in the eastern Transvaal. No territorial authority has been set up.

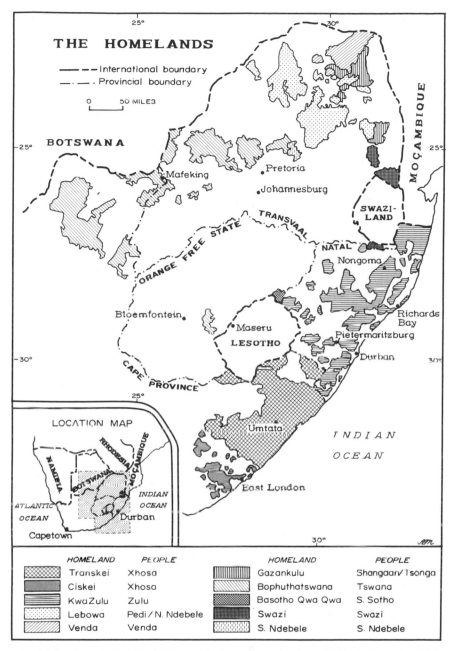

THE HOMELANDS

- — - — International boundary
- — . — . Provincial boundary

0   50 MILES

BOTSWANA

Mafeking

Pretoria

Johannesburg

TRANSVAAL

ORANGE FREE STATE

SWAZI-LAND

NATAL

Nongoma

Richards Bay

Pietermaritzburg

Bloemfontein

Maseru

LESOTHO

Durban

CAPE PROVINCE

MOÇAMBIQUE

LOCATION MAP

NAMIBIA

RHODESIA

MOÇAMBIQUE

BOTSWANA

INDIAN OCEAN

ATLANTIC OCEAN

Durban

Capetown

Umtata

INDIAN OCEAN

East London

HOMELAND	PEOPLE		HOMELAND	PEOPLE
Transkei	Xhosa		Gazankulu	Shangaan/Tsonga
Ciskei	Xhosa		Bophuthatswana	Tswana
KwaZulu	Zulu		Basotho Qwa Qwa	S. Sotho
Lebowa	Pedi/N. Ndebele		Swazi	Swazi
Venda	Venda		S. Ndebele	S. Ndebele

MAP 1.1 THE HOMELANDS. Sources: U.S. Department of State, *South Africa: Homelands* (Washington, 1973), a map simplified from data available 1970-72; Muriel Horrell, *The African Homelands of South Africa* (Johannesburg, 1973), frontispiece "African Reserves in South Africa, September, 1969"; Republic of South Africa, Department of Statistics, *Map 1: Bantu Homelands, 1970*, "White Areas, Bantu Homelands and Districts, 6 May, 1970."

It is difficult to separate the actual state of affairs from proposed consolidations. This map shows the new S. Ndebele homeland, still in process of creation, and the transfer of the Glen Grey and Herschell districts from the Ciskei to the Transkei. It does not show the recent consolidation proposals, especially the proposed reduction of Bophuthatswana and KwaZulu to six and ten blocks of territory respectively. This is, therefore, only an approximation of the present state of affairs.

Table 1.2 South Africa: Population

People	Homeland	Total Population	% of Total Population of Republic	Population in Homeland of Own Ethnic Group	Population in Other Homelands	Population in White Area
Africans						
Xhosa	Transkei	3,930,087	18.32	1,650,825[a]	45,750	1,723,905
	Ciskei			509,607		
Zulu	KwaZulu	4,026,058	18.77	2,057,471	77,480	1,891,107
Pedi	Lebowa	1,603,854	7.47	899,301	101,887	602,666
N. Ndebele	Lebowa	181,748	.84	46,836	23,172	111,740
Subtotal Pedi/N. Ndebele		[1,785,602]	[8.32]	[946,137]	[125,089]	[714,406]
Venda	Venda	357,919	1.66	239,331	11,901	106,684
Shangaan	Gazankulu	737,169	3.43	234,244	158,666	344,259
Tswana	Bophuthatswana	1,719,367	8.01	600,241	10,288	1,108,838
S. Sotho	Basotho Qwa Qwa	1,451,790	6.76	24,189	119,816	1,307,785
Swazi	—[b]	498,716	2.32	81,890	30,130	386,696
S. Ndebele	—[b]	233,021[c]	1.08	—[d]	55,249	177,772
Other	—[e]	318,223	1.48	—[e]	18,902	299,321
Total African		15,057,952	70.20	6,343,938	653,241	8,060,773
Whites		3,451,328	17.48	3,730,951	20,377	
Coloureds		2,018,453	9.4	2,005,325	13,128	
Asians		620,436	2.89	616,995	3,441	
Total		21,448,169	98.0	12,697,209	690,187	8,060,773

SOURCE: Muriel Horrell, *The African Homelands of South Africa* (Johannesburg, 1973), 37–39.

[a] These figures on Xhosa population will be affected by transfers of territory from the Ciskei to the Transkei in 1975.
[b] Homelands have not yet been designated for these peoples.
[c] This figure was stated by a minister on 4 March 1975 to be 283,021.
[d] A figure for the population of the future South Ndebele homeland is not available.
[e] No homeland is planned.

Xhosa are located in two homelands, the Transkei and the Ciskei, separated by a corridor of white settlement. Self-government has been extended to both although the Republic has expressed no objection to the creation of a single Xhosa homeland.

Separate development is based at least in part on a denial of any positive connection between prolonged residence and the acquisition of rights. Architects of the policy are not convinced that the permanent dispersion of Africans throughout South Africa makes it difficult to base rights on polities that the citizen may never have visited. Consequently, in most of the homelands, only a part of the *de jure* population, i.e., the population allocated to a homeland, actually lives there or derives its income from activities in a homeland. (Table 1.3 indicates the dispersion of homeland populations and their relative sizes.) Assuming that coloureds, whites and Asians are residing almost wholly in their own homelands, we find that, among Africans, only the Venda, 1.6 percent of the total population of South Africa, have over

Table 1.3

Percentage Distributions of Ethnic Groups in the Homelands

People	Homeland	% of Each Group in Homeland of Own Ethnic Group	% of Each Group Outside Homeland of Own Ethnic Group	
			Other African Homeland	White Areas
Xhosa	Transkei	54.97	1.16	43.86
	Ciskei			
Zulu	KwaZulu	51.10	1.92	46.97
Pedi	Lebowa	56.07 } 53.00	6.35 } 7.01	37.58 } 40.01
N. Ndebele	Lebowa	25.77 }	12.75 }	61.48 }
Venda	Venda	66.87	3.32	29.81
Shangaan	Gazankulu	31.78	21.52	46.70
Tswana	Bophuthatswana	34.91	0.60	64.49
S. Sotho	Basotho Qwa Qwa	1.60	8.25	90.08
Swazi	Swazi	16.42	6.04	77.54
S. Ndebele		— —[a]	23.71	47.29
Other	— —	— —	5.94	94.06
Total African		42.13	4.34	53.53
Whites		99.46	0.54	
Coloureds		99.35	0.65	
Asians		99.45	0.55	
Total		59.20	3.22	37.58

SOURCE: Muriel Horrell, *The African Homelands of South Africa* (Johannesburg, 1973), 37–39.

[a]No figure is available for the population of the future South Ndebele homeland; it will probably be made up of territory from other homelands and from white areas.

60.0 percent of their *de jure* population living in their own homeland. At the other extreme, only 1.6 percent of all the Southern Sotho live in their tiny homeland. Of the Africans generally, only 42.0 percent live in the homelands, and only half of the Xhosa and the Zulu, the two major peoples, reside in their own homelands. A small proportion of all Africans lives in homelands other than their own, the remainder inhabiting the so-called white areas. Looking at this figure from another perspective, only 600,000 people, or 4.0 percent of the entire African population, would have to be moved to make the existing homelands ethnically homogeneous; to accomplish homogeneity in the white and black areas, however, nearly 9 million people, white and black, would have to be moved. (Only 0.6 percent of the total white, coloured, and Asian populations would have to be removed from the homelands to make them completely African.)

The dispersion of the African population, the dependence of the homelands on the white-controlled economy, and the subordination of Africans in South Africa are long standing. Much of the history of the twentieth century in South Africa has been one of the imposition of constraints on Africans rather than the opening up of opportunities for them. South African whites, although still in a position of overwhelming power, are facing an unsympathetic world outside their borders as well as a restive majority within. In an attempt to manipulate forces of change, they are making limited opportunities available to Africans in segregated political institutions. Limited concessions, however, may contain opportunities unintended by the makers of policy, and the search for such opportunities may be the only strategy available, short of a revolutionary one, to the leaders of politically subordinate groups.

Because the formal changes in political relations are limited and precise, and informal changes are difficult to estimate, a major debate continues as to whether any autonomy has been granted or whether "real" independence is intended. Many doubt the legitimacy and validity of limited self-government, and any independence likely to follow from it. A number of questions must, therefore, be answered before the impact of the establishment and prospective evolution of the homeland governments can be assessed for the Africans of South Africa and for the future of the Republic.

In the following pages we examine the meaning of self-government for blacks in the South African context. What will be the relationship of the South African homelands, individually and collectively, to the dominant government of the Republic? For individual Africans, can the concession of freedom in a juridically independent, but economically dependent homeland provide a meaningful alternative to freedom in the larger Republic? What should the priorities be in order to enhance the political and economic development of the homelands? Today such questions are of more than academic interest.

2

The Context of Political and Economic Development

The existence and configuration of the present South African homelands reflect long-standing conflicts between blacks and whites. Building on the "reserves," the government of South Africa has recently elaborated its policy of separate development in the direction of ultimately creating ten independent African states. It was only with that elaboration, however, that the development of these areas became urgent. Poor, overcrowded, generally lacking in resources, they present a serious challenge to black and white policy-makers in South Africa.

The Territorial Legacy

The location, size, and fragmentation of the homelands are products of the processes of the South African frontier during the nineteenth and their legislative confirmation in the twentieth century. As a result of a triangular conflict between settlers, Africans, and the British government, the policy of defining areas for exclusive ownership by Africans developed in various forms, first as a direct result of imperial intervention and later as a policy adopted by settler governments themselves. What had originally been a policy designed to protect militarily weaker groups became one to minimize the costs of government and to provide dormitories for families of migrant laborers. Consequently, settler governments developed an interest in preserving African landholding, and the internal frontiers of South Africa gradually attained some stability.

Although the policy of reservation secured at least some land to Africans, and, in the case of the former High Commission Territories, a territorial base for future states, fundamentally it was evasive and represented a response of expediency. Neither the imperial power, nor the settler governments, were evolving a policy that would give all people equal access to resources and opportunities. Nor were they ensuring through education that the technological gap between whites, on the one hand, and blacks, on the other, would be narrowed. The job market in modern sectors of the economy soon became racially structured, and education for Africans was left to

7

private institutions with limited power and resources. Frequently the declaration of reserves simply recognized the *status quo* or froze, temporarily, a distribution of land. For a period before 1913, some Africans were in a mildly favored position because they had land reserved to them and could also acquire land outside these reserves, especially in the Cape Province and Natal. The proclamation of a reserve, however, was no guarantee that the reserve would remain intact. Land continued to be taken from blacks and given to whites, sometimes as a punishment for rebellion, or as a means of rewarding cooperative whites.

The Tswana and the Zulu, no less than others, contended for land with colonial and republican frontiersmen. Pushed off the sweet grazing lands of the highveld by the Ndebele and other Nguni peoples, and then by the Voortrekkers searching for fresh pastures, the Tswana moved westward toward the edge of the Kalahari Desert. There they successfully regained some coherence. The voracious appetite for land of Afrikaners from the Orange Free State and the Transvaal led to a steady whittling away of the Tswana holdings. Fortunately, however, for the Tswana, there was a limit. In 1885, in order to forestall further expansion on the part of the Transvaal and the threat of the spread of German imperialism from Southwest Africa, Britain "protected" the largest portion of the new Tswana lands. (It thus provided a subsequent territorial base for an independent Botswana.) Other lands in Tswana hands remained outside the Protectorate but, with the grant of self-government to the Cape Colony in 1872 and the recognition of the autonomy of the Transvaal in 1881, much of these lands were lost. In 1897, for example, the Cape Colony opened Tswana lands to white settlement, partly as punishment for the Tswana rebellion of 1896. The Tswana were thus divided in three: those who remained under British imperial rule in the Protectorate were separated from those under the rule of whites in the Cape and the Transvaal. The Union of South Africa in 1910 brought the Tswana of the Cape and the Transvaal together under a single government without adding to their resources or power.

The Zulu resisted the thrust of whites, but encroachment on their territory was continuous. In the war of 1879, after initial success, they were defeated, their king was exiled, and their kingdom was broken up into separate chieftaincies. Encircled by republican and colonial frontiersmen, the Zulu steadily lost land, especially in the coastal areas most suited to the cultivation of cotton and sugar, later Natal's major crop. Even some foothills of the eastern plateaux — Zulu territory from Shaka's day — were alienated by whites. In 1904 extensive areas of Natal were thrown open to white settlement, the Zulu reserves being immediately diminished by 2.6 million acres; only 3.8 million acres remained.[1] As a result the Zulu found themselves steadily pushed back

1. Shula Marks, *Reluctant Rebellion* (Oxford, 1970), 127.

on to less desirable terrain where water was comparatively scarce, grazing poor, and agricultural conditions harsh.

Neither Bophuthatswana nor KwaZulu is a homeland in any meaningful historical sense, although the Tswana and the Zulu have both lived in these respective areas since the nineteenth century. Both territories contain places of traditional significance to their respective peoples, and both are consequently considered a part, if only a small part, of original, more extensive patrimonies. It would be difficult to find an African leader, traditional or modern, who regards the present borders of the homelands as legitimate, the size of the homelands as sufficient, or the fragmented quality of the homelands as satisfactory.

Bophuthatswana and KwaZulu have never been homelands in any demographic sense. If a homeland is supposed to be the Urheimat, the original gathering place of at least a substantial portion of a people, then neither Bophuthatswana nor KwaZulu qualifies or has ever qualified. Ever since they have been secured to black occupancy, the two homelands have encompassed only a proportion of the Tswana and the Zulu. The remainder have resided upon white-controlled land. At the beginning of this century as many Tswana and Zulu lived outside as lived within their homelands. Today 64 percent of the Tswana and 46 percent of the Zulu live outside their homelands.

Until the coming of the union, although there was considerable variation in law and practice regarding land, each of South Africa's component provinces had set aside areas of exclusive African occupation. Small in the Orange Free State, these areas were more extensive and more fragmented in the Transvaal and Natal; and in the Cape Colony there was the large, consolidated bloc of the Transkei. In 1913 the new government of South Africa began the process of reconciling the different land laws of the provinces, a process that was ultimately to eliminate the favored position long held by Africans in the Cape. In dealing with land, the government accepted the proposals of the South African Native Affairs Commission (1903–1905), which had espoused territorial partition as the only basis for the development of South African society and politics. As far as the commission was concerned, the growth of a mixed society was to be avoided.

The passage of the Natives Land Act of 1913 did not emerge out of a desire to produce the territorial basis of a just, if segregated, society. Instead, it constituted a response to the expressed interests of white farmers, then the dominant group in South African politics, for continued access to supplies of low-wage labor. At the same time a class of South Africans then called "poor whites" was being forced off the land. The act was intended to minimize competition by forbidding Africans to purchase land or to offer themselves as sharecroppers on white-owned land. Certainly the evolution of black-run states was never envisaged, although the reserves were regarded as places wherein "the native way of life," including limited application of indigenous law and governance, could be continued. The primary object of the act was to segregate. The secondary object was to limit the number of African families permitted to reside on white-run farms, particularly in the Transvaal.[2]

The act designated 10.7 million morgen (22.5 million acres), or 7.3 percent of the area of South Africa, as reserves to be occupied and used by and for Africans; these 10.7 million morgen were the "scheduled areas." The crucial contribution of the law involved the distribution of land between Africans and whites. No longer to be left to the forces of the market, land distribution was regulated by law: Africans were prohibited from acquiring land outside the reserves. The act also provided for a commission to recommend additions for a final land settlement, but this part of the act was not carried out. The Beaumont Commission of 1913–1916 recommended areas to be "released" which would have given Africans an additional 8 million morgen, but the Native Affairs Bill of 1917, which embodied the Beaumont proposals, never emerged from a parliamentary committee. Thus the Natives Land Act of 1913 did nothing to consolidate the scattered parcels of what have since become — especially in the cases of the Tswana and the Zulu — fragmented and inadequate homelands.

Since Africans were accustomed to using land extensively, the Natives Land Act dramatically curtailed the traditional African reliance upon the availability of exploitable resources of land. By making no provision for the growth of the reserves commensurate with increased population, the act compelled Africans to employ land intensively both for farming and herding. It also encouraged the able-bodied to offer their services as migratory laborers, or to move permanently to the towns. Moreover, much of the land of the reserves was of deficient quality to begin with, or deteriorated quickly under the pressure of overgrazing. "Though there were tribes and portions of tribes that were well off," a social historian wrote, "the majority lived upon too little land to maintain them as in days of old. Even the . . . traditional allies and favourites of the Government choked upon their land. Such a crowding of men and beasts placed a severe strain upon the land that was left. . . . The breakdown of soil into sand, the replacement of nutritious grass by weeds, the disappearance of trees and shrubs, the scarring of the land could not withstand the pressure upon it of too many men and too many beasts."[3]

These inadequacies of size and terrain, and their human consequences, were widely recognized. The density of population was at least four times

2. Colin M. Tatz, *Shadow and Substance in South Africa* (Pietermaritzburg, 1962), 22.
3. C. W. De Kiewiet, *A History of South Africa, Social and Economic* (London, 1941), 80.

greater (87 ?1 persons per square mile) in the reserves than in the white-controlled rural areas of the Union.[4] The Native Economic Commission of 1932, appalled by what it had seen, testified to the already advanced deterioration of the reserves. "A Native area," the Commission reported in words equally appropriate today, "can be distinguished at sight, by its bareness. . . . Two areas with fertile valleys containing great depth of soil . . . show some of the worst donga erosion in the Union. . . . In the rest of the Union the same causes are at work . . . and they will inevitably produce the same effects in the near future—denudation, donga erosion, deleterious plant succession, destruction of woods, drying of springs, robbing the soil of its productive properties, in short the creation of desert conditions."[5] Many Africans accepted the only option open to them: they moved off the land, flocking to the white-owned lands and the white-dominated cities. "One of the outstanding causes of migration from the reserves," wrote an anthropologist, "quite apart from recruiting, is the appalling shortage of land for native occupation. The Native reserves, at their present low state of development, are both over-populated and overstocked; and as a result more and more people are tending to drift away."[6]

In partial recognition of these realities, the Native Trust and Land Act of 1936 envisaged the acquisition of 7.25 million morgen (15.9 million acres) for Africans, the "released areas" originally recommended by the Beaumont Commission, for a total of 17.7 million morgen (37.2 million acres) of the 142.5 million morgen (289.25 million acres) in the Union (excluding South-west Africa). This transfer, had it been effected, would thus have placed only 12.4 percent of the total area of the Republic in the reserves. The act was also expected to eliminate competition between whites and blacks for land, and, in the areas scheduled to be transferred, whites were to be compelled to sell land to the Native Trust for inclusion in the reserves. "Black spots," i.e., areas of African occupation in the defined "white areas," would also have been eliminated. But returning lands from powerful whites to subordinate Africans was controversial, and the process of transfer was consequently delayed. The intervention of World War II further slowed the handover. By 1945 Parliament had appropriated only £6 million of the originally contemplated £10 million for the necessary purchases, and only about 3 million morgen had been added to the reserves. Sixty percent of the money had

4. Edward Roux, "Land and Agriculture in the Native Reserves," in Ellen Hellman (ed.), *Handbook on Race Relations in South Africa* (Cape Town, 1949), 175.

5. Union of South Africa, *Report of the Native Economic Commission* (Pretoria, 1932), paragraphs 71–74, quoted in H. T. Andrews *et al.* (eds.), *South Africa in the Sixties: A Socio-Economic Survey* (Johannesburg, 1965).

6. Isaac Schapera, "Present-day Life in the Native Reserves," in Isaac Schapera (ed.), *Western Civilization and the Natives of South Africca: Studies in Culture Contact* (London, 1934), 45.

acquired only 40 percent of the land. "It appears," said the chairman of the Native Affairs Commission, "that the European community is not prepared to honour its promises."[7] In late 1974, 20 percent of the quota land of 1936 remained to be acquired.[8]

Recently the issue of land consolidation has once more been prominent, with the government announcing in 1975 yet another final land allocation. The government has repeatedly stated that it will not consider increasing the 1936 quotas.[9] It is not intended that the homelands in total can comprise more than 13.7 percent of the area of the Republic, whenever the process of acquisition, swapping, and "black spot" and "white spot" removal has been completed. Homeland leaders have repeatedly said that they would not consider accepting independence without major territorial concessions. Whether the government will eventually be compelled to make concessions on land in the hope of making independence more acceptable is a question for the future.

Meanwhile, African populations have increased through natural causes and the Republic remains determined to restrict their flow to the towns and to "resettle" at least some Africans in the homelands. Consequently, densities have increased and, overall, the agricultural condition of the homelands has deteriorated. The insufficiencies of the original reserves are now even more pronounced than they were in 1936.

The Physical Setting

Leaders of the homelands have recently been informed of the future extent of the land resources of their territories. The latest consolidation proposals neither alter by very much the arable land and other natural resources available to Bophuthatswana and KwaZulu nor affect their limited access to South Africa's roads, railways, power systems, or seacoast. Moreover, the implementation of these plans will take at least ten years.[10] In the interim the governments of Bophuthatswana and KwaZulu will face difficulties in planning, and homeowners, businessmen, and farmers threatened by removal may be reluctant to invest in or even to maintain their properties.

The basic structure of the consolidated homelands is ruled by four principles: adherence to the total area set aside by the land acts of 1913 and 1936 as distributed to each of the homelands; desire to reduce the number

7. Quoted in Roux, "Land and Agriculture," 174.
8. See *Survey of Race Relations, 1974*, 181.
9. See e.g. *ibid.*, 183.
10. For the latest proposals, see Republic of South Africa, *House of Assembly Debates* (14 May 1975), cols. 5926–5937 (hereafter cited as *House of Assembly Debates*).

of parcels to as few as possible; maintenance of corridors for the Republic's rail, road, power, and communication lines; and continuance of control over existing and planned ports. If present policy is sustained Bophuthatswsana and KwaZulu will remain fragmented. They might gain somewhat more farm land, but existing industries and mines in the new areas would remain indefinitely controlled by whites.

The homelands have limited access to the outside world. Bophuthatswana is far from the sea but it is close to large urban areas, with an arm of the territory reaching to within thirteen miles of Pretoria. Some of its sections also share a border with Botswana. Much of KwaZulu lies along the Indian Ocean and the government of that homeland naturally covets good access to the sea. But the Republic currently plans to limit that access and to maintain the more developed and developable stretches of the coastline (and corridors along the main rail lines) in white hands. Accordingly, only near Umkomaas in the south, near Richards Bay in the center, and in the extreme north might the homeland be permitted direct access to the sea. Richards Bay would remain part of the white-controlled section of Zululand despite KwaZulu's insistence that Richards Bay is and should be its natural port. Without it, although KwaZulu shares potentially valuable land frontiers with Swaziland and Moçambique, the homeland's leaders consider their country virtually landlocked.

In addition to limitations of resources and uncertainties having their origin in the policies of the dominant political system, there are other important structural constraints (discussed at greater length in ch. 6). Residents of all the homelands are dependent fiscally and monetarily on the Republic. They import and export through the Republic and derive most of their consumables from the same source. They are employed prominently in the white sector of the Republic, at least 1.25 million Tswana and 2.0 million Zulu residing there. All the homelands depend almost exclusively upon the Republic for capital and technical assistance. Most of all, the homelands exist without many of the policy options open to former colonial territories. Collectively they are an integral part of the Republic's program of separate development. The segregation of the larger economy — with all of its obviously limiting consequences for growth — is theirs too. In addition to their individual deficiencies, whatever the character of independence each homeland will bear the burden of political and social inequalities.

As potential producers of cash and subsistence crops, both Bophuthatswana and KwaZulu are poorly endowed. Spread over three provinces, Bophuthatswana, the largest of the homelands, captures much local variety within its borders. Bophuthatswana nonetheless is for the most part flat, dry, and unsuited for mixed homestead farming. Most of the homeland lies in a zone of deficient soils, low and unreliable rainfall (twelve to twenty inches over five months), and high temperatures. Around Kuruman, in the west, the land is near desert, and, accordingly, sparsely populated. The heart of the region—near Taung, along the border with Botswana, and north of Rustenburg and Pretoria—receives light rainfall adequate for grazing and on-and-off cropping, but insufficient for settled farming. In fact, there is a close and probably not coincidental association between the northern and western edges of the Republic's maize belt and the southern and eastern bounds of Bophuthatswana. (The small Thaba 'Nchu fragment of the homeland, which is surrounded by the Orange Free State, is better suited to agriculture and herding than most of the homeland.) The homeland's territories are crossed by several rivers (the Great Marico, Molopo, Hartz, Kuruman, and Notwani), but their flows are irregular and do not provide much potential for irrigation. There is a small amount of irrigation at Taung, and in the Bafokeng and Odi II districts springs and streams provide some dependable water. Elsewhere the ground water potential is poor. A number of earth dams and some windmill-fed stock tanks provide water for livestock. The major crops are maize, wheat, vegetables, groundnuts, tobacco, and fruit.

There are nineteen tracts of Bophuthatswana. If and when this number is reduced by consolidation, most Tswana will still find themselves without immediate access to road, rail, telephone, and power facilities. In 1974, for example, there were 397 miles of main roads, only a very small part of which were paved, and several thousand miles of minor roads and paths. Railways cross sections of Bophuthatswana but were designed to serve whites in centers of population rather than Africans in the countryside.[11] Those homeland Tswana who reside in the areas of dense habitation near Pretoria, Rustenburg, and minor towns can depend upon limited bus service, but their rural compatriots must do without. Telephones are few and electricity is virtually nonexistent. Although the most well arranged of all the homeland growth centers is located in Bophuthatswana's Babelegi, near the main highway north from Pretoria to Pietersburg, internal industrial development is still in its infancy.

Bophuthatswana straddles the rich mineral-bearing rock formations of the Transvaal. The Impala and Union mines, near Rustenburg, produce large quantities of platinum. Chrome is mined nearby, and elsewhere in the homeland there are smaller worked deposits of vanadium, asbestos, iron ore, limestone, granite, manganese, salt, and calcite. Prospects for the discovery of exploitable gold and diamonds are good, a major gold-bearing reef having been discovered in 1975. For the most part the present and potential mines are all situated on African lands, but the homeland government has received

11. Republic of South Africa, Bureau for Economic Research re Bantu Development (hereafter cited as BENBO), *Bophuthatswana, Economic Revue, 1975* (Pretoria, 1976), 15–17, 64–65.

no direct benefit from them. Mineral rights are vested in the particular local Tswana-speaking groups (like the Fokeng in the case of the mines near Rustenburg) that control the favored area, in white individuals or companies, or in the Bantu Trust, an agency of the Republic. Exploration and development are regulated by the white-directed Bantu Mining Corporation.[12] Thus homeland governments have received none of the revenues from mining and exercise no control over mineral leasing or exploitation. If there were a transfer of mineral rights to the homeland governments, for Bophuthatswana the resulting income could appreciably improve the standard of living of its inhabitants and provide much of the capital needed for development.

KwaZulu's physical profile is virtually the opposite of Bophuthatswana's. KwaZulu is the most fragmented of all of the homelands, being composed of twenty-nine major and another forty-one minor enclaves scattered widely over Natal. It thus reflects the diversity of that geologically and climatically complex region. Much of KwaZulu is hilly or mountainous and best suited for use as pasture or forest.[13] Temperatures are moderate in winter, except at the highest elevations, and warm to hot in summer. Rainfall is dependable, averaging from thirty to forty-five inches in most of the homeland, and is well distributed throughout the year. Yet the combination of steeply sloped terrain and often heavy showers means that much of the land is susceptible to erosion, especially in those areas where overgrazing and overcultivation have been forced upon the population by increasing numbers.[14] However, the Pongola, the Tugela, the Mzimkulu, the Mkomanzi, and a number of minor rivers and streams provide potential for irrigation.[15]

12. But see C. P. Mulder, "The Rationale of Separate Development," in Nic J. Rhoodie (ed.), *South African Dialogue: Contrasts in South African Thinking on Basic Race Issues* (Johannesburg, 1972), 54. "Mineral rights," says Mulder, "belong to the group in whose area the minerals are found. Already gold and platinum have been discovered in Bantu homelands, and belong to the Bantu nation in question, in this case the Tswana, who draw the mining royalties." Mulder's statement is not accurate in relation to current practice; it may be a statement of objective. See also below, 129, 216.

13. Union of South Africa, *Summary of the Report of the Commission for the Socio-Economic Development of the Bantu Areas within the Union of South Africa* (Pretoria, 1955), 50 (hereafter cited as *Summary of the Report*). The commission, usually referred to as the Tomlinson Commission, estimated 58 percent of the African areas of Natal were unsuited to agriculture.

14. "Statement Summarizing Major Points Emerging During the Proceedings of the Conference: Toward Comprehensive Development in Zululand" (1972), Durban, University of Natal, Institute of Social Research, mimeo., 2. See also Gatsha Buthelezi, "Kwa-Zulu Development," in B. S. Biko (ed.), *Black Viewpoint* (Durban, 1972), 50.

15. For an examination of the resources of the Tugela Basin, see E. Thorrington-Smith, *Towards a Plan for the Tugela Basin* (Pietermaritzburg, 1960). For an appraisal of irrigation generally, see L. P. McCrystal and Catherine M. Moore, "An Economic Survey of Zululand" (Durban, 1967), mimeo., 22.

The northern section of the homeland, between the Indian Ocean and Moçambique and Swaziland, consists of very lightly populated, sandy, reputedly unhealthy coastal flats. Smaller segments are located west of Pieter-maritzburg in the foothills of the Drakensberg mountains, where there is some farming and cattle grazing. In the hilly central Tugela River region cattle and light cropping are the mainstays of subsistence. An expansion of irrigation here would permit more intensive farming. The belt of rolling terrain just inland from the coast includes some sugar cane holdings (most of South Africa's sugar estates are owned by whites) and offers conditions of greater agricultural promise. In some places in the lowveld of northern Zulu-land cotton can be grown. In addition parts of KwaZulu are suited for producing vegetables for urban markets. In the coastal strips and the south-eastern region between the coast and the Drakensberg, pineapples, avocados, and bananas are grown. The mistbelt of the area supports plantations of black wattle, from which tan-bark and tanning extract are produced. There are small African pine and bluegum timber plantations, some experimental sisal and phorium tenax (flax, a jute substitute) estates, and limited fish farming. On dry lands the Zulu now grow corn, sorghum, beans, peanuts, white potatoes and sweet potatoes, tobacco, bananas, and pulses.[16]

KwaZulu's mineral wealth has not been fully surveyed, but is probably limited. There are known deposits of coal, gypsum, limestone, and kaolin. A small tourmaline mine is operating. In 1972 leases were granted for the mining of kyanite and magnetite, and the Bantu Mining Corporation has searched for vanadium and assisted a sand-extraction project near Pinetown. A major coal deposit was found near Nongoma in 1975. An industrial park has been established near Isithebe, north of Durban. Several small fabricating firms have located at this growth point, but there is room for many more.

Like all of the homelands and many less developed countries, KwaZulu has a poorly developed infrastructure.[17] This, as much as any single cause, hinders the development of agriculture and industry in the homeland. Major rail and road arteries run along the coast and north from Durban through the white corridors. A new highway and a new railway bisect KwaZulu from Richards Bay to Vryheid, but both were designed to serve the economy of the Republic. There are 958 miles of road in KwaZulu, of which half are main roads with gravel or tar surfaces. In 1966 Natal had 22 road miles per 100 square miles of territory, but Zululand had only 7 road miles per 100 square miles of territory, figures that are unlikely to have been much altered in the last ten years. There are thirty-seven miles of standard gauge rail lines, not

16. For geographical material, see Monica Cole, *South Africa* (London, 1966); *Summary of the Report; BENBO, KwaZulu, Economic Revue, 1975* (Pretoria, 1976), 16-19.
17. D. Hobart Houghton, "Apartheid Idealism versus Economic Reality," in Rhoodie, *South African Dialogue,* 292.

including the new Vryheid-Richards Bay line, which runs for sixty miles through the homeland.[18] Most of KwaZulu is not yet connected to the national power grid. Few of the population centers within the homeland have extensive telephone service.

Population and Manpower

South Africa expects the homelands to provide the ultimate refuge, though not the regular residence, for all those who speak the indigenous languages of earlier, larger, less crowded "authentic homelands." This allocation will apply even to those who may have stemmed from such homelands generations ago. Consequently, despite limited natural endowment, and, thus far, restricted authority over their own development, the homelands are expected to provide for growing populations without enlarged areas. According to the 1970 Census, there were 600,000 Tswana (predominantly Fokeng, Rolong, Hurutshe, Kwene, Tlokwa, Kgatla, and Tlhaping) in Bophuthatswana and 2.1 million Zulu in KwaZulu. Of the 1.1 million Tswana living outside the homelands, 600,000 or 54 percent lived in urban townships, and 500,000 or 46 percent in the Republic's rural areas. One million Zulu, or 53 percent, lived in urban townships, while 900,000 or 47 percent were located in the Republic's rural areas. Roughly 35 percent of all South African Tswana, and 50 percent of all Zulu lived in the homelands in 1970.[19] (The population of Bophuthatswana and KwaZulu combined is equivalent to about 28 percent of the total population of all the homelands, the citizens of Transkei numbering 1.65 million, or another 10 percent). In the 1970s, even if these two home lands were to be isolated from the Republic, their resident populations would still prove too small to provide sufficient markets or manpower bases for autonomous, internally directed development. By the end of the century, however, the Tswana in South Africa will number about 4 million, the Zulu 10 million. At least 2 million people will inhabit Bophuthatswana in the year 2000. Similarly, within KwaZulu there will be 5 million people or, if the borders are redrawn to include the African townships around Durban and other cities, substantially more. At the same time the white population of the Republic will only be about 7 million; the entire African population — all individually then subjects of homelands — will number 37 million.[20]

18. *BENBO, KwaZulu, Economic Revue,* 74-75; McCrystal and Moore, "Economic Survey," 86.

19. C. J. Jooste, "Background Data" in C. W. H. Boshoff (ed.), *Bantu Outside Their Homelands* (Pretoria, 1972), 10. See the recent full summaries in *BENBO, KwaZulu, Economic Revue,* 20; *idem, Bophuthatswana, Economic Revue,* 18.

20. The growth of the white population includes the addition of 30,000 immigrants per year. The natural rate of increase will fall from about 1.5 percent to 1.2 percent by the year 2000. The African population will grow at about 3 percent per year in the same interval. See J. L. Sadie, *Projections of the South African Population* (Johannesburg, 1974), tables 2 and 8.

This rapid expansion of the African population will generate a corresponding growth in the labor force. In the 1970s the African male labor force has been increasing at a rate of over 100,000 a year. If females are included, more than 150,000 new African workers will seek employment each year of the next decade.[21] Thus, because of the numbers of children already born and the difficulty of reversing demographic trends quickly, the economies of the homelands and the Republic must generate employment opportunities at very high rates to the end of the century if widespread unemployment and extreme discontent are to be avoided. Further, if Africans are to improve their standards of living in real terms, these new jobs must be more productive and higher paying than existing ones. Yet already there is considerable unemployment and underemployment among Africans as well as a backlog of mature workers who seek active employment. South Africa's economic plan estimates a national growth rate, in real terms, of nearly 6 percent—sufficient, it says, to absorb new and hitherto unemployed Africans.[22] With continued separate development, a very substantial portion of this new employment must be generated within or adjacent to the homelands. But to do so implies a shift of private and state expenditures in the same direction and the concomitant relative decline of established urban centers like Durban and Johannesburg, with resulting alterations in white patterns of living and working. Support for separate development and industrial decentralization also means that African workers will need to be increasingly better educated and trained than they are at present.

The anticipated growth in the overall African population, and in the numbers expected to live in the homelands, will put additional pressure upon territories already poorly endowed and limited in size. High and rising population densities, although not necessarily deleterious from the economic point of view, do preclude several obvious patterns of development. Dense populations cannot be expected to revert to primarily pastoral or agricultural ways of life. Bophuthatswana has the lowest population density of all the homelands, with only 61 people per square mile. But most of the homeland is arid, being suited only for light grazing and intermittent cultivation. In KwaZulu there are already 173 people per square mile, the highest density of all the

21. J. A. Lombard and P. J. van der Merwe estimate an annual increase of the male African labor force of about 113,000 annually in the mid-1970s. ("Central Problems of the Economic Development of Bantu Homelands," *Finance and Trade Review*, X [1972], 7 and table 5.) If one-third as many women as men want jobs, this would mean there are 150,000 new African job-seekers every year. The plan for 1972 to 1977 estimated that there would be 6,471,000 African workers in 1977 and that the African labor force would be growing at 2.8 percent per year, or by 181,000 workers at that time. Republic of South Africa, Department of Planning, *Economic Development Programme for the Republic of South Africa, 1972–1977* (Pretoria, 1972), 39.

22. *Economic Development Programme, 1972–1977*, 44–45.

homelands. This is a very high figure for rural Africa and KwaZulu's prime arable land, especially along water courses or in the valleys, holds far higher populations. According to calculations based on the 1970 census, three Zulu districts have population densities per square mile of arable land of more than 3,000 people. Four districts have average densities per square mile of over 400 people.[23] In such circumstances, rural densities per square mile approach the crowded levels of Java and Haiti.

The Tswana have lived traditionally in clustered-site dwellings and are now heavily concentrated in official housing and shanty settlements close to Pretoria, Rustenburg, and Mafeking. Only about 25 percent of the populations of Bophuthatswana and about 10 percent of KwaZulu are officially considered urban, but the statistics seem to underestimate the extent of real agglomeration in both homelands. Even in rural areas, such as those around Taung, concentrated villages rather than dispersed settlements are the rule. In 1976 there were fourteen towns in Bophuthatswana, four with populations between 20,000 and 50,000. Mabopane, near Pretoria, probably numbers over 100,000 if the squatters of adjacent Winterveld are included, and GaRankuwa, eighteen miles from Pretoria and six miles from Rosslyn, is probably as large. Tlbabane and Temba each have about 25,000 people. In KwaZulu there are twenty-three towns, with five more under construction. Umlazi near Durban numbers over 150,000, and three more are in the 30,000 to 60,000 range.[24] Many more Tswana and Zulu live and work in white towns and cities than in the homelands and many of the residents of the rural areas of the homelands commute, migrate, or at least visit the urban centers. A majority of the populations of Bophuthatswana and KwaZulu are thus already living in urban areas or are in close contact with urbanized life.

The age and sex structure of the homelands has significant implications for their economic and political future. One of the major reasons why the homelands have such weak, underproductive economies is that able-bodied men are temporarily or permanently absent in the white areas. High proportions of older men, women, and young children remain behind in the rural areas of the homelands, producing little and relying on remittances from family members working in the Republic. The male:female ratio in Bophuthatswana is .88:1 and in KwaZulu it is .75:1, ratios that underline KwaZulu's greater dependence on migrant labor.[25] If and when border industries are

23. Taken from the 1970 census and reported in Lombard and van der Merwe, "Central Problems," 34, table 9.

24. Republic of South Africa, Department of Statistics, *Population Census, 1970; Population of Cities, Towns and Rural Areas* (Pretoria, 1971), 50; BENBO, *Bophuthatswana Economic Revue, 1975,* 28; *idem., KwaZulu Economic Revue, 1975,* 32.

25. For Bophuthatswana see BENBO, *Bophuthatswana Economic Review, 1975,* 22; for KwaZulu see *idem., KwaZulu Economic Revue, 1975,* 24.

established in number and/or the homelands entice large-scale industry into
their own territories, these imbalances may change. At present, however,
employment opportunities in the Republic draw and are expected to continue
to draw young adult males away from Bophuthatswana and KwaZulu with
a rhythm and on a scale that has only intensified in thirty years.

One measure of the contemporary population imbalance is the adult male
dependency burden (persons up to fourteen years of age divided by males
from fifteen to sixty-four years of age). This proportion suggests how many
young nonproductive dependents an adult male must support with his labor.
It does not include adult females or aged dependents. The average white
male worker in South Africa supports 0.9 young dependents. The average
Tswana male in an urban area supports 1.2 to 1.7 dependents. In the rural
portions of Bophuthatswana the dependency burden grows to 3.5. For Zulu
males the pattern is similar, with a rural homeland dependency factor of
3.3.[26] It is thus obvious that the population composition of Bophuthatswana
and KwaZulu militates against easy development and places a special burden
on the governments of both homelands. For example, both are or will be
forced to respond to the needs of residents who cannot easily pay for the kinds
of costly services — housing, education, medical attention, and social welfare
benefits — for which demand will increase as numbers and expectations grow,
and which yield no immediate economic gains.

The quality, as judged by levels of nutrition and morbidity, as well as the
density and age and sex composition of a population, affects its capacity to
respond to developmental opportunities. Homeland populations lack piped
water, adequate sanitation, and ready access to doctors, nurses, and hospitals.
Judged by the standards of other developing nations, intake levels of calories
and protein are low and deficiency diseases like kwashiokor, marasmus, and
pellagra are common.[27] Even in the cities African children suffer from dietary
shortcomings: one study of an urban sample concluded that 80 percent of
African schoolchildren were undernourished; another study gave a figure of
86 percent as judged by weight.[28] Infant mortality rates in the homelands
are high — at least 128 per 1,000 people, where under 27 per 1,000 is a sign of
a healthy population.[29] The average heights and weights of homeland African

26. Lombard and van der Merwe, "Central Problems," 33.
27. See P. J. Pretorius and H. Novis, "Nutritional Marasmus in Bantu Infants
in the Pretoria Area," *South African Medical Journal*, XXXIX (1965), 237-238,
501-505; F. W. Quass, "The Nutrition of Preschool and Primary School Children,"
ibid., 1137. See also M. E. Edginton, J. Hodkinson, and H. C. Seftel, "Disease
Patterns in a South African Rural Bantu Population," *ibid.*, XLVI (1972), 974.
28. See J. V. O. Reid, "Malnutrition," in Peter Randall (ed.), *Some Implications
of Inequality* (Johannesburg, 1971), 38.
29. J. G. A. Davel, "The Incidence of Malnutrition among Bantu Children,"
South African Medical Journal, XXXIX (1965), 1148. See also Alexander R. P.
Walker, "Biological and Disease Patterns in South African Interracial Populations

children place them in the third percentile when they are compared with American children, although the average heights and weights of African elite children compare favorably with American norms.[30]

Even without the kind of detailed figures that are rarely collected in the underdeveloped parts of the world, it is clear that the human resource capabilities of Bophuthatswana and KwaZulu may be affected by presently irreducible nutritional impoverishments. They, in turn, directly, contribute to retardation and, probably, to an overall energy deficit. "TB (in Bophuthatswana) is like the common cold," wrote one doctor. "If a patient comes in suffering from an ingrowing toenail and you're fool enough to x-ray him, you find he's got TB. . . . Malnutrition weakens the people to such an extent that they catch it as easily as a cold."[31] Thus the future of Bophuthatswana and KwaZulu cannot help but be influenced by the low levels of nutrition and life expectancy that are a feature of homeland life and that, in the short run, affect productivity, receptivity to innovation, and potential political change.

The Political Past

Since 1910 Africans throughout the Republic have suffered the imposition of constraints without the extension of many new rights. The Africans in the Cape have been the most affected: until 1910 they exercised the franchise subject to qualifications of literacy and of property or income; their vote had been important in about twelve constituencies. In 1910 they lost the right (which had never been exercised) to membership in the House of Assembly of the Cape Colony, and their votes were not counted in the allocation of seats between the provinces in the constitution of the Union. In 1930 their vote was further devalued by the extension of voting rights to white women; it was devalued yet again in 1931 when the property and income qualifications for voting were removed for whites only. In 1936 Cape Africans lost the right to vote on the common voters' roll and in exchange, were given three parliamentary seats to be filled by whites.

The impact of these changes on the Tswana and the Zulu was different. The Tswana of the Cape lost such political rights as they had had. Africans, and therefore the Zulu, in Natal before the Union, had had the right to vote, but the conditions were so stringent that in 1909 only six Africans were on

---

as Modified by Rise in Privilege," *ibid.*, XLVI (1972), 1128, where the overall rural Bantu figure is given as 82 per 1,000. The American figure is 20 per 1,000, and the figure for the Netherlands, a low of 13 per 1,000.

30. P. M. Leary and D. Obst, "The Use of Percentile Charts in the Nutritional Assessment of Children from Primitive Communities," *ibid.*, XLIII (1969), 1165-1168.

31. Dr. Donald Mackenzie, head of St. Michael's Mission Hospital north of Kuruman, quoted in "Starvation in South Africa," *Rand Daily Mail,* 11 Nov. 1969.

the voters' roll. The South Africa Act of 1909 therefore affected law rather than practice in Natal. Zulu traditional government had been broken up in the immediate aftermath of the war of 1879, and after the Bambatha rebellion of 1906, their king, Dinizulu, was exiled to the Transvaal, where he died. No major change followed. Indeed, for both Tswana and Zulu, constitutional developments after 1910 notably worsened their positions only if they had acquired rights through residence in the Cape.

The Representation of Natives Act of 1936 gave Africans in the Cape three white members of Parliament, and Africans in the other provinces four white senators, all chosen by a complex system of indirect election. Limited and segregated though it was, the act gave Africans throughout South Africa increased representation in Parliament. While the system lasted, eloquent white spokesmen ensured that some African grievances were brought to the attention of legislators in a way they had not been before 1936. This was small compensation, however, for the disparities between black and white partici- pation in electoral politics. The steady elimination of Africans from political roles held in common with whites without the elaboration of new structures in, and concession of new powers to, the African areas, was a development analogous to the closing to Africans of the market in land in 1913 without at the same time increasing the size of the reserves.

It is the urban Africans who have been most conspicuously disadvantaged by South African constitution making. As in the case of their rural brethren, they originally possessed limited freedom to acquire property in all of the provinces except the Orange Free State. The Urban Areas Act of 1923 exten- ded territorial segregation from the countryside to the towns, and the notion that Africans were "temporary" residents of the urban areas began to find its expression in law. Advisory boards were set up to represent the views of township residents. They were usually under the chairmanship of a white location superintendent and did little beyond noting grievances, having no power to do anything about them. Yet the urban black populations continued to grow, attracted by new opportunities in industry and commerce that, despite the constraints of legal and customary color bars, were preferable to farming in the reserves or working for white farmers. Before 1948 virtually no institutional provision had been made for urban Africans nor were any links provided between the peoples of the cities and the reserves.

When the National Party came to power in 1948 it was able to build upon a long and cumulative tradition of segregation in South African politics and decision-making. From that time it embarked upon a systematic program intended to "retribalize" Africans, to eliminate all participation by Africans, Asians, and coloureds in the disposition of power at national or local levels in the white areas, and to develop new, ethnically-based institutions in the

African areas. These new institutions were ultimately to represent all Africans of a particular ethnic group no matter where they lived.

This institutionalized ethnicity, not of their own making, presented home-land leaders with certain opportunities. Despite their long involvement in an urbanizing economy, the development of a tradition of African, not ethnic, nationalism, and the close links of their homelands to the modern Republic, the Tswana and the Zulu in the 1970s and 1980s may be able to draw upon their own traditions of incipient modernization in the nineteenth century, while avoiding the danger of serving the needs of the Republic more than those of black South Africans. The very emphasis by the government of the Republic on ethnicity, on the historic struggle of Afrikaners, and on the legitimacy of the white presence may encourage the Tswana and the Zulu not only to question the boundaries of the homelands, but to rely upon their past for inspiration and example. There are in both Tswana and Zulu history examples of adaptive modernizing leaders — "conscious social planners" in the case of the Tswana, great military innovators in the case of the Zulu.[32] At certain periods in Zulu history there was considerable mobility and men of talent were able to rise in the service of the king. Reluctantly accepting white rule, Tswana and Zulu entered the modern economy, at the same time preserving some traditional institutions in the reserves. When the logic of apartheid gave them an opportunity to do so, Tswana and Zulu leaders with traditional and modern credentials attempted to use an imposed system to increase the power of their peoples. These new leaders may thus be able to set the politics of their societies in the mainstream of their own traditions at the same time as they struggle for a greater share of South Africa's power and wealth.

32. For details, see Isaac Schapera, *Tribal Innovators: Tswana Chiefs and Social Change, 1795–1940* (London, 1970), 251-257; Max Gluckman, "The Kingdom of the Zulu of South Africa," in M. Fortes and E. E. Evans-Pritchard (eds.), *African Political Systems* (London, 1940), 39, 44-45.

3

The Legislative Framework
of Separatism

In culturally plural societies, especially those dominated by minorities, the maintenance of that domination, and hence of privilege, is inextricably associated with the designation of distinction. Where distinction is easily perceived, as in the case of skin color, barriers to mobility can readily be erected and, if necessary, enshrined in law. In societies with legalistic modes of thought and action the resort to law helps to legitimize the methods employed to maintain the privileges of the dominant group, whatever the observable basis of that group's hegemony.

In the Republic of South Africa observable differences have provided the basis of discrimination, but the bases and precise height of the barriers have long been the subject of intense debate within the dominant group. There has always been tension between those favoring political options presupposing transtribal, or nontribal, affiliation, and those denying any undifferentiated African participation in national life and governance. The integrationist or inclusionist approach, with its many shades of sentiment and varying embodiments in law, was at the heart of nineteenth-century Cape liberalism and Natal segregationism with their assumptions that Africans were to be a part, if a subservient part, of an overall system.

If Africans suffered at the hands of South African legislators, they were at least included in the national political arena. Even when Cape liberals allocated rights and responsibilities with regard to criteria that discriminated against the majority of Africans, they also reserved land for individual African groups, at the same time preserving the territorial integrity of the total society. Furthermore, they were prepared to say that in the fullness of time the processes of development would give a larger and larger proportion of the population full citizenship. It is, therefore, hardly surprising that politically conscious Africans adopted inclusionist positions, even given the limited terms of Cape liberalism. For them the institutionalization of ethnic difference — an exclusionist approach — was a device to ensure their powerlessness.

The ultimate achievement of equality was always anathema to a majority of the white South African population. The exclusionists were never prepared to agree that the achievement of equality in a common society was either possible or desirable. Still adhering to notions of territorial integrity, this group saw the preservation of its power and the maintenance of its identity in the erection of impermeable barriers. Thus the preservation of racial purity and the extention of discrimination in certain key areas was essential.

Until 1948 the refining of the definitions of racial and ethnic differences was unimportant. As in so many plural societies, the "other" was perceived as an undifferentiated mass. In South Africa, whites could therefore oppose simply Africans—blacks or Bantu (and later "nonwhites"). Color, not language or culture, provided sufficient distinction. The purpose of reserving land in the early twentieth century was to secure an overall division between whites and Africans, not to divide whites and particular segments of the African mass. Only later, with the victory of the National Party in 1948, was South Africa governed by a group committed to discouraging ideas of an *African* identity and interest, and the concomitant possibility of solidarity. Africans were to be allocated into and confined in their aspirations to "natural," historical categories. Each of the Southeastern Bantu-speaking peoples (politically separated as a result of the Zulu Mfecane and British and Afrikaner conquests as much as a result of underlying cultural or linguistic disaggregation) was deemed a nation or a nation in embryo. The premises of the South African political system, as interpreted by the Tomlinson Commission of 1955, then came to reside in the twin premises that (a) "the European population . . . has developed into an autonomous and complete national organism, and has furthermore preserved its character as a biological [racial] entity. There are not the slightest grounds for believing that the European population . . . would be willing to sacrifice its character as a national entity and as a European racial group," and (b) that "the Bantu peoples . . . do not constitute a homogeneous people, but form separate national units on the basis of language and culture."[1] Each unit was thus supposed to be an organism that, like the Afrikaner volk, would gain maturity through evolutionary growth.

These definitions are arbitrary. "National entity" and "racial group" are ambiguous terms. Whites may today be a racial group but they are not yet a "complete organism." Whites are permitted to enjoy multicultural nationalism, blacks are not. Moreover, despite the reference to "language and culture," not all of the homelands are linguistically unique (e.g., the Pedi [Sotho] and the North Ndebele [Nguni] populate one homeland) and the Xhosa inhabit two (the Transkei and the Ciskei). Further, elsewhere in the world nations have in many senses been self-defining, but in South Africa

1. *Summary of the Report*, 103; the Bantu Self-Government Bill of 1959, quoted by Gwendolen Carter, Thomas Karis, and Newell M. Stultz in *South Africa's Transkei: The Politics of Domestic Colonialism* (Evanston, 1967), 53.

the state, not individuals or groups, decides. The imperial power, in this case South Africa, has imposed both a territorial and a cultural parameter for each of the new proto-nations. The homelands may therefore be considered nations of convenience (the convenience of a dominant power), and many of their leaders, and numbers of erstwhile citizens, so consider them.

Because the present government of the Republic is committed to deny integration to the African majority, the homelands must be kept distant from South Africa politically, if they cannot be removed geographically. Insofar as possible, they must also be separated from one another until independence. The present elaboration of separate development, with the granting of self-government to nominally homogeneous homelands, and the commitment to grant them independence, may thus be seen as the appropriate culmination of the exclusionist strand of South African political thought.

Even within the integrationist tradition there were deviations that foreshadowed the later articulation of full-scale separate development. Reservation of land provided the territorial base without which the policy would have been a nullity, but it was the elaboration of new governmental arrangements in the Transkei at the end of the nineteenth century that linked new institutions based on British, not African, models with segregated landholding. These institutions were the precursors to a later separation based upon ethnicity and race. In 1894, with the passage of the Glen Grey Act by the government of the Cape Colony, Africans were permitted to enjoy individual land tenure on the same terms as whites in much of the Ciskei and the Transkei. This was intended to emancipate Africans within the Cape Colony and ensure a transition from traditional "unenlightened" patterns of usufruct to "progressive individualism." Accompanying it was the establishment of local councils, first in four and then in all of the twenty-six magisterial districts of the Transkei. These six-man, partially elected and partially nominated councils met bimonthly under the chairmanship of a white magistrate to discuss and advise upon local matters, particularly the allocation of local tax revenues for public works, schools, hospitals, and scholarships. From 1895 the system was progressively extended to the Transkei as a whole and, in 1931, all of the district councils were federated to form the United Transkeian Territories General Council, or Bunga. Meant from its inception to confer some of the benefits of liberalism on Africans and to foreshadow the gradual spread of home rule to other African sections of South Africa, the Bunga, and the Ciskei General Council set up in 1934, remained until 1955 virtually the only working devolutions of authority (no matter how circumscribed) within the South African system.

Presided over by the chief magistrate of the Transkei, the Bunga was composed of the twenty-six district magistrates, three of the six councillors of each district, and three paramount chiefs—108 in all. The Bunga met annually, published its debates, and from the 1930s discussed proposed parliamentary actions affecting Africans in addition to the disposition of £200,000 of tax revenues. Like the African Representative Councils in Northern Rhodesia and Nyasaland, it discussed, advised, and prepared resolutions. In the Transkei case, however, these resolutions were reviewed by the magistrates before being forwarded to the central government. Furthermore, Parliament was not bound in any way to act on them. So the Bunga was a "talking-shop," a useful arena for the ventilation of concerns and grievances, but a powerless body in the broader context of Union politics. Effectively, as members of the Bunga well knew, power lay with the minister of native affairs, who appointed the magistrates and native commissioners in the reserves and approved or named chiefs or headmen. Nevertheless, the African members of the Bunga were not acquiescent: they opposed segregation vociferously and continually, asked for justice in preference to social equality, fought against the loss of voting rights in 1936, sought the extension of the existing franchise to include African women, and often mocked the various land divisions and settlements imposed on Africans by the central government. "What sort of man would he be who came to buy an ox and gave you in payment a horse that was already yours?" a councillor asked in 1936.[2]

In addition to the Ciskei and Transkei councils, in 1936 a Natives Representative Council was set up to represent Africans throughout South Africa. In part this was a concession to satisfy Africans that the new settlement gave them a recognized place in the political system and did not merely rob Africans in general of the right to buy land or Cape Africans in particular of their common roll rights. Chaired by the secretary for native affairs, an administrator, not a politician, the council consisted of six white chief native commissioners and twelve elected and four nominated Africans. The African members used it as a sounding board, but with little practical result, for all of the major African grievances: land, segregation, urban conditions, the state of the reserves, and the very powerlessness of the council itself. It did, however, serve as a forum for *African* opinion and as a place where representatives of separated and voteless people could voice their grievances openly. It was the first and last official body that recognized that Africans had interests in common. However it failed hopelessly to satisfy its African members. In 1946 the council adjourned *sine die,* and in 1947 it rejected new proposals by the Smuts government to make limited changes in the

2. Quoted in Carter, *et al., South Africa's Transkei,* 98. There is another summary in Monica Wilson, "The Growth of Peasant Communities," in Monica Wilson and Leonard Thompson (eds.), *The Oxford History of South Africa* (New York, 1971), II, 87–89.

powers of the council because such proposals were based upon "the principle of permanent separatism."[3]

The new government in 1948 moved rapidly to enact a drastic policy of political segregation. The first change attempted was the elimination of coloureds from the common roll, touching off a six-year constitutional crisis. There followed the first systematic attempt to base African political institutions on ethnic division. In order to "have a basis on which the Native will henceforth be able to give expression to his own inner self to develop his family life and his national life," Parliament in 1951 passed the Bantu Authorities Act. It set up an elaborate new system to give the African an opportunity to "be a recipient of those human rights and privileges for which we are all yearning in this life." Nationalist legislators claimed that they were doing their "utmost to save what can still be saved of the tribal life of the Bantu which embodies the whole basis of his social, political and economic structure."[4] The Natives Representative Council was abolished.

More specifically, the act established a hierarchy of Bantu authorities, tribal, regional, and territorial, with limited legislative, executive, and judicial powers, each guided and ultimately controlled by whites. Members of tribal authorities were to be appointed by local chiefs (all of whom were already salaried government officials) and the local Bantu commissioners (who retained the power of veto). Regional authorities covered two or more tribal authorities and consisted of the members of those subordinate authorities. They could run schools, build and maintain public works and hospitals, improve farming, agricultural, and silvicultural methods, make bylaws, levy taxes, and impose fines. Territorial authorities, defined in more detail by the Promotion of Bantu Self-Government Act of 1959, supervised the regional authorities, taking over their powers and their methods of obtaining revenue, but always to the extent permitted by and with the explicit approval of the governor-general (later, the state president), as advised by the cabinet of the Republic. The authorities were to meet annually.

The Bantu Authorities Act had little immediate impact on local African governance. Chiefs were suspicious, and educated, politicized Africans were unequivocally hostile to it. For them this was retrogressive, patronizing legislation. At first few chiefs and traditional councillors could be persuaded to take advantage of the rearrangements envisaged by the bill. In 1953 the first three tribal authorities were established in the Transvaal, and a few other groups agreed, whether from self-interest or under pressure, in Cape Province and Natal. Not until 1955, however, when the Bunga voted to

3. Colin M. Tatz, *Shadow and Substance in South Africa* (Pietermaritzburg, 1962), 118.
4. J. A. S. Nel and W. A. Maree, members of Parliament, quoted in Carter, *Transkei,* 49.

accept the scheme in principle, did the government succeed in obtaining any significant African support. By that time the Tomlinson Commission had issued its massive report with a call for an acceleration of separate development; representatives of the Bunga may have decided that the proposed new authorities could give Africans the kind of power and arena of control capable of being enlarged over the years. Certainly they had no desire to give up their persistent agitation for a return to the common roll and direct representation in Parliament, but they may have been persuaded that the Bunga had outlived its usefulness.

In 1957 the Transkeian Territorial Authority, composed of chiefs and nominated and elected councillors, replaced the Bunga and became the first day-to-day African government within the Republic. It ran a number of business enterprises and plantations, carried out road and bridge construction, and tried to persuade central government departments and officials to alleviate hardships. Its deliberations were taken seriously; they were not "merely a charade."[5] Even so, its responsibilities and powers were ill-defined and limited and no other African groups followed the lead of the Transkei. If anything, African antagonism to separate development was becoming stronger and more outspoken. There was a successful bus boycott on the Rand in 1957, demonstrations against the treason trial in 1958, riots against the issuance of passes to women, disturbances in the northern Transvaal and the Transkei, and a widespread atmosphere of political ferment that infected at least some of the reserves as much as the cities.

The accession of Dr. Hendrik Verwoerd, previously minister of native affairs, to the prime minister's office in 1958 hastened the translation of ideology into enactment. Given the unrest and anxiety within South Africa, the intensifying hostility of the international arena, the unresolved legacy of the Tomlinson Report, and his own ideological background, it is understandable that Verwoerd should have tried to satisfy a number of political needs with new and comprehensive legislation affecting Africans. Only by giving separatism an expandable framework could Verwoerd and other Afrikaner nationalists have claimed later that South Africa was composed of many nations, white, brown, and black, and that the government was actively promoting the development of all people toward "separate freedom." By dividing Africans into cultural groups, they could assert that the white nation was larger than any one of the "Bantu" nations and should no longer be thought of as a ruling minority. (Today, both Xhosa and Zulu outnumber whites.) The logic of separate development also demanded the elaboration of new institutions of self-government, especially if that elaboration were accompanied by the exclusion of Africans from limited political participation

5. Christopher Hill, *Bantustans: The Fragmentation of South Africa* (London, 1964), 57.

by the repeal of part of the Representation of Natives Act of 1936 and by the exclusion of Africans from open universities.

The Promotion of Bantu Self-Government Act of 1959, however vague and capable of several interpretations, was an elaboration of the Bantu Authorities Act and became the legal cornerstone of subsequent homeland developments. The preamble asserted that Africans formed diverse national units distinguishable by language and culture and could not be considered in any sense homogeneous; that provision should be made for the gradual extension of self-government to the national units; that the units should control land; and that the units should possess a number of executive and legislative prerogatives.

The act accordingly designated eight national units on linguistic and cultural rather than territorial grounds (the Ciskei and Transkei were not differentiated at this stage), with commissioners-general as the representatives of the central government designated to "furnish guidance and advice" and "enlighten the population." It permitted the governor-general (the president since 1961), who appointed the commissioners-general, to transfer legislative powers, as and when appropriate, to the various governmental units. The units, moreover, could govern with powers given to them, and could receive land held in trust under the 1936 legislation. But the act did not define self-government, indicate timetables, enlarge the elective fraction of the envisaged unitary governments, or diminish the central government's continued powers to rule by decree. Respecting certain matters the national executive would henceforth be required to consult the homeland authorities, but only the most far-seeing or totally cynical homeland leader could have derived much comfort from the act, the bitter debate over it in Parliament, and the package of removals and exclusions with which it was associated.[6] Subsequently, however, the act was to be used for the political advancement of Africans at a time when other avenues were closed.

At the time of the passage of the act only the Transkei had a functioning territorial authority. Its subordinate status within the Republic was evident, as was its inability adequately to represent the interests of Xhosa living outside the Transkei. But the force of events within and without the Transkei, and an awareness on the part of some Transkeian leaders of alternative modes of gaining advantages for Africans, precipitated structural changes more rapidly than might have been anticipated or desired by the central government. The Sharpeville massacre in early 1960 compelled white South Africans to become acutely aware of the strength of international antagonism to apartheid. Verwoerd publicly acknowledged its strength and, in 1961 in

6. For the legislation and its relationship to Verwoerd's ideology, see L. E. Neame, *The History of Apartheid: The Story of Colour in South Africa* (London, 1962), 158–161.

order to forestall an almost certain expulsion, retreated further into isolation by removing South Africa from the Commonwealth. South Africa was in the throes of an emergency throughout most of 1960; the African National and Pan-Africanist Congresses were both banned and their leaders detained, banned, or driven underground. In the Transkei, specifically, there were violent protests of local and national grievances throughout 1960 and the first part of 1961. The central government made mass arrests, especially in Pondoland, where legally a state of emergency still exists. Two months later, in April 1961, Britain voted for the first time with the other major powers in the United Nations to condemn apartheid and to work for its moderation. On 10 April 1961 Verwoerd said that "in the light of the pressure being exerted on South Africa," the government would encourage the advancement of self-governing African homelands and would contemplate the provision of independence.

Chief Kaiser Matanzima in 1960 had asked the central government to declare the Transkei a locally controlled African state. On 21 April 1961, apparently to the surprise of officials, a member of the Territorial Authority moved during the regular session that the central administration transform the Transkei into "a self-governing state under control of the Bantu people."[7] Matanzima and his supporters had made a political judgment—that more was to be achieved by supporting separate development than by opposing it; that Africans could not hope to regain representation of any significance in the national arena; and that a large measure of local control might prove an acceptable, if temporary, substitute.

More than a year after making the first overtures, and after intensive political consultations in Pretoria, a committee of whites and blacks, with a majority of officials, slowly drafted a constitution. Despite strenuous and widespread popular opposition in the Transkei, the Territorial Authority in 1962, and the Republican Parliament in 1963, approved the Transkei Constitution Act. It called the Transkei a self-governing territory within the Republic, described its boundaries, and specifically excluded white-controlled enclaves. There were provisions for a flag and a national anthem. Citizenship was restricted to Africans born within the homeland, residents there for five years, persons whose mother tongue was a version of Cape Nguni (Xhosa) and who owed no allegiance to another homeland, and other outsiders whose genealogies led back to other African linguistic groups of the Transkei.

The constitution established a six-man cabinet presided over by a chief minister and a legislative assembly of four paramount chiefs, sixty other chiefs (all chiefs were governmental appointees), and forty-five representatives elected on a basis of adult suffrage. The assembly received a mandate to legislate for education, direct taxation, any and all purely local matters,

7. See Carter, *Transkei,* 26, 113; *Survey of Race Relations, 1961,* 97.

agriculture, local public works, local police and security, courts, welfare, liquor, district councils, and minor issues. The original constitution also reserved a number of powers to the central government: defense, national police and security, harbors, railways, postal and telegraph services, national roads, currency and banking, customs and excise, foreign affairs, and amending the constitution itself. And, as with all subsequent homeland constitutions, bills passed by the assembly had to receive the assent of the state president before becoming law.[8]

During the 1960s South Africa suppressed black- and white-led challenges to the authority of the state, removed more and more larger society privileges from Africans, coloureds, and Asians, and increased the efficiency of its internal security system. For the first five years the state faced various groups desiring major policy changes by constitutional and revolutionary means, although conflict never culminated in prolonged breakdowns of order on a large scale. Even so, the government was frightened. It responded by legislating further limitations on the rule of law, making mass arrests, persistently prosecuting opponents, and detaining leaders and followers without trial for long, renewable periods.

By the middle of the decade the government had demonstrated a willingness and capacity to preserve order at any cost. It had simultaneously manifested a determination to pursue its avowed goals of political and social segregation. The Prohibition of Political Interference Act of 1966 regulated both the political process and access to that process. It prohibited multiracial politics and prescribed the very qualifications of party membership. If many believed that the Sharpeville massacre foreshadowed the collapse of the South African regime, by the mid-1960s it had become even more evident that National Party control of South Africa could be ended only in a distant future, and with great difficulty. In retrospect we can see that confident predictions about the collapse of white rule in South Africa were based upon aspiration rather than any accurate assessment of local conditions.

Equally it became apparent that African political advancement, if any, would occur in the foreseeable future only within the context of the development of the homelands. Matanzima, then widely believed to be a collaborator, nevertheless showed that the logic of separate development could be exploited to African advantage. Making use of the powers conferred by the act, he introduced a measure to provide for the instruction of schoolchildren in English rather than Afrikaans or Xhosa from Standard III. Although contrary to official policy — "mother tongue instruction" is sacred to Afrikaner nationalists — the Transkei made its decision prevail.[9] In 1968, too, the

8. A detailed summary of the act is in *Survey of Race Relations, 1963*, 83-87.
9. Muriel Horrell, *Bantu Education to 1968* (Johannesburg, 1968), 59; Carter, *Transkei*, 161-162.

Transkeian Legislative Assembly, perhaps prodded by South Africa, asked the Republic to prepare the Transkei for independence in the shortest possible time.[10]

Simultaneously the central government attempted to accelerate the implementation of existing legislation regarding the homelands. It also began to prepare new bills in order to enhance the credibility of the homelands and provide for their political growth. The issue of independence, raised by Verwoerd in 1959, began to be discussed more frequently and explicitly. "I established eight [homeland] governments," M. C. Botha, the minister of Bantu administration and development, said in 1970, "not in order that they might sit there and become rigid and bleed themselves to death as governments, but in fact for the purpose of promoting the process of evolutionary political development on the road to their separate independent destinations." During the next year Prime Minister B. Johannes Vorster confirmed the intention of giving complete independence to the homelands, if only at the end of a long road.[11]

Africans, especially urban Africans, at first resisted the creation of homelands as vigorously as they protested against apartheid and separate development. Toward the end of the 1960s, however, leaders in the various potential homelands began to respond to the blandishments and pressures of white officials; some may also have seen potential rewards for all blacks in Matanzima's maneuvering. Whichever, it was more from necessity than from enthusiasm that the leaders of both the future homelands of Bophuthatswana and KwaZulu agreed to follow an accelerated version of the Transkeian constitutional evolution. "Homeland leaders who have accepted separate development," said Chief Gatsha Buthelezi in 1971, "have done so because it is the only way in which Blacks in South Africa can express themselves politically."[12]

Bophuthatswana had accepted tribal and regional authorities (the bottom two steps on the ladder erected in 1951) by the mid-1950s. In 1961, the Tswana Territorial Authority came into being under Chief Tidimane Pilane. Its purview was six large and many small, scattered reserves in the northern Cape and the western Transvaal occupied mostly by Tswana, but also by Xhosa and Ndebele. There were eight (later ten) regional and numerous tribal authorities. Only the Kwena of Mogopa rejected the entire system. The Territorial Authority established a school for sons of chiefs, a teachers'

10. Muriel Horrell, *The African Reserves of South Africa* (Johannesburg, 1969), 3.
11. Botha, in *House of Assembly Debates* (7 Sept. 1970), col. 3505; Vorster, cited in *Survey of Race Relations, 1971,* 29. For a further discussion of South African views on the independence question, see Merle Lipton, "Independent Bantustans?" *International Affairs,* XLVIII (1972), 11, 14.
12. Quoted in Jean Le May, "Black Political Parties Return to S.A.," *The Star,* 12 Aug. 1972.

training college, an industrial school, and an agricultural training center. It sponsored agricultural improvement and stock breeding schemes; encouraged the formation of cooperatives, especially for dairy produce; built feeder roads and erected boundary fences; drilled bore holes; ran a bus service and profit-making liquor stores, and so on. But the Tswana did not receive expanded powers until 1968, when the Department of Bantu Administration and Development was actively persuading other "nations" to form territorial authorities. The new regulations provided for delegation of authority to an executive council, but the Territorial Authority did not become self-governing.

The Zulu, led by Chief Gatsha Buthelezi, of the family traditionally responsible for providing Zulu chief councillors, remained throughout the 1960s essentially antagonistic to the government's pattern of institutional devolution. The first Zulu regional authorities were gazetted in 1959 but resistance to their establishment persisted. As early as 1963 Ingonyama ("Paramount Chief") Cyprian ka Solomon Bhekezulu, who was in favor of the authority pattern, summoned a large meeting of subordinate chiefs to Nongoma in order to promote its acceptance, but Buthelezi asserted that such a momentous decision could only be made after Zulu in both the rural and urban areas were consulted, and other chiefs supported this tactical maneuver.[13]

As of late 1965, in Natal and Zululand 102 "tribes" had requested authorities and 137 either were opposed or indifferent. There were twelve regional authorities, too. Both regional and tribal authorities controlled but a small proportion of the total African area of Natal. In that year, in Buthelezi's own district, officials of the Department of Bantu Administration and Development were reportedly preparing to impose the authority system without local approval. In response, Buthelezi, already the master of ironic joust, said that he was relieved to learn that indigenous acceptance was unnecessary. If the law empowered the government to proclaim tribal authorities, the Zulu should not be asked either to approve or disapprove. Even though he did not think that the Bantu authority program solved South Africa's fundamental problems, he obeyed the law and would cooperate without approving. The majority of the Zulu would remain on record as having consistently opposed authorities as long as they could do so.[14] Late that year, the government gazetted a tribal authority in Buthelezi's Mahlabatini district.

13. See Gatsha Buthelezi, "Independence for the Zulus," in Nic J. Rhoodie (ed.), *South African Dialogue: Contrasts in South African Thinking on Basic Race Issues* (Johannesburg, 1971), 204.
14. *Survey of Race Relations, 1965,* 133-134.

Five years later, Buthelezi was no less intransigent. But he agreed to run a territorial authority after he and other Zulu had been subjected to intense official pressure. He realized that only by making the best of the *fait accompli* could he continue to wield influence and power within the Zulu community and prevent the paramount chief, and his supporters, from organizing the authority on conservative lines in cooperation with the white bureaucracy. The Zululand Territorial Authority thus began to function in 1970, with Buthelezi being unanimously elected by 200 members as its chief executive officer. He immediately called on the central government to demonstrate its sincerity and give the Zulu people a homeland of realistic size and resources: "The plain truth of the matter is," he said later, "that if the South African Government does not deliver the goods on the basis of its own scheme, the Blacks of this country will become even more disillusioned than at present." Furthermore, he said, "I am not prepared to say that separate development is the only hope, but it may be a contribution to the development of the situation. It may be a contribution to the unravelling of the problem, insofar as, if we attain full independence, our hand will be strengthened. Gone will be the days then, one hopes, when people will think of us simply as 'kaffirs.' "[15]

By the last years of the 1960s the government had gone as far as it could with territorial authorities under existing legislation. Thus far the creation of authorities had proved a piecemeal, comparatively uncoordinated, and still tentative process. Only partially could it satisfy what Botha termed South Africa's legal, ethical, and moral obligations constitutionally to advance the "Bantu nations" of the Republic.[16] Now that the government had begun moving all the national units it had so defined toward the territorial authority goal, it faced the possibility of having to legislate separately (as in the case of the Transkei) for an additional eight homelands. In order to avoid this problem, and to give the government greater freedom to devise and proclaim new arrangements, Parliament passed the Bantu Homelands Citizenship Act of 1970 and the Bantu Homelands Constitution Act of 1971. Together these comprehensive bills established a framework for all subsequent homeland arrangements and provided a visible mechanism for harmonizing the older devolutions of authority with current practices and anticipated developments in the newer homelands.

The Bantu Homelands Citizenship Act embodied the government's insistence that all Africans, wherever in the Republic they resided or may have resided over time, had "national" homes, and that those homes were in the

---

15. Gatsha Buthelezi, "End this Master-Servant Relationship," *Rand Daily Mail,* 2 July 1971.
16. M. C. Botha, in *House of Assembly Debates* (7 Sept. 1970), col. 3495.

separate proto-states. The act gave the minister of Bantu administration and development power to provide for the issue of certificates of citizenship so that *every* African would become a citizen of a territorial authority, however remote in time or place his ties to that particular territory might be. According to the provisions of the act, every African born in a particular area, domiciled there, every person using the language of that area or an "associated linguistic group," every person related to a member of such a group, anyone who has identified himself with that population, or anyone associated with such a population by virtue of his cultural or racial background would and must be entitled to the appropriate citizenship. Since an elusive definition of racial identity is a fundamental prerequisite of citizenship, whites, although they might live in a homeland and speak a local language fluently, and perhaps have been born there, could not apply for homeland citizenship. Africans were expected but not required to apply for citizenship.

Allocations and designations of citizenship are made under the act in the first instance by a territorial authority or homeland government, and on appeal, by the minister of Bantu administration and development. The act makes possible the ultimate distribution of citizenship and accompanying identity cards to all Africans; in the future, citizenship is intended to determine and be the basis of participation in political life for all blacks in South Africa and also for the holding of property in the urban areas of the Republic. There is a provision for the granting of homeland citizenship to Africans from other homelands, i.e., Xhosa can acquire citizenship in KwaZulu if the government of KwaZulu agrees. Under the broadly drawn criteria of the act, it will be impossible for an African to say "I know no homeland. We have been in the city so long, there is no basis for giving me a homeland citizenship."

The Bantu Homelands Constitution Act permits the president of the Republic, when advised by the minister of Bantu administration and development, to establish tribal, regional, and territorial authorities, and to grant differing degrees of self-government to indigenous authorities (the word "state" is avoided) without constant recourse to Parliament. The thrust of the act is clear: "It is the firm and irrevocable intention of the government to lead each nation to self-government and independence."[17] As with the Bantu Authorities Act of 1951, the Bantu Homelands Constitution Act distinguishes between the various levels of authority, the tribal bodies on the one hand and the more important regional and territorial instruments on the other. Tribal authorities are to remain closely tied to traditional forms

17. Republic of South Africa, Department of Bantu Administration and Development, *Explanatory Memorandum on the Homelands Constitution Act* (Pretoria, 1971), 1.

(as officially interpreted) of governance, but higher bodies need have no traditional component except insofar as they provide for the participation of chiefs and headmen, adopt the local vernacular as a legislative and administrative tongue, and make an indigenous song the "national" anthem. In Bophuthatswana the Legislative Assembly concludes with the singing of an indigenous anthem.[18] There, too, the mace is crowned by the figure of a leopard and a ring of ox-heads, but it is still a mace, and its function is the same as the mace of the House of Assembly in Cape Town or the House of Commons. There are also national flags with indigenous components, but there is no attempt to base the new polities upon traditional institutions.

The Bantu Homelands Constitution Act decrees no chronological order for the granting of self-government and the establishment of legislative assemblies. Usually, however, assemblies have preceded self-government, the terms of which have been the subject of negotiation between the Republic and an existing territorial authority. Legislative assemblies have been proclaimed statutorily only after the minister of Bantu administration and development has consulted the existing territorial authority. The act empowers assemblies to discuss and pass bills on a list of subjects (the list being in theory easily altered by the minister of Bantu administration and development and the president of the Republic without further scrutiny by Parliament). Homeland legislation must be approved by the state president, who may also refer particular bills back to the original assembly. Furthermore, there are specific exclusions, corresponding to those in the Transkei Constitution Act of 1963. Assemblies are not competent to pass bills pertaining to matters of general security. Military and wider policy powers are beyond their scope, as is the regulation of the manufacture and sale of arms; the entry into each homeland of "persons other than citizens"; foreign affairs; postal service, telephones, and communications; currency and the banking industry; and customs and excise. Homelands may not amend or repeal the Bantu Homelands Constitution Act. Nor are they able to amend their own constitutions without the consent of the president of the Republic..

With any grant of self-government under the act, a territorial authority's executive council automatically becomes a cabinet, councillors become ministers and the chief councillor a chief minister, and directors of departments (so far all white) become secretaries. (In 1974, a black secretary was appointed in the Transkei.) The executive also becomes responsible to the local parliament, being constituted from among the members of the relevant

18. The hymn is *Morena Boloka,* generally recognized as something akin to a Southern Sotho national anthem, which emphasizes Sotho identity, and, unlike Nkosi Sikelela, has no all-African referent. A rough translation is as follows: "Chief [also Lord, God] take care of our people [nation]/ Put an end to wars and tribulations [affliction, oppression]/ Look after it, our nation." Courtesy, Philip Mayer.

legislative assembly. The executive branch retains the customary British-style prerogative over financial matters, being responsible for proposing appropriations to the legislature. Even so, because of the subordinate nature of the homeland system within the larger Republic, budgetary autonomy is limited to control over a revenue fund composed of taxes paid by its resident citizens, taxes on the profits of companies "managed and controlled in the area concerned and in which Bantu have a controlling interest," an annual grant from the central government equal to the cost of functions transferred to the homelands (minus revenues raised from individuals and the salaries of officials lent to the homelands), and such sums as parliament may grant. However, under the enabling act a homeland does not receive all of the taxes paid by its citizens, especially excluding those taxes, such as the sales tax, paid during their sometimes prolonged residence elsewhere in the Republic.[19]

One of the consistent themes in the policy of separate development is the preservation and strengthening of the role of traditional rule in African societies. This policy has been followed because Afrikaner nationalists are themselves conservative and intensely aware of the necessity of preserving their own cultural identity. But presumably the policy is also followed because traditional rulers are assumed to be conservative, especially in wanting, as do most whites, to preserve the existing distribution of power. Thus the homeland constitutions almost invariably include a majority of chiefs. The Bantu Homelands Constitution Act permits the powers of chiefs and headmen to be "varied and withdrawn" only by a "competent authority." In the case of tribal and regional authorities, the indigenous legislative assemblies are deemed "competent." Assemblies, therefore, have the power to withhold recognition from individuals as chiefs and headmen and as members of tribal authorities, but the proportion of members elected is embodied in the constitution, which can only be amended with the consent of the president of the Republic. The act entrenches the powers of chiefs in the Legislative Assembly by making the proportion of nominated and elected members of the assembly subject to outside authority. This restriction was made abundantly clear in 1975 when the government refused to accept an amendment to the constitution of Lebowa that would have created a House of Chiefs, separate from a properly elected legislature.[20]

The act continues the application of the South African judicial system to the territories. Yet, the Republic may transfer courts to territorial authorities on an *ad hoc* basis, and in the future each territory may set up its own high court to replace the local or provincial division of the Supreme Court of South Africa under which lower courts now function in the homelands. (The Transkei has already set up a High Court headed by a white judge from

19. For amendments to these provisions, see 143–144.
20. *Survey of Race Relations, 1975,* 138.

the Eastern Districts division of the Supreme Court.) At the time of transfer, noncitizens (presumably whites) will be exempt from homeland jurisdiction. All citizens of a particular homeland, wherever they may reside, will in a complementary fashion be subject to the courts of their "national" home, a rather complex system of extraterritorial jurisdiction not yet functioning. Even at the time of transfer, however, appellate jurisdiction will remain with the appropriate level of the South African jural system. Thus, the act envisages no major changes in the administration of law. After self-government, homelands will be permitted to amend acts of Parliament so long as the amendments affect their own citizens only; hence, within the framework of separate development there is little to prevent the government permitting, or even encouraging, Africanization of the law.

The Bantu Homelands Constitution Act cannot alone bring a territory to the brink of independence. There are prohibitions in the bill that inhibit a territory's relations with the outside world and define its populace as citizens of South Africa when traveling abroad. Even within South Africa (but outside the homelands), residents of homelands are deemed still subject to South African law and its consequent selective disabilities. Citizens of the homelands, whether or not called "temporary residents," do not have legal rights in the Republic comparable to those of, say, Germans or Italians working temporarily in Britain or resident aliens in the United States. Such migrants, whether long- or short-term, may acquire property and, in certain circumstances, citizenship. In South Africa such possibilities are severely restricted.

Yet, the act contains a phenomenon new to South Africa. It provides a pattern for the constitutional evolution of the homelands and the possible accumulation of power, albeit circumscribed power, by Africans. Moreover, the very existence of the act makes bureaucrats anxious to move all the homelands from stage one (all appointed) to stage two (partially elected legislatures). The act has thus hastened, and legitimized in the mind of Afrikaner nationalists, the process of devolving responsibility to Africans. The fact, too, that the rights of the leaders of the homelands are enshrined in general omnibus legislation also gives an important immunity — of substantial protective value — to the more and more outspoken chief councillors and chief ministers of the homelands.

Under the new legal instruments, Bophuthatswana achieved stage one in 1971, when the thirteen Tswana regional authorities (reduced to twelve) were made subordinate to a reorganized Tswana Legislative Assembly. In 1972, the Bophuthatswana Constitution Proclamation (R 130) declared Bophuthatswana, the "place where the Tswana people abide," self-governing, and provided a method for electing the assembly. This was stage two. The assembly consists of twenty-four elected members and forty-eight members designated by the regional and tribal authorities (primarily chiefs and headmen). The elected legislators represent twelve constituencies, each electing two members, and are chosen on the basis of adult suffrage. The chief minister is elected directly by the assembly. He heads a cabinet of seven ministers appointed by him and approved by the assembly.

Zululand (since 1972 known as KwaZulu), although the most populous of the homelands, was loath to cooperate with the wishes of the Department of Bantu Administration and Development. Yet, during 1971 the central government repeatedly made known its desire that the Zulu should move toward a Transkei-like self-government, perhaps under the leadership of Goodwill Zwelithini, the young Ingonyama and estranged nephew of Chief Buthelezi, who was to be installed later in the year. The Zulu Executive Council and the full Territorial Authority also both asked during the year for a legislative assembly, and finally Chief Buthelezi and the government agreed to discuss a constitution, for the drafting of which Buthelezi relied upon the advice of sympathetic South Africans as well as officials of the Department of Bantu Administration and Development.

In 1972, as KwaZulu ("at the place of the Zulu"), the Territorial Authority agreed upon and received a constitution for stage one (Proclamation R 69) of self-government. It created a nominated and indirectly elected assembly of chiefs and commoners. Each of the twenty-two Zulu regional authorities were to be represented by three chiefs (sixty-six in all). The three chiefs of a tribal or a community authority that was a regional authority also received places. Eventually fifty-five more members will be elected on the basis of adult suffrage, with the number of elected representatives per regional constituency dependent upon the population of each. The urban Zulu are not represented as such, although they can and will vote as from their presumed rural "homes."

Buthelezi managed to gain some concessions during the drafting of this constitution. He won the right to select the members of the Executive Council rather than to have them elected by the assembly, though he is required to present his council to the assembly for approval. He persuaded the members of the authority to swear allegiance to the state president and the Ingonyama only, but to refuse to offer fealty to the Republic's government. That government, after all, was responsible for the passage of the legal paraphernalia of apartheid. Buthelezi told the authority that he was "conscience-bound to disagree with many of the laws made by the Government."[21] The authority also agreed that the Ingonyama should participate only in the ceremonial proceedings of the new assembly, and—unlike the role of paramount chiefs in the Transkei—should have no executive position. In nearly all other respects, bar the 166 rules of legislative procedure but including the scope

21. *The Star,* 12 Jan. 1972.

of the assembly's power, the perquisites of office, and the like, the relevant proclamations put KwaZulu on a footing effectively similar to, if not congruent with, the Transkei and Bophuthatswana. Still, in terms of the Bantu Homelands Constitution Act, KwaZulu, because it has not moved to stage two and has therefore not become completely self-governing, suffers some disability.

The delay in achieving self-government in KwaZulu has been due in part to a political struggle between Buthelezi and the central government. Perhaps because he felt that the shift to self-government involved no major concession of power and resources, Buthelezi used the issue to make a point against the pass laws by refusing to allow voters to register on the basis of the Republic's hated reference books. Instead he has demanded the use of citizenship certificates under the new act, but that maneuver has made political change subject to both the speed with which the certificates are issued by the Department of the Interior, which controls the expensive machinery used in processing applications and manufacturing the identity cards (which include a photograph), and the willingness of Zulu to go to the trouble of getting them. Zulu in white areas, like all Africans there, are understandably nervous about losing rights of residence; Buthelezi has claimed that this anxiety may have inhibited them from applying for citizenship, quite apart from political or economic objections to doing so. Of 2,150,000 people estimated to be qualified for citizenship at the end of 1974, about 600,000 people had applied, and 376,000 certificates had been issued.[22]

It is important to emphasize the limited nature of the changes in the constitutions of the homelands. The legislation of 1970 and 1971 provides no major break with the system established in the Transkei in 1963, the roots of which go back to the Bantu Authorities Act of 1951. What has been achieved *constitutionally* in recent years is the extension of Transkei-type models to the other former reserves. The distribution of power remains much as before, and, if the Transkeian developments are to continue to constitute precursors of change in other African areas, independence is near at hand. Existing legislation does, however, make possible further delegations of authority to Africans not explicitly excluded by the Bantu Homelands Constitution Act, e.g., more departments could be handed over, as in the case of the Department of Health in the Transkei in 1973, and the Department of Health and Social Welfare in Bophuthatswana in 1975. Furthermore, increases in resources are being made to the homelands by allocating money from the Republic's Consolidated Fund and by changing the basis of taxation. But the inequality of power between the Republic and each of its homelands remains. It is an inequality that will clearly not be removed by the homelands' achievement of independence.

22. *Survey of Race Relations, 1975,* 131. For a further discussion, see 55–56.

4

Administration
and Politics

Modern politics in Bophuthatswana and KwaZulu, as in all of the homelands except possibly the Transkei, is in its infancy. The homelands as political communities have not yet exhibited the political dynamics of free societies; it is thus premature to stress the details of internal interaction. This is not to say that these polities are without the real stakes, concomitant rivalries, and the kinds of manipulation and brokerage of power that are seen in older states. It is too early for the lines of cleavage to have become distinct and for personal and local contention to have been translated into identifiable "national" conflicts reflecting divisions of ideology and interest. Consequently, as was often the case in African colonies in the immediate post-World War II period, the politics of the two homelands are dominated more by the personalities of a few individuals than by conflicting ideologies.

This condition is due both to the nature of contemporary homeland society and to the status of the homelands within the South African political system. The homelands possess a limited autonomy and remain almost as much subject to the government of South Africa as they did before being launched on the road to some kind of home rule. Evolving as they have out of territorial authorities—instruments of administrative, not political, decentralization by a domestic colonial power—they cannot yet be expected to display the politics of, say, a British self-governing colony immediately prior to independence. Their legislatures, biased in favor of traditional authorities, are only partially representative of their *de jure* populations. They, and all members of the homeland governments, play defined and restricted roles determined by the constraints imposed by the dominant Republic. At the present time, therefore, the politics of the homelands reflect both a preoccupation with the distribution of power between a homeland and the dominant Republic and a struggle for power between various factions within homeland society. These factions are based partly on personalities, partly on differing views as to the proper role of traditional leaders, and partly on the tactics to be used in confronting the sovereign power.

Client states with extremely limited autonomy, Bophuthatswana and KwaZulu are products of government policy rather than of successful nationalistic confrontation. Because their leaders did not achieve what power they have by gradual processes of accretion, they are unsure of the limits of their autonomy. What the South African government has dispensed it still controls, influences, and, given the inequality of power, could take away. It has transferred responsibility to the homelands only for a few clearly specified governmental functions. Initially all of the homelands began with the same six departments, Finance, Community Affairs (Interior in Bophuthatswana), Works, Education, Agriculture and Justice, but further areas have been transferred to them. Whatever the precise list of functions performed by homeland governments at any one time, they are carried out by cabinets of ministers, each with specific mandates and with responsibility to legislative assemblies, though the conventions of responsible government have still to be developed.

In their departments the ministers are assisted by white officials seconded to them by the Republic. Many of these officials are present throughout sittings of the assemblies and the executive councils. The sovereignty of homeland governments is therefore subject in law to limitations and in practice to severe inhibitions even on the exercise of those powers officially delegated to it. These limitations, moreover, are inherent in the structure of the homelands and result from the thrust of South African policy, past and present, rather than from the failure of African politicians to take advantage of available opportunities. The extent to which Bophuthatswana and KwaZulu can free themselves from such limitations, expand the bounds of their autonomy, and increase their available resources are the key questions of the immediate future, and together become one of the decisive factors on which the success or failure of the South African homeland experiment will be evaluated.

Homeland Administration

The manner in which the South African government has organized the administration of the homelands places great stress upon administrative capacity. For all the expressed desire to develop systems of government that embody the ethos of African society, little concession to the underdeveloped nature of the former reserves, or to traditionalism, is being made in the design of the new administrative departments. Their formal structure closely follows South African and, ultimately, British models. Even the same administrative titles are used. One consequence of this thoroughness is a limited change of personnel and style of decision making at higher levels; until there are many more trained Africans, the homelands will remain dependent for administrative assistance upon the Republic. To some extent the shortage of Africans deemed suited for posts in the governments is caused by the high standards South African white administrators impose on recruits and their reluctance to let loose the reins of administration. It is arguable, though difficult to prove, that more Africans are capable of assuming responsibilities in the homeland governments than are currently permitted to do so. The expansion of indigenous responsibility for, and control over, routine administration is thus more a goal for the future than a present reality. White officials will for some time provide much of the muscle required to translate locally accepted legislation into administrative action.

The dependence of Bophuthatswana upon officials lent by the Republic is shown in the homeland estimates of expenditure for the fiscal year 1975/76. In the Department of the Chief Minister and Finance, which includes the Treasury, the ranking administrative positions in a list of 153 are all held by whites. Of the 22 most senior officials in this department, defining these as principal clerks and above, 10 are whites, nearly all at upper levels of the hierarchy. In the Department of the Interior there are 388 employees, but Africanization has taken place only at the lower levels of the hierarchy; of 23 senior officials, 16 are from the Republic. Virtually all the chief clerks, principal clerks, and senior welfare officers are on loan from the Republic. In the Department of Works the same pattern persists. The senior administrative officials and the technical branches are heavily dependent upon white personnel — all the engineers, surveyors, chief foremen, and principal foremen being white. (There are virtually no trained blacks in these fields.) In the Department of Education, a far greater degree of Africanization has been achieved, but the secretary, chief clerk, and principal clerk are white. The Department of Agriculture follows the pattern of the Department of Works, with the technical posts as well as the higher ranks of the Field Services and the Nature Conservation and Veterinary services being dominated by whites. In the Department of Justice, the senior magistrates, magistrates, and the higher ranks of the administrative section are filled almost entirely by whites. As of late 1974, however, there were 5 Tswana magistrates, and 13 legally qualified Tswana in government service. Twenty-eight had been awarded scholarships and 3 were studying law at a university.

KwaZulu's administration is similar. According to the personnel estimates for fiscal 1975/76, of 91 appointments in the Department of Authority Affairs and Finance in 1974, 70 were held by blacks, all at the level of senior clerk or below, except for the chief executive councillor, the urban representative, and the chairman and vice-chairman of the assembly. Of 704 appointments in the Department of Community Affairs, 657 were held by blacks, including the executive councillor. All of the senior officials were white. Likewise, in the Department of Works, 982 of 1,075 employees were black, but whites held all of the senior administrative and technical positions. For example, of 110 works foremen, 58 were white, unchanged from the previous year. Of the 12 surveyors, 5 were white. In one technical division after another, the estimates show no change over the previous year. In the Department of Education and Culture, the 816 posts were filled predominantly by blacks (805 of the total), but the 6 senior officers of the 57 employed in the general administration of the department were white. The Department of Agriculture employed 3,266 officials, of whom 3,116 were black, but whites again dominated the professional levels. For example, of 29 agricultural officers, 23 were white, unchanged from the previous year. And in the Department of Justice the same pattern persisted: senior administrators, chief magistrates, principal magistrates, and senior magistrates were white; of 24 magistrates, 18 were white, unchanged from the previous year. Looking at Bophuthatswana and KwaZulu together, then, Africanization of the civil service has not yet been realized at the upper levels.[1]

This examination of the most recent estimates can be reinforced by examining those for the fiscal years 1973/74 and 1974/75 as well: table 4.1 gives the overall numbers of officials employed by departments and the number of white officials in each.

During these three years there have been major administrative reorganizations with significant changes in the size of some departments. For instance, the Department of Education in Bophuthatswana expanded from 602 to 5,910 employees, a change due to the transfer in fiscal 1974/75 of 5,279 teachers, presumably from the payroll of the Department of Bantu Education. The Department of Agriculture in KwaZulu expanded from 2,037 to 3,266 employees, due to a shift of Veterinary Services (456) and "Other Staff" (753) in fiscal 1974/75. There also were some reductions. The Department of the Interior in Bophuthatswana expanded by 30 between fiscal 1973/74 and fiscal 1974/75, but then contracted to the former figure of 388 due to the establishment of a Department of Health and Social Welfare. Frequently the expansion of departments has been due entirely to the expansion of administration rather than of services, as in the case of the Department of Works and the Department of Justice in Bophuthatswana

---

1. The three paragraphs above are based on Republic of South Africa, Bophuthatswana, *Estimate of the Expenditure to be defrayed from the Revenue Fund of Bophuthatswana during the year ending 31 March 1976*; Republic of South Africa, KwaZulu, *Estimate of the Expenditure to be defrayed from the Revenue Fund of the KwaZulu Government during the year ending 31 March 1976*. For information on Tswana in legal training see *SAN* 21 Nov., 1974. *SAN* ("South African Newspapers") is a summary of the press made within the South African Department of Information for departmental use.

Table 4.1
Numbers of Officials by Departments in Bophuthatswana and KwaZulu

	Bophuthatswana			KwaZulu		
	1973/74	1974/75	1975/76	1973/74	1974/75	1975/76
Authority Affairs	136 (14)[b]	146 (12)	168 (12)	69 (20)	71 (14)	91 (20)
Community Affairs (Interior in Bophuthatswana)	388 (20)	418 (33)	388[c] (20)	704 (37)	1050 (37)	704 (47)
Works	444 (74)	499 (69)	789 (52)	1789 (150)	1790 (152)	1790[e] (93)
Education	602 (6)	5888 (5)	5910 (5)	651 (13)	651 (9)	816 (11)
Agriculture	327 (72)	418 (46)	417 (47)	2037 (149)	3250 (138)	3266[f] (150)
Justice	148 (29)[b]	288 (50)	298 (46)	388 (64)	388 (64)	415 (64)
Health and Social Welfare	——[a]	—— ——	838 (17)	——[d]	—— ——	—— ——
TOTALS	2045 (215)	7657 (215)	8808 (199)	5707 (433)	7200 (414)	7082 (385)

SOURCES: Republic of South Africa, Bophuthatswana, *Estimate of the Expenditure to be defrayed from the Revenue Fund of Bophuthatswana during the year ending 31 March 1974* and for the years ending 31 March 1975, 31 March 1976; Republic of South Africa, KwaZulu, *Estimate of the Expenditure to be defrayed from the Revenue Fund of the KwaZulu Government during the year ending 31 March 1974* and for the years ending 31 March 1975, 31 March 1976.

NOTE: The number of officials from the Republic is given in parentheses. It is assumed that these officials are white.

[a]The Department of Health and Social Welfare was established in 1975.

[b]The figures given in the estimates for fiscal 1973/74 differ from those given in the estimates for fiscal 1974/75. The latter have been used here.

[c]Some functions were transferred to the new Department of Health and Social Welfare.

[d]KwaZulu does not yet have a department of health and social welfare.

[e]This figure is calculated by carrying over 715 positions listed "Other Staff" in the estimate for fiscal 1974/75, but not included in the estimates for fiscal 1975/76.

[f]This figure is calculated by carrying over 2,174 positions listed under "Other Staff" in the estimates for fiscal 1974/75 but not included in the estimates for fiscal 1975/76.

in fiscal 1974/75. Only in the case of KwaZulu's Veterinary Services in fiscal 1974/75, which employed 65 additional stock inspectors and 407 additional dip tank assistants, does it seem that there was a clearly identifiable expansion of services. The overall impression is one of a great deal of reshuffling of functions between the Republic and the homelands, and between departments within a homeland, combined with the reaching of a plateau in the rate of Africanization. This is particularly noticeable in technical services, where the numbers of veterinarians, surveyors, doctors, engineers, and magistrates in the relevant departments are repeated year by year with virtually no change in the ratios of black to white staff, particularly at upper levels.

South Africa is reputed to contain a reservoir of trained indigenous manpower larger than that of any of the recently independent African countries to the north. Within the overall South African system, however, the distribution of this manpower has been and will continue to be unequal. The governments of the homelands find it difficult to compete economically with opportunities in commerce and industry in the Republic, frequently losing valuable civil servants and teachers. In order to attract Tswana and Zulu home, "to reverse," as the KwaZulu minister of education explained, "the present brain drain to commerce and industry and to countries outside our borders," higher, more realistic salaries are necessary.[2] Moreover, the exercise of responsibility and administrative discretion may appear inhibited by the continued role of whites. In the homelands, as in South African life more generally, it remains virtually impossible to place Africans in positions of authority over whites. There have been exceptions, however. "History was made" in late 1973 when a Zulu was appointed acting principal magistrate for the Nqutu district in northern KwaZulu.[3]

Both homelands have universities designated for them—the University of the North for Bophuthatswana and the University of Zululand for KwaZulu. However these are still small universities offering a limited range of subjects. They are unable to supply the demand for technical people—engineers, doctors, accountants, and management personnel. The total number of African students at universities of all kinds in 1974 was only 7,845 (compared to 95,589 white students), of whom roughly half were enrolled at the University of South Africa, which provides correspondence courses only. For all of South Africa there were 221 African students enrolled in medical school and 21 Africans qualified as physicians at the

2. J. A. W. Nxumalo, speech on the budget, Republic of South Africa, KwaZulu, *Verbatim Report of the First Session of the First KwaZulu Legislative Assembly* (10 May 1974), 196 (hereafter cited as *KwaZulu Debates*); also quoted in *Natal Mercury,* 13 May 1973.

3. *Natal Mercury,* 10 Dec. 1973.

end of 1973. The University of Natal, which was responsible for the primary medical training of Africans, Asians, and coloureds, reported that a total of 188 Africans qualified from 1957 to 1973, an average of about 15 per year. The three universities in homelands—the University of the North, the University of Zululand, and the University of Fort Hare—together granted the following degrees in 1973: 32 postgraduate degrees (Ph.D.s, Masters and honors B.A.s); 263 bachelor degrees; and 70 postgraduate and 176 nongraduate diplomas. In 1957 there was a substantial increase in the upper categories: 54 postgraduate degrees; 354 bachelor degrees; but a decline in postgraduate diplomas (52); while nongraduate diplomas increased to 191.[4] In the ten years before 1973, the University of Zululand produced only 25 science graduates, and has had about 32 Zulu students in legal training each year.

In addition to the imposition by the Republic of high standards for employees of homeland governments, the shortage of Africans suitable for professional positions in Bophuthatswana and KwaZulu is largely attributable to the educational policies of the Republic since 1953. Training programs are now hard pressed to provide candidates capable of meeting many of these levels of achievement. For example, the homelands are being provided with new and complex accounting procedures very similar to those adopted by South Africa itself (see ch. 7). These procedures depend heavily on the services of trained accountants and budget and program analysts, few of whom will in the near future be Africans. Naturally, too, the thorough manner in which the new administrations are being organized by South Africa greatly increases the demand for technically trained functionaries. Thus, although permanent positions in the homelands are limited to local citizens, and whites are to be replaced as soon as possible by blacks (the posts they occupy being officially described as "vacant"), it will be some time before the senior (and controlling) administrative and professional employees in Bophuthatswana and KwaZulu will be Africans.

In relation to personnel generally there seems to be an absence of adequate on-the-job training for blacks and only limited adoption of schedules or procedures for replacing white officials by blacks. This reluctance may be due in part to the unwillingness of officials to devolve power to persons whose ideas, methods, and goals differ from their own. In many situations, prolongation rather than urgency has been the guiding principle. A commentator has argued, not altogether facetiously, that the training period of blacks is exactly equal to the time that must elapse before white equivalents retire. Some white officials expect to be employed for a long time, pointing to the Transkei where whites continued in 1974 to fill about 5

4. *Survey of Race Relations, 1974*, 369, and *ibid., 1975*, 260. For a further discussion of changes in medical education, see below, 120.

percent of the most significant slots in the administration.[5] In KwaZulu, housing has been constructed especially for whites of all ranks close to Ulundi, the future capital.

Given an attempt to maintain administrative standards, the prospects are poor for a smooth transition to an administration with a significant proportion of blacks at every level of homeland administration. Even the supply of black high school graduates is inadequate. There are major inadequacies in the educational structure and there seems to be no overall manpower plan that relates Africanization of the civil service, or even of its lower echelons, to the probable output of the educational system. Moreover, concessions in the employment arena in the Republic only compound problems associated with Africanizing the administrative service of the homelands. Equally, even in those instances in which the attractions of homeland service will prove powerful to a generation of secondary school graduates hitherto denied such opportunity, the governments of the homelands will soon need to compete for recruits with their own growth areas and border industries.

Discipline is another problem. KwaZulu has itself drawn attention to one aspect of this problem — inebriation in the civil service — by publicly dismissing in 1974 six civil servants in the Department of Justice. "The use of hard drink during working hours," reported the councillor for justice, "had reached such a critical level that . . . in one day no less than four Zulu officials at a certain magistrate's office were so heavily under the influence that they were unable to perform their duties." He promised no mercy for officials who "lower the dignity of the Government service by the abuse of liquor."[6]

The administration of Bophuthatswana and KwaZulu is further hindered by the fragmentary and dispersed character of the two homelands and their populations, by the waste involved in servicing and administering noncontiguous fragments of territory, by a sheer shortage of physical facilities and hardware, and, above all, by the consequent need to rely upon the government of the Republic for administrative assistance. Before 1976, Bophuthatswana was better placed than KwaZulu in terms of office space, having been given the buildings of the old Imperial Reserve outside Mafeking from which the Bechuanaland Protectorate was administered until it became Botswana. Mafeking is a white area, however, and a new capital, at first planned at Heystekrand near Rustenburg, is now to be built at Ramitsogo in the Zeerust district. KwaZulu's poverty of office space is indicative of its overall handicap. Ulundi, the future seat of government, was first occupied in 1976. Until then Nongoma was the seat of the legislature, the paramount chief, and the commissioner-general. Chief Buthelezi, the chief executive councillor, lived

5. Jean Le May, "The Homelands in Doldrums," *The Star,* 29 April 1974; *Natal Mercury,* 31 Jan. 1974.

6. Walter Kanye, quoted in *The Star,* 16 May 1974.

at Mahlabatini, thirty miles away over an unpaved road. (When the central government refused to build Buthelezi an office in Mahlabatini, he obtained funds for such a structure from the Evangelical Lutheran Church of West Germany. When several Swiss churches offered to provide him with a Swiss secretary, however, the central government refused her a residence permit. Again in 1976 the government refused to issue a visa for an official from the Oxford Committee for Famine Relief who was to have directed a development project in KwaZulu.[7])

Sixty-six percent of the Tswana and 49 percent of the Zulu live elsewhere at any time, most of them permanently in the white areas. They are thus administered, in many respects on behalf of the governments of the homelands, by South Africa. This is true with respect to the collection of taxes—the so-called quota revenue and any future additional homeland levies—in the urban areas, the administration of education, and the preparation and actual running of elections. Hence Bophuthatswana and KwaZulu must involve South Africa in the voting arrangements for their absent electors. The government of the Republic provides the machinery for voting at magistrates' courts and Bantu commissioners' offices throughout the Republic. In the case of all of the homelands, South African machinery and computers process citizenship documents on which, in the case of KwaZulu, the registration for the homeland's first election will depend. In these and in numerous other major and minor administrative respects, the governments of South Africa and the homelands are still intertwined. Their relationship is bound to remain unequal until the homelands develop financial resources of their own and considerably greater autonomy in policy making than they now possess.

Elections and Parties

Since the passage of the Transkei Constitution Act of 1963, separate development has politicized systems that previously had been administrative entities only. According to British models of representation, the Republic created a legislative apparatus, latterly with a minority of elected members, for the homelands. Elections have also been presumed necessary, although of our two case studies only the voters of Bophuthatswana have gone to the polls. That process precipitated the development of organized political activity within the homeland. Previously, from the establishment of the reconstituted Tswana Territorial Authority in 1968, the Tswana had been governed in several areas by twelve regional authorities, each of which had sent several

7. *Daily News* (Durban), 9 Jan. 1976. Facilities for administration were hardly ideal. Two departments, Authority Affairs and Finance, and Justice, were at Nongoma, the other four in Pietermaritzburg, 150 miles away. Meetings of the Executive Council, at times weekly, required long journeys.

from among their own number to sit on the Territorial Authority. Of the fifty-eight members, twenty-nine were chiefs, seven headmen, and twenty-two councillors.[8] (The members of the regional authorities were themselves appointed by the heads of tribal and community authorities in consultation with the minister of Bantu administration and development.) The Territorial Authority heavily overrepresented rural areas and underrepresented the large urban concentrations. This was a natural result of methods that tied representation to traditional institutions (which rarely link offices and population) predating urban growth. Even so, however much of the representational arrangements of the old authority discriminated against urban dwellers, the new authority exaggerated that imbalance more. It provided equal representation for twelve electoral districts that ranged in population from 22,823 to 225,769.[9] In 1972, each electoral district sent two elected representatives to the new Legislative Assembly, in addition to the members designated by each regional authority. This action, combined with the fact that the designated members were almost entirely from rural areas, gave city dwellers few representatives.

Although elections in the Transkei had necessitated the painstaking enrollment of voters in both the Transkei proper and in the white areas of the Republic, Bophuthatswana chose to avoid the complications and expense that would have been entailed in enumerating voters especially for the 1972 election. It decided to accept reference books as sufficient for the prior identification of voters. All Tswana who desired to cast ballots were asked to register before election day by the simple expedient of having their reference books stamped. At that time they chose a polling station and, with some limitation, a constituency. (Because vast numbers of Tswana live outside the homeland and have always done so, they had to choose constituencies without ever having resided therein, or even in Bophuthatswana.) Since the reference book has been the main administrative method of enforcing influx control laws and tax obligations, potential voters had to be reassured by South African officials (who wanted a high turnout) that persons "without homes as well as those not in registered employment"—serious offenses under the regulations—could nevertheless register. The chief electoral officer even stated that Tswana living illegally in Soweto would not be "endorsed out" of the urban area and returned to (possibly) fictitious home areas if they cast ballots.[10] Nevertheless, there was substantial confusion and anxiety, and the urban Tswana vote proved to be much smaller than hoped for or anticipated by the government.

8. *Survey of Race Relations, 1968,* 146–147.
9. W. J. Breytenbach, "Election in Bophuthatswana," *Bulletin of the Africa Institute of South Africa,* X (1972), 387–388.
10. *The Star,* 22, 29 Aug. 1972.

This limited turnout of urban Tswana greatly favored the list of candidates headed by Chief Lucas Mangope. In 1968, in a secret ballot of thirty-three to nineteen, the reconstituted Tswana Territorial Authority had chosen Mangope, a Hurutshe, to be its first chief councillor. His main opponent, Chief Tidimane Pilane, a Kgatla, had chaired the Tswana Territorial Authority from its inception in 1961. But in 1967, he and Mangope, then vice-chairman, sharply differed over the issue of self-determination, Pilane having begun to urge faster constitutional change and the establishment of a united black multihomeland state.

These sharply held ideological and temperamental differences led to the formation of separate slates of candidates, or "parties," to contest the 1972 election. In late July, Pilane announced the formation of his Seoposengwe (Unity) Party. Mangope countered in August with the Bophuthatswana National Party. Both issued manifestos and constitutions, the Seoposengwe Party needing (the election was scheduled for October) quickly to provide itself with an image distinct from that of the Bophuthatswana National Party. Thus, the leaders of the Seoposengwe Party associated themselves with Buthelezi's attempts to "force the Government to match theory with practice."[11] The party's manifesto accepted separate development *"only* for the implied promises of handing us both our homeland Forefathers' land and particularly for the promise of granting Bophuthatswana its ultimate Sovereign Independence." It proposed to "give top priority in our sense of values as well as first consideration in our programme of development" to equality of opportunity for all Tswana and other homeland residents. It asserted that governments must be elected by "the people." More concretely, the party argued against Mangope's proposed Tswana university and for more attention to adult literacy and free and compulsory education. On economic development, the Seoposengwe Party asked for consultation and a "final say" over mineral exploitation within the homeland and the siting of industrial growth points. Politically, the Seoposengwe Party declared itself a Tswana organization dedicated to uniting all Tswana and at the same time cooperating and associating with other homelands. Pilane specifically called for black unity, complete and integrated consolidation of land, and the total independence of his homeland.[12]

The Bopthuthatswana National Party reaffirmed its acceptance of the *positive* aspects of separate development only. Its platform included a long set of detailed economic proposals and several nationalistic assertions, e.g., that only citizens should qualify for trading rights in the homeland. It demanded to receive all taxes paid by mining companies to the Republic

11. *Ibid.*, 29 July 1972.
12. Seoposengwe Party Manifesto and Constitution, July 1973; *Pretoria News,* 29 Aug. 1972.

for ores won from the soil of Bophuthatswana. But the most important difference between the two parties was their attitude to traditional leadership and ethnicity. Mangope strongly defends the continued involvement of chiefs in political life. "We have been severely criticized," he said, "for the large number of designated members [in the assembly], but we believe we must lead our people from what they know to what they do not know—for the concept of a general election is unknown in our traditional administration."[13] Mangope was responsible for the inclusion of a stipulation in the Bophuthatswana constitution that permits only chiefs to become chief ministers. Pilane has argued just as strongly for a wholly elected assembly in which commoners would play a decisive role.[14] Pilane also favors the incorporation into Bophuthatswana of other African groups (the Ndebele and the Xhosa among others) who are already settled or who may be enticed to settle within the homeland. Mangope, however, is an ethnic nationalist who stresses the rights of Tswana citizens, and he seems to imply that he would like only Tswana to be citizens of Bophuthatswana. For this and other reasons he has been hesitant until very recently to advocate a black superstate or a federation of homelands (see our discussion of Federalism in ch. 5).

Both parties campaigned vigorously, Mangope and his followers within the homeland more than in the cities, from July to October 1972. Only eight of the twelve double-member constituencies were contested, Mangope's party winning the eight seats in the remaining four districts. Thirty-nine candidates stood for the contested sixteen seats, seventeen of whom lost their deposits. Mangope's followers won twelve seats and Pilane's only four. But the Seoposengwe Party candidates obtained 101,800 votes, the winners 268,000, roughly 25,000 and 20,000 votes per seat respectively. (The remaining forty-eight seats were filled by nominees.) Both Mangope and Pilane won sizeable support in their home districts and Pilane seems to have attracted a significant proportion of the urban vote. However, city dwellers hardly cast ballots: whereas 45 percent of the voters in the rural districts went to the polls, only 15 percent of the black voters in Pretoria cast their ballots. Of the 50,000 registered black voters in urban areas, only 4,661 actually went to the polls. Overall, about 400,000 of a possible 800,000 voters cast ballots. Thus, the election demonstrated that Tswana who lived in or near cities were apt to disdain the whole process of separate development and/or to fear for their uncertain status if they actually voted. Taking time off to go to the polls might also have deprived them of earnings. Rural dwellers, more secure and also more attuned to the policies and role of the Territorial Authority, readily cast or were persuaded to cast ballots.

13. Quoted in the *Mafeking Mail*, 26 Jan. 1973.
14. See *Survey of Race Relations*, 1972, 39.

The electoral process must have helped to politicize many Tswana, who saw African leaders vying for support for the first time since the clashes between the African National Congress and the Pan-Africanist Congress in the late 1950s. The addition of elected members probably made Mangope's control of the government of Bophuthatswana more secure and, in the eyes of some urban Africans, more legitimate. At the same time, although both parties were new and their personnel therefore inexperienced, an organized opposition had been created that could enliven debates about the use of legislative and executive power in the homeland. The election was followed, however, not by increasing rancor between these two parties, but by a growing dispute within the ruling Bophuthatswana National Party.

The conflict centered around disputes between the two personalities who dominated the cabinet—Mangope and Chief Herman Maseloane, minister of the interior. For a time relations between the two men had been close and, from their public statements, there was little major disagreement between them. Both talked in moderate tones of the government of the Republic. Both at times attacked "terrorists" and both expressed strong nationalistic feelings. When Mangope went overseas in May 1973, Maseloane acted for him, but, after Mangope returned, signs of conflict became apparent.

Mangope apparently felt that Maseloane had attempted to undermine his authority in discussions with the central government and by machinations within the ruling Bophuthatswana National Party. Mangope moved first, in February 1974, against S. Mogotsi, the party's organizing secretary. He ousted Mogotsi, this unilateral action being approved by vote of party executives of 112 to 86. Yet members of the Executive Council criticized Mangope's leadership and also voted favorably on a motion of confidence in Maseloane.[15] In March, when the homeland assembly met, members attacked Mangope for moving against Maseloane. He was also accused of controlling the Bophuthatswana Development Fund by claiming the power to appoint all its trustees for life. By this time Chief James Bogosing Toto, the minister of agriculture, had publicly supported Maseloane and the majority party in the assembly was decisively split. Through the commissioner-general, Mangope asked the president of the Republic to remove Maseloane from the homeland cabinet and, during a hastily called week-long recess of the assembly, the commissioner-general strenuously attempted to reconcile the opponents. Finally, however, Mangope consolidated his position and, by a vote of 60 to 7, the assembly demonstrated its confidence in Mangope's leadership.[16] However, the two ministers remained in the cabinet

15. *Hoofstad* (Pretoria), 18 February 1974; *The Star*, 19 February 1974; *Mafeking Mail*, 22 February 1974. All translations from the Afrikaans press are by Jeffrey Butler.
16. *Pretoria News*, 8 April 1974; *Mafeking Mail*, 19 April 1974.

and at first Mangope was able to expel only V. A. Maqondoze, the chairman of the assembly, from his membership of the executive committee of the party. Maseloane and Toto successfully appealed to the courts for injunctions. For a time Mangope unwillingly accepted this anomalous position but late in the year he abandoned the Bophuthatswana National Party and took his loyal ministers and legislators into the newly organized Bophuthatswana Democratic Party.[17]

Mangope was thus initially forced to live with unresolved conflicts that stemmed from a peculiar provision of the Bophuthatswana constitution. Chief ministers could not demand the resignation of ministers. Nor apparently could they resign themselves and reconstitute an entire cabinet. Instead, the chief minister was forced to await the pleasure of the constitutional monarch—the state president—or, practically speaking, the minister of Bantu administration and development. When the central government refused to oust a dissident, or simply wished to temporize, a homeland government would have its decision-making capacity severely reduced by having to retain a cabinet of political incompatibles. In April 1975 this situation was finally resolved in Mangope's favor. By Proclamation 84/1975 the chief minister received a plenary power of dismissal: "The Chief Minister may, for reasons which he may deem sound and cogent, . . . remove any other Minister from office." Maseloane and Toto were expelled four days later.[18]

KwaZulu has not yet held elections. They have been delayed because Chief Buthelezi and the Legislative Assembly have refused to permit reference books —"symbols of oppression"—to be used as identifying documents for voters. Thus the usual progression to stage two of autonomy, uninterrupted and rapid in the other homelands, has been slowed dramatically here. At the second stage a homeland becomes partially self-governing and is permitted to amend certain kinds of South African legislation for implementation within the homeland area or as it affects its citizens wherever they may be in South Africa. (Security, defense, trade, and foreign relations are excluded.) Buthelezi has scorned the advantages of stage two, calling them "mere trappings," but in 1974 the KwaZulu Legislative Assembly showed that it was not prepared to wait.[19] By unanimous vote it called for an election even if citizenship certificates had not been obtained by all Zulu. The assembly wanted to end what some of its members called an "exercise in frustration." Apparently contrary to Buthelezi's wishes, the assembly proposed to request the government of the Republic to move KwaZulu to stage

17. *Mafeking Mail*, 7 June 1974; *Star Weekly*, 10 November 1974.
18. *Survey of Race Relations, 1975*, 135.
19. Quoted in *Natal Mercury*, 17 May 1974.

two without elections. Nearly all of the other homelands had achieved stage two and tiny Basotho Qwa Qwa had done so prior to a poll. But the Department of Bantu Administration and Development continued to insist on an election.[20]

In 1975, however, Buthelezi claimed that he had twice suggested to the assembly that reference books be used for electoral registration but had been turned down. In addition, perhaps with tongue in cheek, he suggested that there were practical difficulties: because KwaZulu was "such an unconsolidated Dalmatian-skin type of thing," it had not been possible to demarcate electoral divisions. In what one newspaper regarded as a "surprise change of policy," Buthelezi announced that he would seek an amendment to the constitution in May 1976 to permit the use of reference books for the registration of voters. He anticipated an election before the end of the year.[21]

Lack of elections has not delayed the development of vigorous politics in KwaZulu. The divisions are complex and not easily subsumed under the labels "traditional or modern," "capitalist or socialist," or "urban or rural." Major differences have arisen over how to and who should respond to official policy initiatives, whether any progress is possible by cooperating with the authorities, and what role traditional groups, particularly the Ingonyama and those around him, should play. These conflicts have been immensely complicated because of the central government's unwillingness to remain aloof, making no secret of its hope that traditional institutions and leaders would begin to play more than decorative and symbolic roles. In 1968, when Ingonyama Cyprian ka Solomon died, Prince Goodwill Zwelithini, the heir apparent, was only eighteen years-old; Prince Israel became regent on the assumption that he would exercise authority until Prince Goodwill turned twenty-five. However, in 1971, shortly after Buthelezi had begun to lead the Zulu politically, Goodwill insisted upon assuming the paramountcy. The government of the Republic had previously met with Goodwill and, pursuing its open support of traditionalism in the homelands, had presumably encouraged him to provide a countervailing influence. At Goodwill's installation the minister of Bantu administration and development, M. C. Botha, spoke of the dangers of undermining the status and position of the Ingonyama. "No member of your government," the minister said, "should consider his own position to be more important and more exalted than that of the Paramount Chief."[22] Buthelezi promptly called the minister presumptuous and patronizing, and ever since has railed at each South African intervention in Zulu affairs.

20. *Rand Daily Mail*, 9 May 1974; *Comment and Opinion* (Pretoria), 29 Nov. 1974.
21. *Sunday Times* (Johannesburg), 6 July 1975, quoted in *Survey of Race Relations, 1975*, 131; *Star Weekly*, 14 Feb. 1976.
22. M. C. Botha, quoted in *The Star*, 3 Dec. 1971; *Sunday Times* 5 Dec. 1971.

Buthelezi's impressive combination of traditional and modern claims to legitimacy, and his own political skills, enabled him to outwit the maneuverings of the traditionalists and their backers throughout 1972 and 1973. Indeed, at the end of 1973 Goodwill acknowledged Buthelezi's success by driving in a convoy of Zulu dignitaries to the Durban airport in order publicly to greet Buthelezi upon the chief's return from meetings in Ethiopia. In 1974 Goodwill went farther. "I give full support to my Government, led by Chief Buthelezi," he said. "I am just not prepared to become involved in politics."[23]

But the issue has remained alive, leading to another confrontation between Buthelezi and Goodwill and renewed accusations of the involvement of whites in Zulu politics. Buthelezi responded by laying a complaint with the police under the Prohibition of Political Interference Act of 1968. Once more the issue was resolved for the time being: in January 1976, before the Legislative Assembly, Goodwill signed a categorical undertaking to "withhold myself from any participation in any form of politics and from any action or words which could possibly be interpreted as participation in politics."[24]

Organized opposition to Buthelezi in the modern sector, but backed by traditionalists, surfaced in 1972 when a group of city dwellers formed the Zulu National Party. Led by Lloyd Ndaba, sometime editor of *Africa South,* a newspaper that had attacked Buthelezi and may have been supported by the central government, the party counted among its backers Prince Israel, Prince Patrick, Prince Clement, E. B. Tshabalala, a Soweto tycoon, and A. W. G. Champion, the Zulu political leader from the days of the Industrial and Commercial Workers Union in the 1920s. The party fought an Urban Council election in Umlazi, but lost badly.

Umkhonto ka Shaka (Shaka's Spear), a second opposition party, was organized in late 1973 to oppose Buthelezi. In favor of separate development and against Buthelezi's notion of African solidarity, claiming "Zulus would be swamped," Umkhonto was led by Prince David Zulu, Chief Charles Hlengwa, Abel Mhlongo, Lloyd Ndaba, and a few others associated with the discredited National Party. They all met on several occasions with a member of the Republic's Bureau of State Security and, by early 1974, it was assumed that Umkhonto was backed financially by the bureau. Goodwill disowned Umkhonto and, at its 1974 sitting, the legislature censured Chief Hlengwa, the speaker, so severely that he withdrew a motion of censure and left the assembly in disgrace. Later he lost his position as chairman of the Umbumbulu Regional Authority, an action caused by the resignation of twenty-five of its twenty-six members. As a result Hlengwa immediately lost his seat in the assembly.[25]

23. *Natal Mercury,* 25 May 1974.
24. Copy made available by Thomas Karis; *Star Weekly,* 20 Dec. 1975.
25. For details, see *Natal Mercury,* 1,3,7,13 May and 12,19 June 1974; *The Star,* 21 April and 7 May 1974.

Two other parties were formed after the demise of Umkhonto. Uvulamehlo Izimtuphuthe, of Clermont, a retired separatist church leader, organized the Zulu Labour Party, with a sparse membership. He pledged his support to Buthelezi, however, and — paradoxically — was against the participation of chiefs in politics. Champion, A. E. Buthelezi of Dassenhoek, and Lawrence and Paulos Nxele were reputed to be the founders of another party, the Voice of the People, which was announced in 1974. It was opposed to any ban on political parties.

Buthelezi's hand has been strengthened by these comparatively inept attempts to compete with him openly. He has often spoken of the inappropriateness of organized opposition within the KwaZulu political system, arguing that traditional politics were consensus politics and in particular that the Zulu should remain loyal to their past. The assembly agreed to this proposition in 1974, passing a motion to ask the minister of Bantu administration and development to empower KwaZulu to control or forbid parties prior to independence.[26] In May 1975, the minister stated in Parliament that the KwaZulu government had in fact requested the cooperation of the South African government in prohibiting political parties among the Zulu people. He said that "the formation of political parties . . . and . . . the activities of such parties . . . are natural corollaries of democracy. . . . The holding of free elections, of which the Chief Executive Councillor has often spoken, is hardly reconcilable with the banning or control of political parties in general."[27] This sparring did not prevent Zulu politicians from attempting to minimize their own political factionalism. In mid-May details were issued of the founding of Inkatha YakwaZulu, "a national cultural liberation movement," open to all Zulu, whose president would also be chief minister of KwaZulu. Only members of the organization would be eligible to stand for election to the Legislative Assembly. After some negotiations over the powers of the central committee in relation to the assembly, the constitution of Inkatha YakwaZulu (subsequently called Inkatha YeSizwe) was accepted by the assembly.

If elections are held in KwaZulu in 1976, as promised, and the organization is functioning vigorously, it may be extremely difficult, if not impossible, for opposition parties to run candidates at all. However, in view of the refusal of the South African government to agree to a ban on opposition parties, the claim to a monopoly of candidacies will not have the force of law, and opposition groups may be able to contest elections. Consequently, the experience of Bophuthatswana may be repeated, and in order to mobilize voters behind an official slate Buthelezi may use Inkatha YeSizwe for electoral

26. For Buthelezi, see *The Star*, 28 July 1971. For the Legislative Assembly, see *Rand Daily Mail*, 8, 18 May 1974.
27. *House of Assembly Debates*, 2 May 1975, col. 5361.

purposes, thereby institutionalizing his appeal to the Zulu masses and raising the stature of little known candidates. It has been suggested, however, that Buthelezi sees Inkatha ultimately as an African, not merely a Zulu, organization. He may envisage it as a possible successor to the banned African National Congress.[28] The organization may, therefore, function in two ways: as a means of mobilizing Zulu votes within KwaZulu politics and at the same time of contributing to the black nationalist cause.

Buthelezi's only serious opposition within KwaZulu could come from a politician as articulate and militant as himself. Barney Irving Dladla, KwaZulu's first councillor for community affairs, began openly challenging Buthelezi's leadership in early 1974. A former teacher and businessman from Estcourt and a sometime member of the African National Congress, he helped to found the Pan-Africanist Congress. Now fifty-one years-old, Dladla became prominent during the industrial strikes in Durban and Richards Bay in early 1973. At that time Zulu workers looked to him for support and guidance. Always articulate, he became their spokesman. During the textile strikes in Durban at the beginning of 1974, Dladla was again prominent. He negotiated on the strikers' behalf without consulting or waiting to receive instructions from Buthelezi's cabinet. As a result, Buthelezi transferred responsibility for Zulu labor affairs to Solomon Ngobese, KwaZulu's official urban representative (see below), and furthermore suggested that his government should remain officially aloof from labor disputes in the white areas of the country.

The growing rift between Buthelezi and Dladla became public during the 1974 sitting of the assembly. Buthelezi demanded a pledge of unequivocal support from each of the members of his cabinet and chastized Dladla for daring to criticize his decisions. At an afternoon sitting Buthelezi repeated his request for a pledge of allegiance and members of the cabinet arose one by one to express their confidence in Buthelezi's leadership. Dladla sat still, staring into the distance. Later Dladla counterattacked, complaining of persecution. (Under the KwaZulu constitution, executive councillors can be dismissed only by a resolution of the Assembly on the recommendation of the chief executive councillor.)

Clearly there was an intense rivalry. Both Buthelezi and Dladla are strong personalities and they have disagreed on a number of policy matters. Dladla had long differed with Buthelezi and others over the kinds of developmental tactics to be followed in the homeland. On many occasions Dladla had apparently taken decisions regarding development without the consent of the cabinet. With regard to labor recruitment within the homeland, Dladla wanted to charge employers per contracted worker, a form of tax on labor hitherto unknown within South Africa. In Addis Ababa in 1973 Dladla had

28. *The Times,* 14 March 1976.

objected to the way in which Buthelezi presented KwaZulu's stand on separate development to a conference of Americans and Africans. Free enterprise-oriented, Dladla has espoused large-scale industrial development. Buthelezi, on the other hand, has favored smaller scale operations. Because he differed from Buthelezi over the kinds of developmental tactics to be followed in the homeland, Dladla had long criticized the efficiency and motives of the Bantu Investment Corporation, a body with which Buthelezi has continued to work, though not without friction. Dladla opposed the corporation's monopoly of certain business areas. Most of all, Dladla had angered his colleagues by initially taking decisions regarding homeland growth and urban strikes. "When there is a fire one must act quickly to extinguish it," Dladla replied in extenuation.[29]

At mid-year, after the controversy between Buthelezi and Dladla had intermittently boiled and simmered, reconciliations being followed by fresh recriminations, Buthelezi transferred Dladla from the councillorship of the Department of Community Affairs to a similar position as head of the Department of Justice. The cabinet censured Dladla for talking out of turn. Then Dladla resigned from the cabinet, only to retract that resignation a few days later. He promised to continue to disagree with his colleagues, accused Buthelezi of dictatorship, claimed that Buthelezi was against the formation of black trade unions (because they frightened foreign investors), and implied that Buthelezi was corruptly benefiting from the construction of a house.[30] Although he had finally signed the pledge of loyalty to Buthelezi, their differences were as intense as ever. Eventually, in late August 1974 the assembly removed Dladla from the KwaZulu cabinet by a vote of seventy-eight to zero.[31] But such bitter disagreements cannot be buried in homeland politics. When KwaZulu holds elections Dladla and his mostly urban backers will doubtless provide opposition for Buthelezi.

The Legislatures

Insofar as their mandates permit, legislative assemblies make the law for Bophuthatswana and KwaZulu. The narrowness of their scope is obvious from an examination of their debates, especially on the estimates (or budget); although in time the assemblies may mature institutionally, at present they tend to ratify legislation without extensive informed discussion. Both also meet only twice a year for sittings of short duration (once in regular session,

29. Quoted in *Natal Mercury*, 22 May 1974. For the controversy, see *ibid.*, 14, 15, 21 May and 13, 17, 22, 25 June 1974.
30. *Ibid.*, 29 June 1974.
31. *Rand Daily Mail*, 29 Aug. 1974.

usually a second time in special session). In format and procedure they are Western, with sergeants-at-arms, maces, and chairmen and vice-chairmen. The government and the opposition parties face each other on parallel benches, in Bophuthatswana meeting in the Montshiwa township community hall near Mafeking, in KwaZulu sitting until 1976 in a school hall in Nongoma. The proceedings are extremely formal, the members arriving dressed as for the stiffest state occasion.

When the elected Bophuthatswana Legislative Assembly met for the first time in late October 1972, its members chose Chief Mangope as chief minister by a vote of sixty to eight (for Pilane), with both the government and the opposition obtaining support from the nominated representatives. On the second day of the sitting the Bophuthatswana Flag Bill passed laboriously through the various parliamentary stages: second reading, committee, and then the third reading. Everything had painstakingly to be translated from the speaker's tongue into one of the other two of the assembly's three official languages (Tswana, English, and Afrikaans). There was hardly any discussion except for a short, irrelevant speech at the committee stage. The Payment and Privileges of Members Bill followed. During the committee stage, the minister of the interior attempted successfully to amend the bill in order to deny remuneration to the chief whip and assistant whip of the opposition if the numbers in opposition fell below half of the majority. Members of the Seoposengwe Party curiously failed to react. The first session continued in this desultory vein for five days, the proceedings being covered in fifty-one pages of the assembly's published debates.

Taken together, they, and the proceedings of subsequent sessions, demonstrate the natural inexperience of the Tswana legislators. The presiding officers were nervous and several of the ministers read speeches written out in full by their white departmental secretaries. The level of debate was correspondingly low. There was some skirmishing on points of procedure and, during the presentation of the estimates, specific complaints (in particular about the hiring of white officials). It is hardly surprising that one reporter noted that there was much "fidgeting" among members and frequent appeals for attention.[32]

In the 1973 session there was, however, a spirited debate on a motion of no-confidence. It was moved by Chief Pilane, leader of the opposition of eight members, but he carried the debate largely on his own. In 1974, when the disunity of Mangope's Bophuthatswana National Party became explicit and public, Mangope found himself under attack by some of his own followers, as well as the official opposition. The discussion degenerated into a slanging match.

32. *The Star,* 2 Nov. 1972.

The KwaZulu Legislative Assembly functioned at first in a matter-of-fact manner. Because of the need for frequent translations (many of the traditional members understand only Zulu), the proceedings were extremely time-consuming. They were usually dignified and formalized and, until the disputes between Buthelezi and Dladla, there was little real debate. Indeed, motions were piled on motions in a bewildering sequence. However, Buthelezi rarely missed a parliamentary opportunity (especially with the press in attendance) to make known his disdain for white "guidance." He dominated the whole, having demonstrated his abilities in 1972 by guiding the long and detailed KwaZulu draft constitution through the assembly. Then his recommendations and amendments, even those seriously limiting the role of the Ingonyama, were approved without arousing traditional opposition. Conflict within the traditional elite of Zululand has yet to achieve its fullest expression in parliamentary maneuvering or debates.

The major, and unavoidable annual task of British style legislatures, is the consideration of the estimates and the appropriation of revenue. Although ch. 6 contains a lengthy review of budgets, and of expenditures and sources of revenue (with tables), it is important here, in order to understand the relevant policy constraints, to anticipate that discussion in outline.

The budgets of both homelands have demonstrated a steady but unspectacular growth in homeland activity. In both areas expenditures approximately doubled in the three years prior to 1975, with a slightly greater relative increase in KwaZulu, an increasing rate of growth in Bophuthatswana, and a constantly high rate of growth in KwaZulu. The proportion of revenue spent in each department shows differences between one homeland and another, but within each homeland considerable stability over the three years.

Until the fiscal year 1974/75, the homelands obtained revenue from taxes, fees, and licenses directly under their control and sums voted by the Parliament of the Republic.[33] The amounts from the first source have risen substantially since 1972, but funds from the Republic have increased far more. In addition, budgetary shortfalls were made good by large sums voted by Parliament. In the 1974 budget, additional grants to homelands went up by 50 percent, the largest single increase being R20 million to KwaZulu. The homelands, therefore, received roughly half of their total revenues from an appropriation debated every year in the all-white Parliament. As expenditures on Africans can be a sensitive matter in South Africa, both Bophuthatswana and KwaZulu have been dependent upon the Republic's government, the goodwill of which reflects the forces of white politics. That dependence is likely to continue because the government firmly resisted suggestions in Parliament in 1975 that homeland governments be consulted over the

33. At the end of 1974 Vorster announced changes in homeland financing. See 143–144 below.

amounts to be paid to them. A deputy minister replied that such a change would amount to giving homeland governments a say in the affairs of the Republic.[34]

Bophuthatswana presented its first budget as a self-governing entity early in 1973. A. J. Raubenheimer, then the deputy minister of Bantu administration and development, opened the session with an attempt to allay disappointment over the size of the Republic's contribution to the budget. "Money is not the only requirement for the development of a country," he said. "It also requires the devotion and zeal of its people."[35] When Mangope introduced the estimates, the import of Raubenheimer's statement was evident: instead of the R29 million requested by Mangope, expenditures were set at R18 million, 30 percent of which would be derived from revenues collected and controlled by the homeland.

Mangope had originally planned a considerable increase in his government's responsibilities. "Unfortunately," he told the legislators, "I have to report that we have very little funds available for capital and other development." It has become "impossible to do much extension of capital works like the erection of buildings in townships, schools, roads, and other development works."[36] Mangope complained vehemently about the failure of the Department of Bantu Administration and Development to provide more than a token increase in resources although the Republic derived substantial returns from platinum and other minerals mined in Bophuthatswana — for which the homeland received nothing. When Vorster suggested changes in the basis of taxation of mines in the homelands, Mangope welcomed the change: "The question of revenue from the mines has long been a sore point with us." Furthermore, because of the way in which whites serving in the homeland were paid from quota revenues, "more money," said Mangope, "went out of the homeland coffers to pay whites who generally earned more than Africans."[37]

Faced with a serious shortfall, Mangope's predicament exemplified the problems that self-government has created for African leaders: it removes whites as targets and places unpleasant administrative tasks in black hands. In the budget debate of 1973 and after, Mangope and his colleagues appealed to their people to pay their taxes on time: Maseloane warned Tswana that failure to pay taxes was "a crime." To tide Bophuthatswana over temporarily, the assembly authorized the government to borrow R1.5 million from the

34. Republic of South Africa, *House of Assembly Debates* (10 Feb. 1975), cols. 468, 533.

35. Republic of South Africa, Bophuthatswana, *Debates of the Bophuthatswana Legislative Assembly*, 13 March 1973, 26. (Hereafter cited as *Bophuthatswana Debates*).

36. *Mafeking Mail*, 23 March 1973.

37. *Rand Daily Mail*, 20 March 1973.

Republic to alleviate the shortage of teachers.[38] But additional taxation could not be avoided. In 1974 the assembly decided to levy R2.5 on Tswana citizens wherever they resided, the tax to be collected by receivers of revenue in the Republic and by other homeland governments.[39] The tax by itself will do little to diminish the interdependence of all the homelands and South Africa, nor will it provide a substantial source of revenue. Bophuthatswana is, therefore, still limited in its freedom to initiate new programs.

A study of the KwaZulu assembly's budgetary sitting in 1973 only reinforces the limitations placed on homeland initiatives. When introducing his budget Buthelezi said that he had been forced to trim his estimates when he finally heard what the size of the parliamentary grant was going to be. As this is the only portion of the budget that varies appreciably, its size determines how enterprising and ambitious homeland governments can be. Buthelezi made clear the limits on his freedom to initiate. "The stage where we are is such that all programs of development are dictated to us by the Central Government." KwaZulu controlled only 23 percent of its total revenue, and therefore Buthelezi was going to impose a new tax of R3 on Zulu men over eighteen years of age. But he estimated that it would raise only R1.75 million, 2 percent of total revenue, in the fiscal year 1974/75.[40] A year later he seemed to have trimmed that estimate, saying he expected to collect R1.0 million in the first year. He hoped that the amount would rise to R1.5 million and then to R2.0 million.[41]

Buthelezi's resources entirely under his own command thus remain limited. And the spectacular rises in the estimates are misleading if they are taken as indices of development. As in the case of Bophuthatswana, teacher salaries were raised by 17 percent, a rise that absorbed more than half the increase in the educational budget. Furthermore, the high rate of inflation, and the attempt by KwaZulu to narrow the gap between white and black wage rates, leave little room for real growth in services.

At this stage the legislatures of the homelands exist primarily to approve decisions made by the Republic and, to a lesser degree, by their own leaders. The scope of legislation passed is narrow, sometimes dealing with the symbols of public life. Members are not yet used to holding their leaders responsible for acts of state by the use of such devices as parliamentary questions, although the use of motions of no-confidence is growing. In more experienced and autonomous parliaments, discussions of legislative proposals are often detailed and technical, especially during the committee stage. In Bophuthatswana and KwaZulu discussions have been brief and perfunctory, partly

38. For Maseloane and the loan, see *Mafeking Mail,* 25 May 1973.
39. *Ibid.,* 26 April 1974.
40. *KwaZulu Debates* (1973), 109.
41. *Star Weekly,* 2 March 1974.

because the procedure is new to most members, partly because the membership played no part in formulating proposals, and partly because the members are unaware of the role an assembly could play. As yet they therefore have little real stake in the proceedings, and that stake is not likely to grow until the resources available are large enough to make choices — and therefore genuine conflicts of interest among Africans — more real.

Executive Councils

Bophuthatswana, having reached stage two of self-government, has a cabinet of ministers; KwaZulu, still in stage one, has an executive council of executive councillors: ministers and councillors have roughly analogous departmental responsibilities. If the councils follow the British models on which they are ultimately based, they will exercise a collective responsibility for their legislative and administrative acts. But the conventions of responsibility have been slow in developing in the two homelands because it is not yet clear what control leaders have over the composition of their councils. Dissident ministers in both homelands have proved extremely difficult to discipline and eject. Although the leaders appear to dominate the assemblies and their executives, they are not fully in command of their followers.

The councils meet regularly, usually weekly, and include the department heads (ministers), the chief ministers, and the secretaries (in KwaZulu they are called directors). So far the latter have all been whites, transferred from the Republic. They refrain from participating unless requested to do so.

In addition to Mangope, the Bophuthatswana cabinet consists of N. T. Matseke, Interior; Chief B. Motsatsi, Works; M. Setlogelo, a commoner, Education; T. M. Molathwa, another commoner, Health; Chief V. Shuping, Agriculture; and Chief Thipe Victor Makapan, Justice. Molathwa and Setlogelo are each over forty years old. Setlogelo, a Rolong from Thaba 'Nchu, was a teacher. Makapan, for many years until 1966 an interpreter employed by the Republic's Department of Information, became a chief in late 1972. He has completed ten of eleven courses for a B.A., presumably by correspondence from the University of South Africa. The other university-educated member is Molathwa, who obtained a B.Sc. in hygiene at Fort Hare. He was then employed by the Institute of Family and Community Health in Merebank, Natal, became a health inspector in Kimberley, and in 1964 returned home and opened a general store in Taung. The chiefs have strong traditional roots and tend to emphasize the Tswana character of their government. As a cabinet, it is more "nationalistic" and less overtly politicized than its counterpart in KwaZulu.

The KwaZulu executive councillors are Walter Kanye, Community Affairs; Chief Everson Xolo, Works; James Alfred Walter Nxumalo, Education; Chief

Owen Sithole, Agriculture; and Jeffrey Mthethwa, Justice. Although Xolo
is only thirty-five years-old, the other councillors are in their mid- and late
forties, and Nxumalo is sixty-five. Nxumalo has a teacher's certificate, and,
after being educated at St. Chad's, Ladysmith, obtained his B.A. through
the University of South Africa. He was a supervisor of schools, then an
inspector, a position he held for several decades until joining the council in
1972. Chief Xolo attended the school for the sons of chiefs in Nongoma.
Kanye attended school at Marianhill, Pinetown, became a clerk at a gold
mine for more than two years, and assumed the position of assistant secretary
of the nonlegal African Mineworkers Union. As a result, he lost his job in
1946. Kanye then obtained a position with a bus company, becoming one
of its first few African inspectors before 1950, when he left to work with his
father on a coal mine in Natal. There he held a clerical post until 1958, when
he became secretary of the Usutu Tribal Authority. In 1971 he was elected to
represent the Nongoma Regional Authority on the Zulu Territorial Authority.
At the time of the formation of KwaZulu's first cabinet, he held the Agriculture portfolio, but since Sithole lived near Pietermaritzburg, where the
Department of Agriculture was housed, Kanye and Sithole swapped coun-
cillorships simply to limit the distances that they would each have to travel.
Mthethwa, who succeeded Dladla in the council, is a businessman from
Msinga.

Urban Representatives

Since so much of the population of Bophuthatswana and KwaZulu is resident
in the Republic, and thus is "extraterritorial," the governments of the homelands may delegate their obligations and some of their responsibilities to
subcabinet officials known as urban representatives. They were provided for
in the Promotion of Bantu Self-Government Act of 1959, originally being
appointed by and acting as agents of the government of the Republic. They
were meant to replace existing elected urban African advisory boards, but the
boards were instead superseded almost everywhere by elected Urban Bantu
councils, which function separately from arrangements made for and with
the homelands. Earlier, too, the representatives were conceived of as "am-
bassadors" from the homelands to their peoples in the cities, but the analogy
is inaccurate. In fact, they do not represent one government to another, but
rather a homeland's authority to its nominal citizens. The analogy would be
useful only if, say, American diplomats abroad had no other function than
to look after the interests of their own country's citizens.

The role of urban representative has come to be partly consular (collecting
and trying to deal with grievances and attempting to intervene with official
urban bodies on behalf of citizens), and partly political (working to improve
communications between urban Tswana and Zulu and their governments).

The most recent estimates, those for the fiscal year 1975/76, for Bophutha-tswana provide for one urban representative and three assistant urban representatives, the latter an increase of two over the previous year. The urban representative has a salary—indicative of the importance attached to the position—higher than any other homeland employee except the top two civil servants and the chief minister. The assistant representatives serve in Pretoria, Soweto, the Reef towns, and Welkom in the Free State gold fields. (There are two unpaid representatives in Cape Town and Bloem-fontein.) They are full-time personnel and are provided with a car, an office, and clerical assistance. One of their major tasks is to obtain revisions of incorrect ethnic classifications. The representatives thus appear regularly before Bantu Affairs commissioners as advocates. Recently, too, their responsibilities have been increased with the establishment of Urban Tswana boards appointed by the representative at meetings for Tswana. Cities are to have boards of seven members, small towns boards of five. The chairmen are appointed by the representative in consultation with the board.

Solomon Ngobese, KwaZulu's first urban representative, mayor of Umlazi, and a former oil company employee, was appointed in late 1973. The yearly salary voted him, R5,000, R2,000 more than that voted by Bophuthatswana for its urban representative, was also higher than that for any other KwaZulu official except the chief executive councillor. The urban representative is supposed to provide the main channel for inquiries and complaints from Zulu citizens in the Republic. He is charged with investigating matters relating to resettlement and education. After the conflict between Dladla and Buthelezi, Ngobese was also given the additional responsibility of looking after the interests of Zulu workers in the cities.

In 1975 Gibson Joseph Thula became the KwaZulu government's principal urban representative. In 1976 he had three deputies. Thula, a former teacher and social worker who had served as vice-president of the Black Social Workers Association of South Africa from 1965 to 1967, and had then worked in public relations for a large liquor company, was based in Soweto. His deputies were responsible for Umlazi (Durban), Orange Free State (gold fields), and Transvaal (also Soweto) problems. Thula was also active as a publicity chairman of Inkatha YeSizwe, the Zulu National Cultural Libera-tion movement. By 1976 Thula divided his time as the principal urban representative of KwaZulu between assisting Zulu who had problems with the bureaucratic or security machinery of the Republic and representing Kwa-Zulu to the leaders of urban black (and white) South Africa.

White Officials

The homelands still depend in many ways upon the cooperation of the central government. Departments other than that of Bantu Administration and

Development, e.g., Water Affairs, Public Works, Transport, and the Postal Administration, remain responsible for many services in the homelands. Officials are seconded from central governmental service, not hired on contract by the homelands. They are therefore far more responsible to their old than to their new masters and, consequently, there is a considerable range in the quality of the service they render. Many officials are punctillious; others have led Mangope, Buthelezi, and other legislators to complain. For example, in June 1974 Mangope reacted vehemently to delays and misdirection of salary checks to teachers, accusing unnamed officials of acting "deliberately to prove that Blacks were incapable of running their own affairs." He then generalized the attack. "For years we have been going cap in hand, begging Whites who are only interested in [an] 'inconvenience allowance.' "[42] Members of the KwaZulu Legislative Assembly have said that the appalling condition of their roads was due to uncooperative and inefficient officials in the Department of Works.[43] Both Buthelezi and Mangope have reacted strongly to what they regard as meddling by whites in homeland politics. But given the overall framework, the institutions and policies within which both officials and homeland leaders operate, the conduct of officials has not been the major issue.

The official representatives from the Republic to the homelands are the commissioners-general. Created by the Promotion of Bantu Self-Government Act of 1959, these officials were meant to "furnish guidance and advice . . . promote the development of . . . consult with . . . [and] enlighten the population."[44] Thus, in these paternalistic terms, the commissioner-general of a homeland was intended to represent not only the central government to a homeland, but also the Republic to the *people* of the subordinate "national unit."

Their mandates are complex; the commissioners-general are frequently placed in awkward positions because in practice they are not always the channels of contact between the homelands and Pretoria. Mangope and Buthelezi, and their cabinets, frequently deal directly with the South African prime minister or his associates. Administratively, too, the major tasks of coordination and policy making are between homeland departments and the state's Department of Bantu Administration and Development. It is not clear when the commissioners-general are used as a channel of communication and when they are not. They play no part in the summit conferences of homeland leaders and Republican ministers. Their position is as anomalous as is

42. *Mafeking Mail,* 7 June 1974. Presumably Mangope referred to a special allowance paid to white officials serving in the homelands.

43. *Natal Mercury,* 10 May 1974.

44. Quoted in Gwendolen Carter, Thomas Karis, and Newell M. Stultz, *South Africa's Transkei: The Politics of Domestic Colonialism* (Evanston, 1967), 54.

that of the urban representatives. They are not diplomats representing one government to another, and unlike the urban representatives, they have no special responsibility for the interests of citizens of the Republic who may be "temporarily" in the homelands.

The commissioners-general are usually loyal politicians of the second rank who have long taken an interest in African affairs or who have grown up in a particular area and hence have a command of an African language. They tend to hold their posts for a long time. The veteran was Hans Abraham, the first commissioner-general in the Transkei, who played a forceful, hence controversial, role there. On at least one occasion before he retired in 1973, the Transkei government requested his removal. Once he referred to Africans as "heathens," which led Mangope to demand an apology from him.[45] P. H. Torlage, commissioner-general to the Zulu and Swazi national units, a former leader of the National Party in Natal, spoke Zulu. Dr. T. S. Kloppers, a medical practitioner, commissioner-general to the Tswana for thirteen years, was succeeded by Senator Gerhardus A. Wessels in 1973. Wessels was for a long time chairman of the National Party Senate group on Bantu affairs. He speaks and writes Zulu, Xhosa, and Swazi, and said on his appointment that he aimed to master Tswana in "three to six months." He has long urged the teaching of African languages in white schools.[46]

It is difficult for commissioners-general to avoid becoming involved in the politics of the African communities to which they are accredited; indeed their mandate would almost require them to do so. In March 1974 Wessels became deeply involved, almost certainly against his wishes, in the clash between Mangope and Maseloane. When the Legislative Assembly opened, a motion of no-confidence in Mangope was proposed by Maseloane and Chief Toto, and both of them, with the chairman of the assembly, took their motion to the commissioner-general. According to Maseloane, the commissioner-general had tried to act as a peacemaker before the assembly began, but Mangope had insisted on taking the matter "to the people." When a legal question arose as to Mangope's competence to remove Maseloane as a chairman of a regional authority, the Department of Bantu Administration and Development, at the suggestion of the commissioner, sent an opinion, which denied Mangope's contention, to the secretary of justice of Bophuthatswana; the opinion was then read out in the assembly.[47] A commissioner-general can, therefore, easily be drawn deeply into conflicts among Africans, particularly if he should appear to be taking sides. Although Wessels has apparently been able to avoid such a charge in Bophuthatswana, his counterpart in KwaZulu, Torlage,

45. *Die Transvaler* (Johannesburg), 19 March 1973.
46. *Ibid.*, 9 June 1973; *Pretoria News*, 15 June 1973.
47. *Hoofstad*, 22 March 1974; *Rand Daily Mail*, 27 March 1974; *Mafeking Mail*, 19 April 1974, May 24, 1974.

was criticized by Buthelezi early in 1973 for working too closely with the Ingonyama and thus against the elected leader of the Zulu.

The range of a commissioner-general's activity is wide and can involve humdrum matters of administration. At times he acts as a channel of complaints. In KwaZulu, Torlage tried hard to make himself accessible to and known by Zulu. He had his office in a large new brick and stone building outside Nongoma. In his conference hall, where the walls are decorated boldly with photographs of historically important Zulu, he met official delegations. He saw individuals "off the street," too, and referred their problems to the proper authorities. Charting a course between interference and availability, Torlage tried to avoid infringing upon the purview of officials in departments or those of homeland leaders.

The commissioners-general have no legislative role except to transmit measures passed by assemblies to the relevant Republican minister. In turn, the ministers send them on to the president, who promulgates or denies them. So far no measures passed by the assemblies of Bophuthatswana and KwaZulu have been refused, but the assemblies have passed nothing controversial except for educational matters. The departments, especially that of Bantu Administration and Development, seem to have encouraged commissioners-general to speak often to homeland and urban audiences on the future of separate development. Torlage, for instance, in 1972 told Africans in Germiston that Zulu needed more opportunities for employment, not additional land. "What is the use of more land," he said, "if the people living there have no work? . . . It now rests with you to create new opportunities for work in the homelands." He urged urban Africans, because of their knowledge of the West and accumulated skills, to go "home."[48] In 1973 Torlage made another round of visits to Springs, Germiston, and Soweto. To meetings of 500 and 800 people he spoke of "building bridges to the homelands." In KwaZulu, Torlage has been active in attempting to smooth the path for these "returnees" but with limited success: local people frequently distrust urban outsiders who have in many cases never before entered a homeland. They do not want newcomers, with their "know-how" and Western ideas, to usurp commercial or other local economic opportunities.

The commissioners-general have no control over the civil servants who staff the administrative machinery of the homelands. It is these officials, not the commissioners-general, who are in a position to exert great influence, even control, in many areas of policy. The secretaries (directors) provide the staff and, in some departments, the line functions, irrespective of these tasks being performed by subordinate whites or blacks. In relation to their ministers these officials "caution, advise, and warn," and make information

48. Quoted in *The Star*, 14 June 1972.

available on matters of fact and procedure. They cannot and do not command. But of course they could withhold evidence, fail to make inquiries, and inhibit the actions of ministers generally. However, most of these senior officials have been careful to play their roles as administrators properly. But however impeccable their behavior, they control the making of the new civil services. They remain responsible for recruiting, training, and reporting on those who will replace them. Africans do not yet appoint persons to supernumary positions, where blacks are trained to work side by side with the whites who are leaving. Furthermore, the white administrators are also paid by the Republic and their salaries do not appear on the local estimates. (This device has the advantage, from the Republic's point of view, of not publicizing within the homeland assemblies the disparities between the salaries of whites and blacks.) The most important effect is that neither Bophuthatswana nor KwaZulu yet has any control over the individual salaries, the total salary bill, or the output of the whites sent to serve it.

5

Leadership and Policy in the Emerging Homelands

The leaders of independent Africa dominate the political affairs of their own countries and peoples; the preferences of presidents or generals are more influential than the deliberations of elected legislatures. Consequently, patriotism is in many places equated with loyalty to a ruling party or a particular head of state. Some states are still governed by the politicians who, as nationalists during the colonial period, wrested power from Britain or France. Their direction of the anticolonial movements provided a legitimacy that was carried over into the period of postindependence and still persists. It reflected and still almost everywhere reflects the notion that strong undivided leadership is essential if the new states are to succeed in a potentially hostile and much more powerful world. The Republic of South Africa provides this external reality for the homelands, and their chief executives, like the earlier anticolonial nationalists, dominate their cabinets and legislatures. This dominance is to some extent a function of their own personalities, but the system of separate development, and the nature of the relations between the dependent proto-states and the powerful Republic, also encourages the exercise of power by a prominent few.

Since the homelands are subordinate polities, their political dialogues take place primarily with the dominant power. They focus upon the redistribution of power and resources and about how and when that redistribution will take place. Thus, it is incumbent upon the individually weak homelands to support their own men of stature in their dealing with the dominant Republic, a characteristic exaggerated by the novelty and non-African form of the homeland legislatures.

Since they also sit infrequently and are still constitutionally weak, the assemblies offer few constraints upon the actions of determined and able chief ministers. In their early debates members worried that criticism in the assemblies could weaken the hands of their leaders and unnecessarily divide the embryo states. The leaders of the homelands thus have a freedom of action with regard to the assemblies that they cannot yet expect with regard to solving the problems of their peoples. They control only specified areas of policy and command few resources. Nevertheless, as Matanzima did originally, Mangope and Buthelezi have adroitly made use of the limited opportunities available to outspoken leaders by the logic of the policy of separate development. As chief executives of recognized political entities they have a freedom to speak critically that is rare for blacks within South Africa. The future of South Africa and its homeland policies could depend upon the extent to which it remains possible for leaders like Mangope and Buthelezi to articulate grievances and persuade the rulers of South Africa to improve the quality of life for all blacks.

Both Mangope and Buthelezi have attacked the South African social order as a whole and policies that affect their homelands in particular. Restrained in tone, Mangope has made his impact with the cutting edge of resolute understatement. Buthelezi has been strident, ironic, and importunate. The press, especially an English language press disillusioned with the official parliamentary opposition, has regarded Mangope and Buthelezi as "good copy." It has thus helped to shift the question of the homelands from the periphery to the center of South African politics. Mangope and Buthelezi address themselves as much to the white electorate and its leadership as they do to their own peoples; a large proportion of their speaking takes place before English- and Afrikaans-speaking whites. They are, therefore, contributors to a South African debate involving more than their own homelands. Thus far successfully, they have gambled on the South African government's inability to hamper their activities without laying separate development open to the taint of cynicism and hypocrisy.

Constitutionally and politically, Mangope and Buthelezi have been placed in positions of considerable complexity. Holding great authority in relation to their own peoples, as shown by the weakness of organized opposition to them in the homelands, they spar in an entirely new way (for South Africa) with white rulers who have an increasing interest in ensuring the credibility, outside, as well as inside South Africa, of a contrived system. In 1975, too, as the Republic energetically sought to ensure détente in southern Africa by negotiating with Zambia and ending white rule in Rhodesia, so the success of separate development became more essential than ever before. Antagonizing the homelands, or slowing the pace of their political and economic growth, could deleteriously affect the relations of the Republic with black Africa. For the same reasons the government of the Republic began in 1975 to accede to some of the improvements in the South African social order demanded by homeland leaders.

Short of eroding their own power—indeed for the purpose of buttressing it—South African whites recognize the need to cooperate with the leaders of their black homelands if they are to enhance the likelihood of stability throughout southern Africa. From the overthrow of the Caetano government in Portugal in 1974, South Africa has sought to buy time with space: i.e., to postpone a radical redistribution of power at home by accepting change in Moçambique, or even assisting it in Rhodesia. But events in Angola have increased the pressures on South Africa to achieve both a resolution of the long-standing dispute with the United Nations over Namibia, and to create a political order at home that would restore to South Africa some legitimacy internationally. Détente and separate development are complementary components of present South African policy; détente may not be achievable, even after the resolution of conflict in Rhodesia and Namibia, without drastic changes in the policy of separate development.

Homeland Leaders

Homeland leaders, especially Kaiser Matanzima of the Transkei, Cedric Phatudi of Lebowa, Hudson Ntsanwisi of Gazankulu, Lucas Mangope, and Gatsha Buthelezi have become major figures in South African politics despite the limited powers and poverty of their proto-states. Mangope and Buthelezi are poles apart in manner and method, but they have both learned to operate within, and to publicize, the constraints imposed on them by the South African system. Their demonstrated determination and magnetism enables them to dominate their own homelands, and so to represent the views of their peoples with force and conviction. By so doing they are able to urge the central government to narrow the gap between promise and performance. They have done so, as have other homeland leaders, by exploiting the rhetoric and logic of the policy of separate development, decrying inconsistencies, alternatively being moderate and radical and angry and restrained, and by welcoming concessions and demanding reasonable further progress.

Lucas Mangope

Chief Mangope was born in 1923 at Motswedi, north of Zeerust in the Transvaal. His father, a chief, sent him away to a school run by the Community of the Resurrection, an Anglican monastic order of which Trevor Huddleston is the best known member. Mangope indeed credits Huddleston with a large measure of direct influence on his own life. In 1946, after more than a decade in schools run by the order, Mangope obtained a senior certificate (equivalent to an American high school diploma) from the community's St. Peter's School in Rosettenville (Oliver Tambo, a major ANC leader, long in exile, was a schoolmate), and then a junior teaching diploma at the Diocesan Teachers' Training College near Pietersburg. Meanwhile, he had been advancing in traditional rank, having become the leader of the Mathlatlhowa regiment of his own Tswana group. Between 1947 and 1949, he worked in the Department of Native Affairs. But in

1951, he returned to school, attending Bethel College near Lichtenburg in order to obtain his Higher Primary Teachers' Diploma. Having taught primary school in the 1940s, during most of the 1950s he taught in a secondary school in Motswedi (serving for several years as its principal) and in other secondary schools in Mafeking, Potchefstroom, and Krugersdorp.

By this time Mangope had become more heavily involved in administration and politics. When his father died in 1959, he became chief of the Motswedi-Barutshe-Boo-Manyane tribe and joined the Zeerust Regional Authority. He was appointed to the Bantu Education Advisory Board and the Advisory Council of the University of the North. When the Tswana Territorial Authority was formed in 1961, he became vice-chairman, advancing to chairman in 1968 and chief minister in 1972 with the evolution of his homeland. In these positions he steadily gained stature, employing solid, and until recently, undramatic qualities of patience and persistence in the pursuit of his own and Tswana ends. Much of his strategy has been based upon the acquisition of medium- or long-term rather than short-term results. A professed admirer of the doggedness of Afrikaners, Mangope well knows that endurance and integrity are essential if his objectives are to be achieved. Moreover Mangope, no less than other homeland leaders, knows that it will be difficult as well as essential for power to be redistributed in such a way that the economic and social development of his proto-state is least compromised.

Mangope has a significant advantage in his dealings with the Republic that is shared by few of the other homeland executives. He is fluent in Afrikaans, the language of negotiation and employment as well as the predominant foreign language for Africans of those portions of the western Transvaal and the northern Cape where most Tswana reside. As a school teacher Mangope specialized in the teaching of Afrikaans, his pupils one year even proving more proficient than all others in the Transvaal examinations. For this effort Mangope was awarded a trophy that is still a source of pride. Afrikaner journalists delight in his employment of their language and his ability to speak eloquently and knowledgeably of Afrikaner history. Sometimes, too, Mangope has praised the candor and trustworthiness of Afrikaners. He is a believer in reconciliation. He has rejected the white supremacy policies of the opposition United Party and criticized the Progressive Party (as it then was) because of its espousal of a qualified franchise.[1] He has condemned idealistic radicals, and once collected funds from his people for the "fight against terrorists." He urged his followers to attend festivals celebrating the tenth anniversary of the establishment of the Republic.

1. *The Star,* 20 Oct. 1971; *Die Transvaler,* 6 Nov. 1972. The Progressive Party combined with the Reform Party to form the Progressive Reform Party in 1975.

Like other homeland leaders, however, he has reacted to the altered climate of opinion in South Africa. In 1973, while deploring terrorism, he warned that bargaining had to be resorted to; "time is running out" he said. Soon after the Portuguese coup of 1974, he said: "Things will never be the same again in South Africa since the events in Lisbon." Linking the "certainty" of increased terrorism along the borders with the frustration and anger of "my own people" and the increasing militancy of young blacks, he put the issue starkly. "Can he [the white man] expect us to help him defend this country—and we are more than willing to do so—without knowing what our rights are?"[2]

However strong his criticism, Mangope's tone is always restrained. He frequently expresses an understanding of the Afrikaner predicament, even before audiences with whom it might not be particularly welcome. At an Institute of Race Relations conference he praised former Prime Minister Verwoerd's perseverance and vision: "He has brought us more years of precious time to sort things out than we are willing to give him credit for."[3] Given this record, it is hardly surprising that until mid-1973 the Afrikaans press lauded Mangope as a supporter of separate development. It is clear, however, that Mangope's visit to the United States in 1973 exerted a profound influence on him. After his trip he came into direct conflict with Prime Minister Vorster, who had threatened to prevent white opposition parties from inviting homeland leaders to their congresses. Mangope was forthright: "I am not going to be muzzled," he said, "not even by Caesar himself."[4]

Mangope's policies and public statements had grown increasingly critical from about mid-1972. On the occasion of the grant of self-government to Bophuthatswana in June 1972, he reminded a Tswana and Afrikaner audience that he had repeatedly affirmed his support for "the positive aspects of the policy of separate development with the emphasis on development." Under his guidance, the first annual congress of the Bophuthatswana National Party "accepted and firmly supported those aspects of separate development they regarded as positive."[5] But in his capacity of chief minister, now able to speak to white, especially Afrikaner, audiences, Mangope has raised major questions candidly. Before an audience of white students at Stellenbosch University he called for real sacrifices on the part of whites. "If it is really our honest intention to allow the policy [of separate development] to succeed then it is surely time for the whites to make some sacrifices," he

2. *Rand Daily Mail*, 13 Sept. 1973; *Oggendblad* (Pretoria), 29 May 1974; *Star Weekly*, 13 July 1974.
3. Lucas Mangope, "The Political Future of the Homelands," South African Institute of Race Relations (Johannesburg, 1974), mimeo., 2.
4. *Hoofstad* (Pretoria), 25 Sept. 1973).
5. Quoted in *Rand Daily Mail*, 2 June 1972; *Mafeking Mail*, 2 March 1973.

said. "I mean real sacrifices. Of course I understand only too well that the idea of voluntary sacrifice is the most difficult thing to sell to a privileged electorate. But that does not alter in any way the hard facts of the situation which has been reached in our history."[6] Early in 1973 he decried whites who remained unaware of the anger and bitterness that discrimination caused among blacks. After the proposed Bophuthatswana budget was drastically reduced by the Republic, he criticized separate development as such, but with a less abrasive tone. "It is my experience that most of the criticism of separate development has merit." He reminded the Department of Bantu Administration and Development that every time "Pretoria fails to fulfill the promises implicit in separate development it undermines the position of homeland leaders committed to the policy."[7]

It is impossible to decide the extent to which the utterances of homeland politicians, particularly those statements that are addressed to Republican authorities or to sympathetic journalists, are tactical in origin. In 1973 Mangope began to question the whole political basis of separate development. He shifted his emphasis from the necessity of collaboration, and from complaints about failures to perform, to an attack on the refusal of South Africa's rulers to consider devising a workable, single political system capable of embracing all the peoples of South Africa —the major premise of separate development. "Naturally," he concluded, "I would prefer to see social and economic equality in South Africa together with one-man one-vote participation for my people in the central political system. However, this is clearly out of the question right now."[8] "I don't think there is a better policy [than separate development] for the whites, but it is not so for the blacks. This is my opinion based on the way in which it is being carried out."[9]

Yet Mangope has courted Afrikaners and used their institutions as possible models for Tswana. He has appealed to leading Afrikaner industrialists for their assistance in establishing for Africans a *Reddingsdaadbond,* an organization set up in the late 1930s to promote Afrikaners in economic life. In his assembly he said that he envisaged his Tswana university as one to be modelled on Rand Afrikaans University, an Afrikaner institution.[10]

Mangope's recent speeches place him much closer in tone to Buthelezi, by whose example he has undoubtedly been influenced. On his return from the United States in 1973, Mangope suggested that South Africa pay

6. Quoted in *Die Vaderland* (Johannesburg), 12 Oct. 1972.
7. Quoted in *The Star,* 25 Jan., 27 March, and 28 March 1973; *Rand Daily Mail,* 29 March 1973.
8. Quoted in *The Star,* 26 Jan. 1973. Reiterated in Mangope, "Political Future of the Homelands," 5.
9. *Hoofstad,* 23 Jan. 1974.
10. *Mafeking Mail,* 19 April 1974.

Bophuthatswana R240 million over twenty years because its people "had never been paid adequately for their labor."[11] In 1976, in explaining his willingness to negotiate with the South African government over independence, he repeated the demand for compensation for the Tswana people, who by the "sweat of their brows" had helped enrich South Africa.[12] He has always justified cooperating with the Republic on the ground that separate development offers a means of gaining concessions for Africans. But the rate and magnitude of those concessions has disappointed him and he has deplored the way in which the policy has been implemented. Insisting by implication on an undivided South Africa, he has said, "In the country of our forefathers, and of our birth, the sharing of power is our inalienable right." In 1974 he protested at meddling in "matters of purely local politics" by Republican officials and reiterated his demands for substantial concessions of money and power "to ensure meaningful progress towards equal opportunity for people of all races in South Africa."[13]

Without substantial returns, Mangope (and Buthelezi) acknowledge the impossibility of winning over younger Africans, especially students, most of whom are hostile to separate development in all its forms. In these circumstances, where the caution of the dominant power precludes substantial immediate satisfaction of the expectations of their peoples, homeland leaders must skillfully orchestrate their rhetoric and activity. This is a performance at which Mangope has become particularly adept, stating major demands in tones of studied moderation that make his rare displays of anger all the more impressive.

Gatsha Buthelezi

Buthelezi's rise from comparative obscurity to national and international prominence has been rapid. From his reluctant acceptance of the position of chief executive councillor of KwaZulu in 1971 he has become a forceful spokesman for Africans generally, and one of the most frequently quoted men in South African public life. Consequently, his genius both for the artful isolation of inconsistency and the generous search for accommodation—for ways in which to make major concessions to the anxieties of whites—has been given ample exposure in the daily press. Without that coverage he could not have so captured the imagination of many whites. As a result, he has hastened the growth of a new kind of oligarchic, multiracial politics in which leaders of all white opposition parties, except those of the far right, have held discussions with him and with other homeland leaders. His efforts have also helped to bring the leaders of the homelands together politically and to

11. *Rand Daily Mail,* 13 July 1973.
12. *Ibid.,* 2 Feb. 1976.
13. Mangope, "Political Future of the Homelands," 5; *Star Weekly,* 6 July 1974.

force the pace of homeland political development. In all of these endeavors Buthelezi's charisma and self-confidence have provided a critical personal ingredient.

Chief Buthelezi was born in 1928 at the Ceza Mission Hospital near Nongoma, thereafter being taken, as was customary, to the royal kraal of his uncle, Ingonyama Solomon. There he grew up with others of princely lineage, including his cousin Cyprian, a subsequent Ingonyama. One grandfather was a chief councillor to the Ingonyama Cetewayo. The other, on his maternal side, was Ingonyama Dinizulu. The young Buthelezi went to primary school in Nongoma and to Adams College, the famed American-founded mission high school in Amanzimtoti, and then to Fort Hare University College. He studied history and native administration, but never completed the course. On the occasion of a visit to the college of a governor-general, he participated in a demonstration against an intrusion by "the rubber stamp of oppression." At first suspended, Buthelezi was expelled just before his final examinations. Only later could he complete his degree, at the University of Natal. He had hoped to go on to study law, but the pressures of family obligation were strong. On the insistence of Princess Constance Magogo ka Dinizulu, his mother (who remains influential today), he returned home. In 1953, aged twenty-six, he succeeded his father as head of the 20,000-member Buthelezi clan, with its headquarters at Mahlabatini. The white authorities were so concerned about his potential for leadership and trouble-making, however, that they confirmed him as chief only after a five-year probation.

Relations between the clan under his leadership and the government of South Africa have never been cordial. Buthelezi and his people resisted the implementation of the Bantu Authorities Act of 1951 — not without material cost. In a bold gesture early in the next decade, they even accepted a R320,000 agricultural betterment scheme only on condition that they themselves should pay for it (at a tax of R20 per person over two years). This may have been Buthelezi's idea. There was internal opposition, however, and only R10,000 was ever collected. The promised improvements should therefore have been defaulted, but, a second time, the government offered to pay for them. This time the tribe, in a voice echoed many times more recently by Buthelezi, said haughtily that if the government were impatient it could make the improvements on its own, "but the tribe would not accept [them] of its own accord."[14] Still later, the tribal leaders offered to implement the scheme, but only around Mahlabatini, where Buthelezi lived. There the betterment could be observed by the entire tribe. The government would not, in the end, accept this reluctant and conditional assent.

14. Quoted in *Rand Daily Mail,* 19 June 1970.

Buthelezi and his followers remained obstructionist throughout the 1960s. (During the same period he was one of Ingonyama Solomon's closest advisors.) Only in 1968, after South Africa forcefully made its wishes known, did they finally agree to the establishment of a regional authority at Mahlabatini. Buthelezi became its chairman, making it widely known that he and his people, having never been consulted about the implementation of the Bantu Authorities Act, were merely obeying the law. "The Buthelezi tribal authority," he said, "feels that it is not under any obligation to register any acceptance or objection to the proclamation of the regional authority for the district, as the tribal authority is already fully cooperating with the department in the implementation of the Act."[15]

Since his expulsion from the college of Fort Hare, Buthelezi has managed to speak his mind without falling afoul of white authority. This says as much for his adroitness as it implies the government's awareness of his abilities and potential. He has tried on numerous occasions to deflect policy and to take advantage of mistakes made by officials. One of his stratagems is to make absolutely clear where power lies — as he did in the case of the regional authority at Mahlabatini, and as he did early in 1973 when he refused to discuss plans for land consolidation because his people had not been consulted about them. He is not deferential in fact-to-face contact with cabinet ministers, but he observes the courtesies of political combat. Unlike his ideological forbears, such as Chief Albert Luthuli, he is able to say much for which they were banned and detained, evidence both of the strength of his position and of a change in the political style of South Africa's rulers. But in his dealings with the government he has some serious handicaps. Unlike Mangope he speaks no Afrikaans and cannot similarly charm Afrikaners while simultaneously disagreeing with their policies; Buthelezi moves essentially among English-speaking whites and blacks hostile to separate development. He has close personal ties with members of the Progressive Reform Party and is a staunch member of the Anglican Diocesan Committee for Zululand. His multiracial prayer breakfasts extend this last dimension of Buthelezi's personality. He has criticized the United Party, and its plan for a federated South Africa — which should endear him to the government — but he has consistently excoriated all those, whoever they are, who would seek to perpetuate white supremacy in South Africa.

Buthelezi frequently replies to official pronouncements with asperity — in tones still not customarily employed by blacks when talking of and to whites. He reminds his listeners of the absence of choice for an African leader working within a system so dominated by the power of whites. He also urges progress. "When a man is reaching for the moon, we cannot be expected to move towards self-determination at oxwagon pace," an ironic use of an

15. Quoted in *ibid.*, 19 June 1968; *Survey of Race Relations, 1969*, 131.

Afrikaner cultural symbol. His strategy is to push incessantly, issue after issue, for the accelerated development of black interests within and without the homelands. He espouses multiracialism, professing to welcome whites in KwaZulu even if blacks remain unwelcome in the rest of South Africa. Buthelezi also has for many years preached nonviolence. "I have not deviated from my path of nonviolence" he said in 1975, "in spite of all the violence arrayed against us, as the powerless and voiceless people of this land. . . . Our people can never meet violence with violence, even if one assumes some wanted this. . . ." Yet "the whole system under which we are ruled as Blacks is structured on violence. It is a form of violence to forbid my children to go to a school of their choice because of their colour. It is a form of violence that I cannot enter the Post Office at Nongoma [through] a door reserved for Whites. . . . The influx control regulations and pass laws are a form of violence. . . . The whole colour bar system is based on violence and violence is used every day to enforce it."[16] Nevertheless, Buthelezi's stands on these and numerous other issues are less significant politically than the ways in which he enunciates them.

Although his is not the only African voice in South Africa—separate development has raised a veritable cacophony—he is the most widely known and admired of the black leaders, not merely among his own people, but among Africans generally. Although his very use of the platform provided by the government has led to his being attacked as a "stooge" by Africans inside and outide South Africa, he has indubitably become a "national" figure, looked to not only by most Africans, but by many in all the other groups in South Africa.

It is because Buthelezi so persistently addresses himself to the problems of South Africa, as well as those of KwaZulu, that he appeals to Africans and whites outside the homelands. He has raised the morale and enhanced the pride of all Africans. What may be termed his major constituency—urban blacks of many ethnic groups and liberals of all colors—works and lives outside his homeland. Politically, this is both his greatest strength and his greatest weakness, but of his popularity there can be little question. After touring the towns of the Reef with Buthelezi, a leading correspondent wrote of his inordinate, charismatic appeal. "At Kagiso, Ketlehong, Duduza and Mamelodi, Africans received him with a warmth I have rarely seen accorded to any other politician in this country. . . . In Soweto . . . Chief Buthelezi was cheered by thousands."[17]

16. Gatsha Buthelezi, "Report Back to the Reef Africans on the Conference of Black Leaders with . . . Vorster . . . 1975," mimeo., 29; *Natal Mercury,* 11 May 1974.
17. Tim Muil, *Natal Mercury,* 29 Oct. 1973. See also Lawrence Schlemmer and Tim J. Muil, "Social and Political Change in the African Areas: A Case Study of KwaZulu," in Leonard Thompson and Jeffrey Butler (eds.), *Change in Contemporary South Africa* (Berkeley, 1975), 120-121, for an opinion poll.

Buthelezi speaks with freshness on the issues of the day, frequently showing an acute sense of timing and a sense of irony welcome in tense and otherwise humorless political exchanges. Although sometimes a poor speaker, especially when reading from a prepared text, he has that dramatic attribute called presence. He is also proud and temperamental, "There are moments of brooding . . . glimpses of chilling pride, times when the cheeks are puffed out with anger or when the mouth is large with laughter, and just when you think he is all extrovert . . . you become aware that this is a very private man."[18]

Policies and Programs

Mangope and Buthelezi are not faced with the comparatively simple problem of wresting autonomy from a reluctant, distant, and reasonably benevolent imperial power that has lost the will to rule and can withdraw from overseas commitments without risking major political disquiet at home. On the contrary, they face an entrenched, cohesive oligarchy fearful of the consequences of change. They thus need to identify the intentions of their rulers and to modify them. By a lengthy process of defining and redefining the rationale for separate development and the terms on which the homelands should and will survive, Mangope and Buthelezi with some urgency are attempting to make separate development work for Tswana and Zulu. Without additional power and resources both Mangope and Buthelezi may become discredited and lose their legitimacy. Thus their attitudes and actions on specific issues reflect the unavoidable tension between the constraints of a patron-client political system and the imperatives of modern political leadership.

That tension is exacerbated by serious handicaps in the field of communication. Not only are homeland populations poor, dispersed in fragmented homelands, in cities, and on white farms, but the homeland governments do not yet control the effective dissemination of information. In a country with a largely illiterate population, radio is especially important, but in South Africa it is controlled by the state. Radio Bantu, an organ of the South African Broadcasting Corporation (SABC), concentrates on entertainment, and insofar as it deals with political issues at all, it propagates views favorable to the Republic. Occasionally, homeland leaders are interviewed on the radio, but they do not have regular access to it. It is not merely that homeland leaders lack such access: commentators on news programs directed to whites have attacked homeland leaders, and Radio Bantu programs have cast what Buthelezi, for example, has regarded as "slurs" on the policies of KwaZulu.

The African press in South Africa is limited and mostly owned by whites. Generally it takes a politically cautious line. The English newspapers, as an

18. Tim Muil, "Gatsha the Conciliator," *Natal Mercury,* 15 Sept. 1973.

opposition press, have for a long time given coverage to African affairs, but usually only where they impinge on politics. Recently three newspapers — the *Rand Daily Mail, The Star*, and the *Natal Mercury* — appointed correspondents to deal with the homelands. More and more newspapers, including Afrikaans ones, have appointed reporters, some of them African, to deal with African affairs at greater length than has been customary. The African readership of English newspapers is large and that of African newspapers in English is growing, especially in urban areas. But there is virtually no circulation of newspapers in African rural areas, nor can any of these newspapers serve the practical political needs of homeland leaders or of their governments.

This lack of a range of media normally available to leaders in developed societies has been more keenly felt by Buthelezi than by Mangope. Buthelezi has threatened to use Radio Zambia or Radio Tanzania to disseminate his ideas, and he has tried to establish a broadcasting service of his own. In late 1973, however, the South African government refused to allow KwaZulu to open its own radio station on the grounds that the South African Broadcasting Corporation already provided a special service for Zulu.[19] Buthelezi has also considered establishing a weekly newspaper, to be called *Iswi Lomnyana (The Black Voice)*, to interpret "ourselves and our actions as Blacks." The journal would publish articles on federating the homelands, language problems, modern medicine, the role of the church (Buthelezi is a devout Anglican), black traders, biographies of Zulu and Xhosa businessmen and cabinet members, and studies of the liberation of Africa north of the Zambezi. "We wish" he said "to introduce our people to unadulterated news of what goes on in independent Africa."[20] In the context of contemporary South Africa, this is a radical program, with its appeal to Nguni and to Africans as blacks, and the attempt to publicize both the history and the present-day activity of independent Africa. Much of the literature on independent Africa, both scholarly and polemical, is unavailable in South Africa.

Until homeland leaders control media of their own, they will have to exert what influence they can over contemporary affairs through the English and Afrikaans press. Buthelezi has been adept at using an opposition press only too willing to help him. He was the first African politician to institute press conferences after meetings of the KwaZulu Legislative Assembly or Executive Council, and he frequently arranged for the appearance of articles on current issues. "I talk a great deal to newspapers" he said "because they are my only propaganda medium. I do not have the SABC."[21] From September 1973

19. *The Times*, 22 Sept. 1973. See also Schlemmer and Muil, "KwaZulu," 118.
20. Quoted in *Rand Daily Mail*, 17 March 1973.
21. Quoted in *Die Vaderland*, 8 Feb. 1973.

Buthelezi began writing a regular twice monthly column entitled "Through African Eyes" for the "morning group" of newspapers—the *Rand Daily Mail* (Johannesburg), the *Natal Mercury* (Durban), the *Daily Dispatch* (East London), the *Eastern Province Herald* (Port Elizabeth), the *Cape Times* (Cape Town), and the *Sunday Times* (Johannesburg). He has, however, not been limited to exposure in the opposition press. Afrikaans newspapers frequently send reporters to interview him, and though they are critical both of his attacks on the government and the liberal company he keeps, they acknowledge his skill as a politician and the legitimacy of many of the points that he makes.

The efficacy for the homelands of this dependence on media controlled by others is not easy to estimate, though it is clearly of value to individual homeland leaders and to the newspapers concerned. For the homelands the benefits are indirect and long term: frequent exposure of black leaders speaking in anything but deferential tones is accustoming whites, English as well as Afrikaans speakers, to black politicians *inside* South Africa using the platforms made possible by separate development. As long as the press in South Africa remains comparatively free, homeland leaders can make their claims on the conscience of South Africa's rulers publicly, appealing in fact to constituencies other than those that they officially represent. Without this means of expression, homeland leaders would be far weaker in negotiation with the Republic because the grievances of their people would be less widely known. Furthermore, few of the policies being discussed would have been subjected to an explicit African response. The willingness of the press to publicize such responses forces those in authority to acknowledge or deny grievances, and, often, propose remedial action. Publicity may, in fact, encourage give and take, and progressively change the relation of patron to client states from one of administrative command to one of political bargaining.

This constant discussion of issues and canvassing of alternatives may well play a major part in initiating change in the direction of mitigating the inequalities of power. Homeland leaders are interested in the whole range of political issues and would clearly like to make these matters of negotiation soon.

Federalism

Federalism has its attractions for many South Africans. Whites who oppose the present government have seen the uses to which a unitary constitution can be put by a stable, ethnically-based party representing a minority of the total population but a majority of the racially defined ruling group. Politically active blacks who hope to achieve a redistribution of power peacefully see in federalism a realistic device that could allay the fears of the dominant white electorate. Proponents of federation or confederation envisage some kind of institutional linkage of the black homelands with the white-dominated heartland. Such an arrangement would inevitably enhance the potential power of the homelands and provide a broader forum for the political aspirations of blacks. In particular it could define the relations between the various political units more precisely instead of leaving formally independent homelands dependent upon the informal goodwill of a powerful neighbor that no longer rules.

Buthelezi discussed the redistribution of power at the national level as early as 1971. He then proposed a national convention of all races in order to seek a political "modus vivendi." But Vorster rejected the idea, claiming that he did not believe in "umbrella bodies." In a 1973 meeting with the prime minister, Buthelezi made similar suggestions with the same result. During the same month, however, in response to pressure from the United Nations, South Africa agreed to consider establishing a multiracial council for Southwest Africa (Namibia). Buthelezi and prominent Afrikaner nationalists asked why South Africa should not also create a multiracial council.

Early in 1974 Buthelezi reminded an intellectual audience that separate development presented an ideal opportunity for the construction of a federal edifice "in which Black and White fulfillment can be justly reached." According to his scheme separate autonomous black- and white-run states would be linked federally and would cooperate on matters of common concern.[22] "It seems obvious," he said, "that a federal formula of the kind that raises the whole issue of power at the centre should be avoided. . . . It should be possible to establish a common machinery for certain matters without raising the hardy annual of demand for control of a central Parliament. This issue, which bedevils any mutual understanding and mutual confidence, could at least be postponed for several generations. During that time," he continued, "mutual confidence could grow to a point where agreement could be reached at the centre as well." If the Republic were prepared justly to establish constituent independent states (presumably with territory and resources greater than the present homelands) then interracial tensions would be reduced and South Africa could decrease its expenditures on defense. Under this scheme the central federal authority would still control fiscal matters in order to "preserve the essential dynamism of the South African economy." Influx control and pass laws would disappear, but in the heartland blacks would still be "guests." There would be state as well as a common federal

22. Later Buthelezi addressed the technical problem. "It is true that, legally speaking, States must be in existence before they federate. But my argument is that we were not consulted at the time of union, and we can [make] reparation for this gross omission by looking at the new formula for a future South Africa together, with no party expecting any other to swallow holusbolus what they have dreamed up unilaterally." Quoted in *Natal Mercury,* 9 May 1974.

citizenship, and each of the states would control its own internal affairs, make its own constitution, and so on.

Except in terms of the economy, external defense, and foreign affairs, Buthelezi envisaged a comparatively weak federal, more a confederal, government. "It should be possible," he concluded, "for Homelands policy to be used as a basis of a formula for the South Africa of the future." But South Africa would have to move quickly and boldly to establish its credibility. Subsequently, Buthelezi told the KwaZulu Legislative Assembly that federation had been proposed in good faith. "In spite of all that happens to us we still love our country too much to want to see it destroyed."[23] Speaking during the same month, Mangope said that he would welcome the gradual strengthening of federal ties in the economic sphere, in terms of security—federation "would serve as a formidable bulwark against aggression, terrorism, and infiltration"—and in the educational and cultural spheres as well. An educational and cultural federation could promote "higher training standards," especially at the university level, and the "best spirit of good neighbourliness."[24]

Federating the homelands themselves has also appealed to African leaders. Buthelezi and Matanzima have proposed a federation of their territories that could serve as the nucleus for a political association of all of the homelands. Matanzima has even suggested federating with Lesotho and Swaziland. Although not as yet enunciated in any detail, these proposals accurately reflect an awareness by blacks of their relative powerlessness—of their being divided instead of united. Joining the Transkei and KwaZulu, and thus 37 percent of the total *de jure* population of South Africa, is a rational response to the perceived limits of separated self-government and to the contemplated future constraints placed upon the relations of homelands with other homelands. "It seems, as far as politics are concerned, the majority of White people unite on fundamental issues, although they have different backgrounds and languages. We would be fools if we didn't follow the good example they have set," said Buthelezi. On a platform in Cape Town he and Matanzima both pledged themselves to "black unity."[25]

A federation even of all of the homelands would be an alliance of the weak against the strong. As a legitimating device it would recognize the validity of a single black nation counterposed against the white nation that, despite

23. Gatsha Buthelezi, "White and Black Nationalism, Ethnicity, and the Future of the Homelands," The Alfred and Winifred Hoernlé Memorial Lecture, South African Institute of Race Relations, Johannesburg, (Jan. 1974), mimeo. Buthelezi said that he had made most of the same suggestions in writing to Vorster in March 1973 without receiving any reply. The final quotation is from *Natal Mercury,* 9 May 1974.

24. Mangope, "Political Future of the Homelands," 7.

25. Quoted in *Rand Daily Mail,* 4 April 1972 and 19 Feb. 1973; *Die Transvaler,* 15 Sept. 1972.

a deep cultural division, rules South Africa. A black federation could also be consistent with the policy of separate development, but it has been South Africa's avowed aim to divide, not unify its blacks. The minister of Bantu administration and development made it clear in 1973 that the homelands would need the cooperation of the Republic if any federal union were attempted prior to independence.[26] In 1974, when the leaders of the homelands backed a federal solution to the race problem of the Republic "within a single economically indivisible country," the prime minister said that blacks could rule their enclaves but whites would continue to rule South Africa.[27] Even so, the central government has not prevented the leaders of the homelands from acting more and more in concert.

Late in 1973 both of these federal notions were explored by eight of the nine homeland leaders (accompanied by a retinue of seventy councillors and advisors) in an unpredecented "summit" meeting at Umtata. They agreed to federate their own states after independence. Matanzima said that they wanted "one black nation and not weak tribal groups divided along ethnic lines." Ntsanwisi, the chief minister of Gazankulu, said that black freedom was of paramount importance. "We must deemphasize all things that separate us and rather emphasize those things which unite us." Buthelezi promoted both a federation of blacks and his pet scheme of federating multiracially. At one point he made a "papal appearance" on a balcony of the Transkei Hotel to give a clenched-fist, black-power salute to the cheering crowds below. Hailed by Matanzima as the "Lion of the East," he told them that "we are doing the same thing as the banned African liberation movements, but we are using different methods. Through this unity, as sure as the moon is in the heavens, we shall liberate ourselves. With power and with God on our side we shall overcome."[28]

Buthelezi's fervor, if not his form of words, was shared by all the black leaders at Umtata. Mangope initially subscribed to the conclusions of the summit. Within a week, however, he had declared that the decision to move toward federation was "shooting at the moon." Federation, he said, would not come about in his lifetime. And he criticized the press for giving too much publicity to Buthelezi.[29]

Mangope had long been cool to the idea of a black superstate. The peoples of the Transkei and KwaZulu are Nguni, speaking mutually intelligible languages. Together they comprise over half of the African population of South Africa, whereas the Tswana comprise only 11 percent of the total.

26. Botha, quoted in *Die Transvaler*, 16 Feb. 1973. But see Schlemmer and Muil, "KwaZulu," 132.
27. *The Times*, 18 Nov. 1974.
28. Quoted in *The Economist* (17 Nov. 1973), 66; *The Times*, 9 Nov. 1973.
29. Quoted in *Natal Mercury*, 19 Nov. 1973.

"Swamping" is a sensitive issue among Tswana, having been raised publicly by Maseloane, and Mangope was subject to some internal pressure on this issue both before and after the summit conference.[30]

As an ethnic nationalist, Mangope naturally fears for the autonomy of the Tswana. "I have been entrusted," he once said, "with the task of serving the Tswana people, and, therefore to do what I regard is in the best interests of Bophuthatswana, and nothing else."[31] Chief Pilane, however, has consistently been in favor of black unity and claims to have raised the issue of federation in 1967. "I was called to Pretoria," he said, "where I was given a tongue lashing by officials of the Department of Bantu Administration . . . [and] warned never ever to think that Africans of this country could work together politically."[32] Mangope is closer to Maseloane than to Pilane on this issue. "Separate development," he has said, "has stimulated the sense of identity of the Tswana people, and I regard that as a positive aspect of separate development. . . . We are completely aware that we will be a minority group in a federation with the governments of larger groups, and we shall not like being in a minority."[33] Both before and after the summit he stated his preference for federal ties to neighboring Botswana, rather than to the other black homelands, a preference that Vorster welcomed in 1975.[34] Nevertheless, throughout 1974 and 1975 he joined Buthelezi, Matanzima, and the others in joint meetings and took part in the formulation of joint approaches to the government of the Republic.[35] Temperamentally and philosophically inclined to go his own way, Mangope has not always done so.

In such discussions federation has at least two meanings: (1) institutionally it is an arrangement linking established governments and, (2) politically it is a synonym for black unity. Although Mangope has sometimes been hostile to federation in the latter sense, he has not been invariably opposed to federation as an institution, provided Tswana interests could be preserved — the classic stance of small and weak states. In 1973 he said that he preferred some kind of multiracial council capable of ironing out difficulties in the practical implementation of separate development prior to any federation. But later he began to favor federation in the form of a redistributive device: "The positive aspects of separate development could be revived if the home-lands could form a federation with white South Africa, a federation of real

30. *Mafeking Mail,* 29 March 1974.
31. Quoted in *Die Transvaler,* 15 Aug. 1972.
32. Quoted in *Rand Daily Mail,* 10 Aug. 1972.
33. *Die Transvaler,* 19 Nov. 1973.
34. *The Times,* 17 Feb. 1975. The Government of Botswana officially wishes no ties to an independent Bophuthatswana.
35. Mangope, "Political Future of the Homelands," 6.

equality where all were represented in the federal authority."[36] He declined to participate in a multiracial conference on federation held immediately after the summit, but he associated himself with Buthelezi's position in favor of federation in early 1974. When he was attacked in the assembly shortly thereafter for allegedly going beyond his mandate in calling a summit conference, he linked the issues of federation and independence. The conference did not bind the Tswana people, he said, and if Tswana were thinking of independence, leaders would have to think about independence as well as federation. "Even after independence we may have to federate with white South Africa for economic and defence matters."[37]

Mangope's position is complex, and his caution is based partly on a concern for Tswana identity, partly on a temperamental inclination to go his own way, and partly on political pressures within Bophuthatswana. His apparently foot-dragging stance has not reduced his willingness to take common action with other homeland leaders. He played a major role in convening the historic first summit of black leaders; he takes part in formulating joint approaches to the government of the Republic; and he agrees fundamentally with Buthelezi in seeing federalism (however the definition of it fluctuates) as a device for redistributing power and resources. The differences between him and Buthelezi stem ultimately from his perception of himself as the leader of a people who are a minority in a double sense, i.e., as a political minority suffering discrimination in the existing social order and as inevitably a minority in the new society that would follow any major redistribution of power.

It is clear that independence and federation are closely related in the minds of Buthelezi and Mangope. For Buthelezi they tend to be mutually exclusive alternatives, believing as he does both in multiracialism and in the essential unity of South Africa. In a major speech in Soweto to 10,000 Africans in March 1976, he called for an abandonment of separate development and for majority rule.[38] Mangope, on the other hand, has followed the Transkei in opting for independence. In November 1975 he called a special meeting of Tswana chiefs, headmen, and their representatives—not a meeting of his party or his assembly—at which a resolution was passed in favor of independence. Five days later he secured a majority at the annual congress of the Bophuthatswana Democratic Party, and ten days later, by a party vote, secured the assent of the assembly.[39] In February 1976 at a meeting of 450

36. *Rand Daily Mail*, 15 March, 1 Aug. 1973; *The Star*, 27, 31 March 1973; interview with Rotberg and Butler, New York, 15 April 1973.
37. *Mafeking Mail*, 29 March 1974.
38. *The Times*, 14 March 1976.
39. *Survey of Race Relations, 1975,* 135.

Tswana in Soweto, he disclosed that he had discussed independence with the government, including compensation for low wages in the past, protection of Tswana in South Africa along the lines accepted by the European Economic Community for each other's nationals, and more land. On the same day, both opposition parties attacked him for supporting independence.[40] For Mangope, federation is a condition to follow independence, if at all. For Buthelezi, independence is to be avoided altogether.

Land Consolidation

Of the tangible matters at issue between the Republic and Bophuthatswana and KwaZulu, land consolidation and the acquisition of land illustrate better than any other the extent to which homeland leverage is still limited. For at least sixty years the availability of good, arable land has been a major grievance of the Tswana and Zulu. The Native Trust and Land Act of 1936 promised some amelioration of existing difficulties, but those promises have never been completely fulfilled. Now that the logic of separate development assumes and decrees that these homelands will have to provide for a growing number, perhaps even a growing proportion, of all Tswana and Zulu, there is less land available per person than ever before. Yet land is a sensitive subject for blacks as well as for whites, and is seen by many as a precondition for the economic and political development of the homelands.

The central government has long been aware that Bophuthatswana and KwaZulu are too small, too fragmented, and too poorly endowed with arable land to provide for a rising standard of living and increased agricultural productivity. The Native Trust and Land Act aimed to add to their areas and reduce their fragmentation, but essentially it only rationalized an existing system of reserves. It did not provide, and was not intended to provide — as homeland leaders point out — a territorial base for embryo nations. Nor did the Republic's consolidation proposals of 1972 and 1973 ameliorate the problem. Representing unsatisfactory compromises from both planning and geopolitical points of view, they pleased few. The journal *Woord en Daad* ("Word and Deed"), the mouthpiece of the Afrikaanse Calvinistiese Beweging (Afrikaans Calvinist Movement), was outspoken in criticism of the government. The proposals, it said, "led to serious doubts about the credibility of the policy of separate development and the honesty of the Government, and consequently of the whites."[41]

Because the Republic's proposals for consolidation conformed only to the

40. For both meetings, see *Rand Daily Mail*, 2 Feb. 1976.
41. Quoted in *ibid.*, 13 July 1973. The *Mafeking Mail*, 18 June 1973, was also critical. "This is a long, long way from pleasing anybody," it said of the Bophuthatswana consolidation scheme.

overall land totals of the 1936 act, there was no prospect that they could satisfy the homelands. Land is, after all, both an ideal and a real issue. It has the historical overtones of conquest and deprivation, and the present-day starkness of distress—of overcrowding, poverty, and enforced resettlement. Yet the suggested consolidations provided for little redress or relief, the promised reduction of Bophuthatswana to six large blocs and KwaZulu to ten coming without any substantial addition to the area of the homelands and with serious disruptions to the current settlement patterns of both blacks and whites. Moreover, when introducing the proposals, the government could give no precise indications of their timing and/or their cost. "I cannot," M. C. Botha told Parliament, "even give a rough estimate of the time or the money involved."[42] At the 1975 level of central government expenditure for white-owned land being transferred, all of the hectares scheduled to be handed over to blacks should be purchased by 1990. A rapid, generous consolidation into single homelands would have been of considerable value to the South African government for public relations purposes; a delayed and limited consolidation was of little value at home or abroad.

When Botha announced the consolidation proposals for Bophuthatswana in 1973, he conceded that Mangope would "probably be a little disappointed."[43] The segments of the homeland would be reduced from nineteen to ten and a total of 352,000 hectares of African land (94,000 in the Transvaal and 258,000 in the Cape) would be given to whites. In return Bophuthatswana would receive 605,000 hectares of white-owned land (218,000 in the Transvaal and 387,000 in the Cape), for a net gain of 254,000 hectares. More than 120,000 Tswana would have to be uprooted and moved. Upon his return from a visit to the United States in 1973, Mangope was more than a little disappointed. He denounced the proposal as a sham. Chief Maseloane had voiced the same sentiment when the proposals were announced.

Earlier Mangope's government, supported by Pilane, had put forward its own consolidation scheme that involved the shift to Africans of many millions of hectares of white-owned land, the transfer to black rule of a half million whites, and the annexation of the white towns of Kuruman, Taung, Warrenton, Vryburg, Delareyville, Lichtenburg, Mafeking, Koster, Rustenburg, and Zeerust. Mangope made it clear that he had no objection to whites staying in the homelands and becoming citizens. The result was a unified parallelogram stretching from Warmbad, north of Pretoria, to the border of the Orange Free State, near Christiana, and westward north of Postmasburg to the border of Botswana. The northern border of the homeland would be Botswana. In size, this consolidated territory would be larger than the

42. Botha, quoted in *The Star*, 28 April 1973.
43. Quoted in *ibid.*, 26 May 1973.

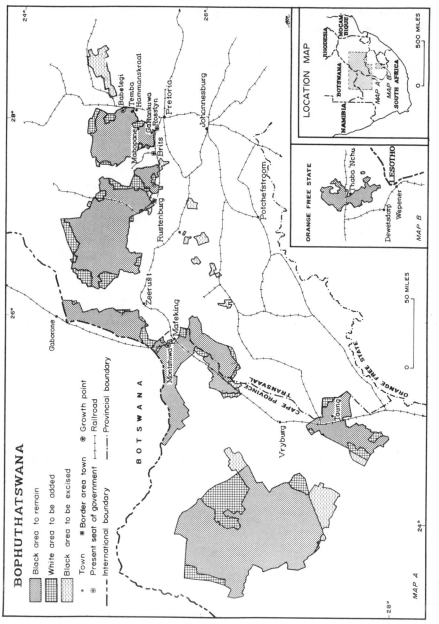

MAP 5.1. PROPOSED CONSOLIDATION OF BOPHUTHATSWANA. Sources: Republic of South Africa, BENBO, *Bophuthatswana Economic Revue, 1975* (Pretoria, 1976); Muriel Horrell, *The African Homelands of South Africa* (Johannesburg, 1973).

Orange Free State. Mangope said at the time, "I do not think that we would be satisfied with anything less as a basis for independence."[44]

For KwaZulu the complicated process of rearranging the map includes the transfer of 300,000 hectares of African land to whites and the addition of 463,000 hectares, including only 227,000 hectares of the lands promised in 1936. Of the land offered to KwaZulu, 239,000 hectares are to be taken from state-owned territory, the remainder, presumably the more arable lands, are to be purchased from white farmers. The net gain to KwaZulu is 163,000 hectares, including the R100 million Jozini Dam irrigation scheme on the Pongola River. (The Jozini project is itself controversial, experts being unsure of the fertility of the Makatini flats, which are meant to be irrigated by the waters of the Pongola. Swaziland has also demanded compensation for upstream flooding to be caused by the dam. At the moment the project has been stalled and the dam has not been allowed to fill.) Although the Republic has agreed to transfer white-settled Port St. Johns to the Transkei, the consolidation proposals deny KwaZulu the port city of Richards Bay and a potential port on Sordwana Bay. They also deny KwaZulu the income-producing Hluhluwe game reserve, but transfer the Umfolozi game reserve to the homeland. During the election campaign of 1974, the deputy minister of Bantu administration and development indicated that Eshowe, once the administrative capital of Zululand, could eventually be transferred to Kwa-Zulu, but he was overruled by Vorster at another political meeting. Moreover, some of the proposed consolidations consist of the artificial connection of enclaves by long isthmuses. As the united Party's leader in Natal commented, the proposals promised fragmentation, not consolidation. "This," he said in Parliament, "is a debate about partition."[45]

Buthelezi had rejected similar consolidation proposals throughout 1972 and early 1973. No plan made by whites without intensive consultation with Africans could, he made clear, hope to meet with Zulu favor. Nor could the wholesale dislocation of Africans be justified unless whites were equally affected. When the provisional plan was issued he said that no government of KwaZulu could possibly allow its name to be associated with the upheaval of 133,000 Zulu for the sake of a meaningless consolidation. "If the Government is going to move these people, it is not with our co-operation. We prefer that they are left alone and not uprooted until a plan is produced which is acceptable to all races in Natal." He went on: "The world can now witness that we were not consulted in these plans, that we reject them, and that what is allocated to us by Whites is done by naked *baasskap* because all that matters to the Nationalist Government is White supremacy."[46]

44. See *ibid.*, 14 April 1973.
45. Radclyffe Cadman, quoted in the *Sunday Times* (Johannesburg), 10 June 1973.
46. Quoted in *The Star,* 20 April 1973.

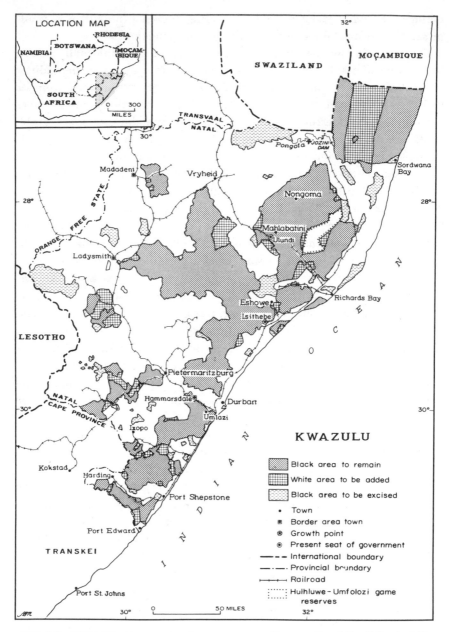

MAP 5.2. PROPOSED CONSOLIDATION OF KWAZULU. Sources: Republic of South Africa, BENBO, *KwaZulu: Economic Revue, 1975* (Pretoria, 1976); Muriel Horrell, *The African Homelands of South Africa* (Johannesburg, 1973).

Buthelezi objected strongly to the Republic's retention of Richards Bay. "If the . . . Government seriously wanted KwaZulu to be a viable state," he pointed out, "then Richards Bay should be our port so that we have an outlet to the sea and a possibility of getting anywhere near economic viability."[47] (*Woord en Daad* agreed. "How did the Trekkers and the old Transvaal Republic not strive and struggle for an outlet to the sea? How bitterly unjust did we not find it . . . ?")[48] Various Zulu spokesmen and several white politicians also noted that the consolidation proposals had allocated the best African-owned sugar cane areas to whites. Blacks, said a United Party legislator from Zululand, who had "farmed sugar cane for generations," absurdly were being moved to new blocks of land where "growing sugar was impossible."[49] Two academic observers reported that the proposals would not improve KwaZulu's economic base or give it real prospects for "meaningful independence. . . . A politically independent KwaZulu that is not enlarged, enriched and consolidated will be a thoroughly nonviable state, overly dependent on White South Africa, impossible to adminster and burdened with a depressing man–land ratio."[50]

Dladla joined Buthelezi in condemning the suggested plan. "The present generation of Whites," he said, seems "determined to dispossess us of everything that constitutes wealth in order to keep us in semi-slavery conditions." Specifically deriding plans to remove Africans from lands along the Drakensberg escarpment and the upper Tugela River, he said that it was time that whites are "told in no uncertain terms that we, as Black people of this country, deserve a fair distribution of land." If, he went on, "the Government is prepared to move 100,000 people in order to please 90 farmers and gain a few votes from the United Party, we want them to know only the barrel of a gun will move us from our land and heritage. . . . We will not rest until justice is done to the Black man." Later Dladla rejected a specific portion of the plan with blunt words. "The Government wants to strip us of our land and force us on to barren land which will compel us to work for farmers. The Government is making our people into cheap labour units and we will not tolerate this."[51]

The debate over these proposals took three years. The issue became a major one with the publication of the first proposals in mid-1972, the final proposals being accepted by resolution in Parliament only in May 1975. Long before this date Buthelezi, using the stratagem of refusing to be

47. Quoted in *ibid.*, 20 Jan. 1973.
48. Quoted in *ibid.*, 12 June 1974.
49. Cadman, quoted in *ibid.*, 17 Feb. 1973.
50. Alan C. G. Best and Bruce S. Young, "Homeland Consolidation: The Case of KwaZulu," *South African Geographer*, IV (1972), 68–69.
51. Quoted in *The Star*, 9 June 1973. See also Dladla, again quoted in *Natal Mercury*, 27 Dec. 1973.

associated with proposals on which he had not been consulted, urged Vorster to stop the limited consolidation of KwaZulu. "Since no meaningful consolidation would be achieved," he said in March 1973, he was against the plan. He could not accept the responsibility of moving thousands of people. "We asked . . . the government," he told the press, to "drop its policy of trying to consolidate KwaZulu . . . [instead] of trying to lead us to independence as a state in separate blocs."[52] Vorster's reaction to Buthelezi's dissatisfaction was conveyed to President William Tolbert of Liberia. KwaZulu, Vorster said bluntly, would never be consolidated into a single territory, even though the process of consolidation would continue.[53]

Only after being satisfied with regard to land, Mangope and Buthelezi have reiterated often, can attention ever be given to independence. Without sufficient land, independence would be a mockery. Mangope has called for "a more fair and just sharing of the land." The 1936 Act, he has said, in no way provided for future independent sovereign states. "Any continued references to this act in the context of Homeland consolidation has the taste of a dishonest subterfuge, and will do untold harm."[54] "We will not be eager to receive independence," Buthelezi said, "if it will be in the spirit of 'Since you want independence, take and starve.'" He later made it clear that the Zulu were not so "naive as to participate in a scheme to defraud us by asking for so-called independence, before land consolidation and without [the] purchase of foreign territories within our boundaries."[55] He said that the Zulu had never wanted South Africa to be chopped up into homelands, but since they had been they should realistically reflect former territories.[56] Subsequently, at a meeting of homeland leaders in late 1974, everyone (except Matanzima) explicitly rejected independence for their territories until they had been consolidated and provided with a viable economic infrastructure.[57]

The issue between the government, on the one hand, and the homeland leaders (except Matanzima), on the other, had not been resolved when the consolidation proposals were accepted by the Republican Parliament in 1975. At issue between them was the government's insistence on linking land to the ethnicity and the race of the groups and individuals who were to own it. Hence the homeland leaders have repeatedly pressed, as an alternative to independence, for a federation of properly consolidated homelands that would be based on territorial, not on ethnic and racial criteria. At a summit meeting with the prime minister in January 1975, Buthelezi reiterated the link between consolidation, independence, and political rights. Homeland

52. Quoted in *The Star*, 31 March 1973.
53. *The Times*, 17 Feb. 1975.
54. Mangope, "Political Future of the Homelands," 5.
55. Quoted in *The Star*, 14 Sept. 1971; *Rand Daily Mail*, 26 April 1972.
56. *The Star*, 5 April 1975.
57. *The Times*, 18 Nov. 1974.

leaders, he said to a huge gathering in Soweto, "did not want the homelands to be given independence as they were now. . . . They would remain poor states forever dependent on crumbs from the Pharoah's table." Unless the homelands were enlarged and properly consolidated, the only alternative was for Africans to be represented in the central Parliament.[58] In April he emphasized the egalitarian and historical bases of the claim to more land: "Either South Africa converts to one man one vote or it fully recreates the former homelands as consolidated economically viable units."[59] But the proposals went through Parliament essentially unchanged. They gave little comfort to the homeland leaders, and apart from achieving a considerable reduction in the number of homeland fragments, did little to alter the territorial bases of the respective homelands. If the territorial settlement remains as set out in 1975 proposals, the Republic's government may find that major concessions in other areas of policy will be necessary if separate development is to remain credible.

Industry and Commerce

Since the homelands are seriously underdeveloped, alternative modes of growth must be provided if static or declining trends in agricultural produc- tivity are to be arrested. In an industrializing society like South Africa there are more options than there are in purely agricultural or pastoral societies. Yet it is precisely the limitation of so many of these opportunities — the control of the movement of labor and differential access to credit, markets, and education — that so hinders African development. Official barriers to invest- ment of white capital in the homelands contribute to this backwardness, although the barriers have been lowered steadily since 1968. Moreover, even if there were no barriers, capital would still have to be lured into the home- lands with the kinds of incentives — railway rebates, inexpensive premises, tax holidays — now being offered by the government of the Republic to entrepreneurs in and out of white South Africa. Although originally favoring border industries to growth inside the homelands, the central government now encourages both forms of development.

Mangope and Buthelezi naturally prefer industrial growth within the homelands to development outside their borders. They would also like to abandon the government's "agency" system, according to which entrepreneurs receive medium-term leases to sites within the homelands and are required ultimately to promote the takeover of their enterprises by Africans. Mangope and Buthelezi support the unfettered inflow of whites and their capital on a direct basis, but, if sufficiently utilized, the agency method also has potential advantages. Several homeland leaders have in this connection

58. *Star Weekly,* 15. Feb. 1975; *Survey of Race Relations, 1975,* 27.
59. *Star Weekly,* 5 April 1975.

allowed their names and faces to be used by South Africa to advertise investment opportunities in the homelands. Throughout 1974 and 1975 the
advertisements appeared in prestigious overseas newspapers and newsweeklies.
"Make no mistake, we're not the only people you help when you start your
factory in our country," said one version, quoting Buthelezi. "First and
foremost, you'll be helping yourself." Matanzima assured apprehensive
capitalists that nationalization of investment or impediments to the free
remittance of profits were both impossible. "South Africa is the only country
where you can participate in the profit-potential of Africa without capital
risk," he was quoted. Together with Phatudi, the chief minister of Lebowa,
and Chief Wessels Mota, the chief executive councillor of Basotho Qwa Qwa,
they urged foreigners to site their factories and service industries exclusively
in the black homelands.[60]

Buthelezi has also denounced the withdrawal of foreign capital from South
Africa in other overseas advertisements. "What we need is not disengage-
ment," he said, "but full foreign participation in South Africa's overall
economic development to create more jobs, higher wages and better training
opportunities. I am no apologist for apartheid, but a realist who knows that
a job may make the difference between living and starving for many Black
families in South Africa."[61]

In addition to investments on the most advantageous terms possible, the
leaders of the homelands naturally want to negotiate those terms themselves
rather than having to accept what South African agencies offer. Mangope
and Buthelezi specifically wish to diminish the role within their own homelands of the Bantu Investment Corporation. Neither has affection for its
policies, Buthelezi having accused the corporation of neglecting Zulu
development. He has challenged it either to accept Zulu representation on
its board or "for God's sake let them get their hands off our money."[62]
Mangope and Buthelezi have both urged the central government to establish
Tswana and Zulu development corporations to replace the Bantu Investment
Corporation and to be responsible solely for the promotion of economic
growth in the two homelands. They wish these new corporations to be
representative of the ideas of Tswana and Zulu, and not of whites. (The
Xhosa Development Corporation has been unpopular in the Transkei because
it is dominated by whites and because it rarely consults the leaders of that
homeland.)

60. Full page advertisement in *The Economist*, 27 April 1974. The same, or
virtually identical, advertisements appeared in *The Times, New York Times,
Washington Post, The Sunday Times* (London), and many other newspapers and
journals.
61. *The Washington Post*, 26 Sept. 1973.
62. Quoted in *Rand Daily Mail*, 9 July 1971.

Mangope and Buthelezi were responding to the demonstrated dissatisfaction of their peoples with the actions of the Bantu Investment Corporation. In 1974, D. P. Kgotleng, a member of the Bophuthatswana Legislative Assembly, complained that the corporation had neglected to advertise businesses when they failed and fell into the corporation's hands: "This policy must not be applied only when it is in favor of Whites. It should also be applied when it is in the interest of Blacks."[63] In the same year the corporation, with the approval of the government of KwaZulu, tried to sell its wholesale grocery operations in Umlazi to a white-owned private firm. But the Umlazi Traders' Association and the Zululand African Chamber of Commerce protested vigorously and the sale was rescinded. The businessmen of KwaZulu made it clear that they would no longer support "ventures which were allegedly for the benefit of the Zulu businessmen but without the involvement of the Zulu traders at a decision-making level."[64]

In mid-1975, the Bantu Investment Corporation announced that it was forming the Bophuthatswana National Development Corporation, and Bophuthatswana thus became the first homeland to have its own investment institution. (The Xhosa Development Corporation has since 1968 encouraged Xhosa businessmen in both the Transkei and the Ciskei.) The board of directors of the new corporation was to be composed of five Tswana members named by the Bophuthatswanan government and five white directors selected by the South African government. A similar corporation was to be set up for KwaZulu. Buthelezi reacted strongly, protesting the exclusion of homeland cabinet ministers and the low proportion of blacks as members.[65]

Above all Mangope and Buthelezi decried investment strategies prepared for Bophuthatswana and KwaZulu without consultation with themselves or the homeland assemblies. On his return from the United States in 1973, Mangope had welcomed the passage of legislation facilitating investment but in 1974 he deplored the lack of consultation with homeland leaders. "People will absorb and implement change only to the extent to which they take part in it."[66]

"Give the Zulus the right," Buthelezi has said, "to make their own decisions, and development will follow." He sees no reason why KwaZulu should not obtain loans from overseas similar to those received by Malawi from South Africa. "People," he spoke of foreigners, "tend to laugh off separate development if they are told that none of the homelands has any machinery to negotiate with industrialists and overseas agencies." Pretoria must no longer insist upon prior approval of foreign aid, he said, or upon its being processed

63. *Mafeking Mail,* 14 June 1974.
64. *Natal Mercury,* 10 April 1974.
65. *Survey of Race Relations, 1975,* 148.
66. *Ibid., 1973,* 211.

through the Republic rather than its being channelled directly to a homeland.[67]

The Urban Dimension

One of the major objectives of separate development is the creation of clearly defined political orders, each with its own territory and each sovereign in its own area. But the presence of a majority of South Africa's blacks in the white-controlled heartland compromises that policy and provides homeland leaders with a legitimate claim to speak on behalf of urban blacks.

In early 1975 the summit meeting of homeland leaders and the Republican government was devoted to the position of urban blacks. Buthelezi made a major address on the subject soon after, explicitly adopting the form of a parliamentary representative speaking to his constituents and speaking throughout of himself as an African, not a Zulu leader. "A Report Back to the Reef Africans . . ." was a challenging speech, acknowledging limited progress and asking urban Africans to let their leaders know what they felt future strategy ought to be.

The relationship between homeland leaders and the urban Africans is a complex one involving serious problems for both sides. By working within the policy of separate development, however reluctantly, homeland leaders expose themselves to the attack that they are "stooges" and are serving Republican, rather than African, ends. This is a particularly serious issue for urban Africans who clamor for rights where they live today, not where they, or their ancestors, formerly lived. By speaking on behalf of urban Africans, the homeland leaders inevitably compete with the black leaders who are again appearing in the cities and who have yet to be given an institutional base comparable to those of the homeland leaders. Thus, on occasion, urban blacks have denied that they are represented by homeland leaders and have appealed for homeland status to be accorded to cities like Soweto — an appeal that the government has firmly denied. In 1973, P. M. Lengene, former chairman of the Soweto Urban Bantu Council, pointed to the fact that the majority of homeland assemblies were appointees of the government. "Do you call this a Government of the people or a Government appointed by the central Government? Do you expect the black people to have confidence in such a Government?" After the second summit meeting in January 1975, blacks, often members of Urban Bantu councils, criticized the homeland leaders for excluding urban blacks from their "team" to meet the Prime Minister."[68] It was doubtless in response to this kind of criticism that Buthelezi spoke so strongly in his "Report Back." "Some blacks," he said,

67. Quoted in *Rand Daily Mail,* 17 July, 22 Dec. 1972.
68. *Star Weekly,* 3 Jan., 15 Feb., 5 April 1975.

"baited in the main by the white press, took it upon themselves to question our credentials for speaking for our people here. . . . I dispute that there is any blackman who is not acquainted with the whole impact of black oppression."[69]

Neither Mangope nor Buthelezi has yet been effectively challenged in their own homelands or in the cities. Urban leaders have not yet developed a political or institutional base comparable to that of the homeland governments, partly because government policy has been hostile to the development of an urban African political system. At a "Black Renaissance Convention," organized by black theologians near Pretoria at the end of 1974, there was considerable debate on homelands and the policy of separate development, both of which were attacked, particularly by delegates from the South African Students' Organization and from the Black Peoples' Convention. One former homeland minister was prevented from speaking, after the passage of a motion labelling him as a "protagonist of separate development."[70] And in February 1976 Mangope was bluntly told by T. J. Makhaya, mayor of Soweto, "We in the urban areas are not interested in splinter groups in the Black nation—we want homeland leaders to represent all the interests of all the Black people of South Africa."[71]

Mangope and Buthelezi have not been backward in seizing opportunities to intervene forcefully on behalf of their subjects. Buthelezi has long been an articulate advocate of the rate for the job, and both he and Mangope have advocated higher wages and the right to strike. In an angry exchange with white industrialists in 1973, Mangope demanded that they pay minimum wages to their employees of R80 a month, a figure approximating the then-recognized poverty datum line.[72]

The wave of strikes that engulfed Natal in 1973 offered a major test of homeland external relations. As 60,000 Africans withheld their labor in Durban, Dladla, then KwaZulu's councillor for community affairs, intervened in their behalf and, by his presence, made KwaZulu's interest in improved wages and conditions of service widely known. When 500 workers struck the aluminum smelter at Richards Bay later in the same year, he appeared at the plant and indicated that requests for Zulu labor would in the future be channelled through his office, a threat to the established order that was reinforced during the textile strikes in Durban in 1974. However, the KwaZulu government does not yet control the recruitment of labor.

69. Buthelezi, "Report Back," 6.
70. *Rand Daily Mail,* 17 Dec. 1974; Report on The Black Renaissance Convention, held at Hammanskraal, 13–16 December 1974, mimeo.
71. *Rand Daily Mail,* 2 Feb. 1976.
72. *Pretoria News,* 17 March 1973.

South Africa has not openly challenged these homeland initiatives. In fact, it has pursued a more flexible course. As a response to the wave of industrial unrest, South Africa passed legislation for the first time making it possible, under stringent conditions, for Africans to bargain collectively—but not to establish formal trade unions—and thus, legally, to strike. The homelands were thus associated favorably with a limited expansion of the rights of urban Africans. As Harry Oppenheimer, chairman of the Anglo-American Corporation, commented in 1974, the policy of separate development had had effects probably not foreseen. "Far from bringing about a real separation between black and white, it was simply bringing about a situation in which tribal authorities would play an increasingly powerful role in relation to industry in the white-controlled urban areas."[73]

Even more striking, in 1974 and 1975 the leaders of the homelands began bargaining as a group directly with the government of the Republic for improvements in South African life. As a result of what were described as "brutally frank" discussions between Vorster and Botha and seven of the homeland leaders in early 1974, the Republic promised to reexamine the utility and validity of influx control and pass law regulations, and to appoint a committee jointly with the leaders to investigate the fairness of African tax contributions to the revenues of the Republic. Although there was no immediately positive result of this meeting, and the members of the tax committee have yet to be appointed, a second meeting between Vorster and the homeland executives took place early in 1975. The homeland leaders demanded that blacks be allowed to own homes in white urban areas; that the rights of black traders be increased; that influx control be abolished; that black physicians in government service receive the same pay as whites; that the power of black urban councils be strengthened (Buthelezi urged the government to declare Soweto a black homeland); that the homelands be permitted to decide upon the medium of elementary school instruction for their "citizens" in white South Africa; that ethnic residential grouping in the African townships be abandoned; that Africans be permitted to form trade unions; and that political prisoners be released and exiles be allowed to return home. Vorster only agreed, however, to reconsider restrictions on African businessmen, to think about removing some of the inequities in the existing influx control arrangements, and to consider ending the ban on property leasing by Africans in the urban townships.

Because Vorster offered contingent rather than tangible concessions, his pledges of reform in some areas of hardship caused by the apartheid system disappointed the homeland leaders. He had earlier contended that the policy of the Republic was differentiation, not discrimination. Discrimination, he

73. *The Times,* 9 May 1974.

had told the leaders of the homelands, would be removed but political power must and would remain in white hands. Power shared was power lost.[74]

Buthelezi, the most outspoken of the leaders in Cape Town, stormed out of the 1975 meeting and handed the press a copy of a memorandum that he had read to Vorster: "We have been prepared to endure abuse" he had told Vorster, "in the hope that the government's policy may be a road to real fulfillment for Blacks. If this road . . . is leading only to a cul-de-sac, then our only alternative is to seek fulfillment not in unreal 'separate freedoms' but in . . . the only seat of power which is Parliament." He went on. "I feel that it is my moral duty . . . to point out, the only logical alternatives we have, if we do not want our people to resort to civil disobedience and disruption of service in this land. Not that I intend leading my people in this direction at the moment [a phrase the Prime Minister was quick to condemn], but . . . I should point out that if no meaningful change is forthcoming for them . . . this will come as a logical alternative. . . . I cannot be expected to successfully ward off the venting of pent-up frustrations . . . if the government continually fails to offer [my people] anything meaningful." The time to "deliver the goods" had come. Otherwise disaster could not be avoided. The next day Buthelezi said that blacks must discuss "other means of taking the initiative and impressing their demands upon the Republic."[75]

These threats—only an escalation of Buthelezi's characteristic stridency—may have fallen on closed ears. But four months later the South African government announced a series of reforms. Henceforth urban Africans could "own" their homes, if not the land on which their houses were situated. This ownership consisted of thirty-year leases only, but it overturned the Republic's formerly rigid refusal to give any semblance of permanency to the stay of blacks in the white heartland. All residential security for blacks was hitherto supposed to be available only in the homelands. Moreover, the thirty-year leaseholds can be bequeathed or sold. Since 1967 black residents of the sprawling dormitory townships that surround South Africa's major cities could only rent a home, month by month, with no security of tenure. If they lost their jobs, they could be evicted immediately. If they died, their widows and families had to leave. Additionally, Vorster said that urban traders were to be permitted to deal in a wide range of commodities previously excluded. Instead of being restricted to the sale of "essential day-to-day needs," they were to be allowed to sell furniture, open department stores and banks, and so on. Black businessmen were now to be permitted to own their own premises, to enter into partnerships or companies, and to establish more than one type of business. Black physicians, lawyers, and other professionals

74. *Ibid.*, 18 Nov. 1974.
75. Buthelezi, "Report Back," 20–21; *African Research Bulletin* (1–31 Jan. 1975), 3495.

would, for the first time in nearly a decade, be allowed to open consulting rooms in the black residential areas. In October, however, the concessions on property rights were qualified by requiring applicants to take out homeland citizenship. This restriction was strongly attacked. Ntsanwisi said that homeland leaders had not been consulted about the change, and had certainly not suggested it.[76]

Despite the limited nature of the changes announced, South African ministers clearly regard the summit meetings as an institution capable of development. Botha linked the concessions directly to the earlier discussions with the leaders of the homelands. "Good results," he said, came from "constructive dialogues" with the leaders and were "proof of the government's sincere intentions, in accordance with its principles and policy, to come forward with further adjustments."[77] In so doing the Republic openly recognized the necessity of further concessions and the increasing importance of the homelands at a time when South Africa was attempting to enhance its credibility in Africa. It might be argued that recognition of the homelands by outsiders is one of the major objects of the détente policy; recognition could hardly be gained if the homeland leaders were seen to have minimal impact on policy. Although influx control and other forms of apartheid have not as yet been reformed, nor the sensitive question of black political rights in the South African heartland discussed seriously, Vorster has unquestionably given the leaders of the homelands renewed opportunities to negotiate with the government and influence the trend of future policy.

Education and Manpower Training Policy

The African areas of South Africa have long suffered from educational as well as economic neglect. The peoples of the homelands are thus conscious of the need for better educational facilities and particularly for training that will allow them access to better paying jobs in the homelands and the Republic. The leaders of the homelands are as aware as were their counterparts in colonial Africa of the crash measures that will be needed to overcome the vast educational deficits of their states. Without such measures, accelerated political and economic development will be impossible.

Compared to whites in South Africa, the educational disparities of Africans are glaring. In 1973/74 South Africa expended for education about R29 on each African child, R110 on each coloured child, R141 on each Asian child,

---

76. *Survey of Race Relations 1975*, 26, 82–3; *Star Weekly*, 6 Dec. 1975. After the Soweto riots of 1976 the central government withdrew the homeland citizenship requirement for urban leaseholds.

77. *The Times*, 7 March 1974, 23, 25 Jan., 3 May 1975; *The Economist*, 1 Feb., 10 May 1975.

and R483 on each white child.[78] School for white South African children is compulsory and free, and school books are provided without charge. For Africans schooling is voluntary (there have never been sufficient places to make it compulsory) and, in relation to African incomes, expensive, although recently there have been moves to abolish the shocking inequity of making African parents pay for school books. If the educational equipment and physical facilities available to whites are compared with those available to blacks the disparity becomes even more glaring. As Buthelezi reminded a university audience, "while South Africa violates the ideals of Western culture, it poses simultaneously as the bastion of Western standards in Africa. . . . The [unequal] spending on education . . . is not for most South Africans a question of conscientious scruple."[79]

Mangope and Buthelezi have frequently noted the lack of resources devoted to African education. Both homelands budget large proportions of their expenditures on primary and secondary training, although they are finding it difficult to increase the quality of education given. In 1973 Mangope told his assembly that 40,000 extra Tswana children would qualify for additional school places; they would require 900 new teachers and classrooms, even averaging 40 children per class. How were the staff and buildings to be provided? By 1973 educational spending in Bophuthatswana had risen sharply, comprising one-quarter to one-third of the homeland budget. In the same year education accounted for the second largest proportion, about 23 percent, of KwaZulu's R46 million budget. Only the amount devoted to works was larger. By the fiscal year 1975/76, the amount budgeted had risen to R18.5 from R10.7 million, although the proportion going to education was only 20 percent of total spending. In 1974 KwaZulu's councillor for education reported that the homeland lacked 1,000 classrooms and had a serious shortage of teachers. He doubted if his department could attract "the right kind of degreed teacher" until salaries, determined by the government of South Africa, were raised substantially.[80]

Throughout the 1950s and early 1960s the Republican government centralized its control over African education. At the beginning of 1954, responsibility was given to a division of the old Department of Native Affairs, and in 1958 this unit became a separate department. Power over education had been held by the four provincial governments and by a large number of

78. *Survey of Race Relations 1975,* 214. The figures for African children are based on those in "white areas." If the figures included homeland children the disparity would be even more glaring; if expenditure on education were related to population rather than school population, the disparity would be more glaring still.

79. Quoted in *Die Transvaler,* 26 Aug. 1972.

80. For expenditure on education in Bophuthatswana and KwaZulu, see Table 6.6. For Nxumalo's speech see *Natal Mercury,* 15 May 1974.

church organizations representing South African and external denominations. The movement of authority was not exclusively upwards, however, for integral to the government's program was the devolution of some control to school boards and committees consisting of appointed representatives of the local African communities. There was a good deal of resistance to this reorganization, however, since the entrenched interests gave way with little grace; on the other hand, the central government did little to ease the transition and, in the process, extinguished some of the brightest fixtures of private African education. In particular, vocational and technical training, adult education, and university education were severely retarded. The advancement of the homelands has suffered as a result of critical shortages of trained manpower.

At present it is not clear what the ultimate division of educational responsibility will be among the local committees, the homeland departments, and the Department of Bantu Education. The homelands exercise only a circumscribed control over educational budgets and policy. There exists, however, a *bona fide* division of power between the department, the homeland governments, and the local committees and boards. At least for the present, the Department of Bantu Education will continue to control the rate and direction of educational expansion and will possess reserve discretionary power to intervene in virtually all details of the operation of schools, including the ability to bar or dismiss an individual teacher without a hearing or statement of cause. As the autonomy of the homeland departments increases along with their ability to manage their own affairs, it will become less likely that these reserve powers will be exercised capriciously. The specific tasks of the department include development of syllabi, administration of examinations, issuance of certificates, determination of educational methods, guidance of professionals, and maintenance of standards. Educational finance, which since 1972 has been a charge against the Republic's general revenue account, remains subject to the white Parliament, although it now flows through the homeland governments. There exists an appointive Advisory Board for Bantu Education consisting of fifteen African educators and citizens who meet with the policy makers of the department.

The homeland education departments are responsible for building and maintaining school buildings, employing and paying teachers, furnishing and equipping buildings, and controlling school boards. At present, white secretaries head the education departments of Bophuthatswana and KwaZulu and most of the senior inspectors are white. In the homelands, local school committees oversee each community school. In KwaZulu, they are composed of five members elected by parents and four named by the circuit inspector.[81]

81. *Bantu*, XXII (July, 1975), 12-13.

Within the homelands, training of specialized kinds is carried out by the Department of Bantu Administration and Development (African agricultural extension officers); the Department of Bantu Education (primary, secondary, teacher training, and vocational); the Bantu Investment Corporation (management and business skills); the semiautonomous universities (academic and professional training); private firms (on the job, apprenticeship, and subsidized training); and private groups. The governments of Bophuthatswana or KwaZulu do not yet control, although they may influence, the decisions taken by these organizations.

As is the case with other aspects of resource management for development, control over education and training rather quickly passes beyond the homeland government into the formal and informal networks of the white governmental system. If the homelands' educational policies are to be coordinated with the human resource requirements of the South African region, this coordination will have to take place at the upper levels of the white bureaucracy. The Bantu Investment Corporation's industrial development program, the growth of border industries, and the expansion of the core economy are generating demands for more and better trained black manpower that far exceed the present capacity of homeland and other training agencies. So long as there is no comprehensive manpower policy for the South African regional economy, the individual homelands will experience difficulties in determining their training priorities. Any steps that they take can be vitiated by programs adopted by other homelands, the Republic in its training of urban blacks, or even by foreign states such as Lesotho. Parallel training schemes may generate oversupplies of labor in some fields and insufficient supplies in others.

KwaZulu has established a KwaZulu Planning Committee to oversee economic, educational, and social planning. The committee is chaired by Buthelezi and includes the six directors of the KwaZulu departments, representatives of government development corporations, and several consultants from outside the central government, among them Professor Lawrence Schlemmer of Natal University and Lawrence P. McCrystal, a professional planner. Its role as a planning body is unclear, because its effective scope is limited to those educational and training programs under the homeland's jurisdiction. Only agencies of the Republic are in a position to develop a regional manpower policy and implement it, presumably after consultation with the homelands and adjacent countries. The minister of Bantu education is also the minister of Bantu administration and development, but there is little formal overlap between the two departments. The Department of Planning makes only broad African labor force and employment projections in drawing up its annual six-year plan. The Decentralization Board has responsibility for guiding the reallocation of industry and jobs to border areas. Then there is a high-level, interagency committee to coordinate training and labor policy. Nonetheless, South Africa has no national manpower policy.

A good deal of growth in African education has taken place in the past ten to fifteen years. Most of the problems of African education are as much the result of the rapid expansion of enrollment and the woeful shortage of money, teachers, and schools as they are of any failures of vision or execution on the part of the responsible officials. Table 5.1 illustrates how rapidly the South African black school population has increased. From 1955 to 1973 the African population rose by 61 percent, but student enrollment more than tripled in the same period. The numbers of schools and teachers have not, however, fully kept pace. The supply of teachers has risen to an index of 265, and the student–teacher ratio has deteriorated from about 40:1 in 1950, to 46:1 in 1955, and to 58:1 in 1967; the ratio was also 58:1 in 1973. The number of schools has nearly doubled since 1955.

In order to squeeze the maximum number of students into the available facilities, many schools have gone to double sessions, especially in the early

Table 5.1
Homelands and Republic:
African Schools, Teachers, Pupils, and Population, 1955–1973

Year	Schools		Teachers		Pupils		Population	
	No.	Index	No.	Index	No.	Index	No.	Index
1955	5,801	100	21,974	100	1,013,910	100	10,386,000	100
1956	5,198	89	22,557	103	1,103,243	109	10,633,000	102
1957	6,322	109	25,499	116	1,259,354	124	10,890,000	105
1958	6,906	119	25,931	118	1,344,783	133	11,158,000	107
1959	7,335	126	26,110	119	1,409,425	139	11,437,000	110
1960	7,718	133	27,767	126	1,506,034	149	11,727,000	113
1961	7,997	138	27,828	127	1,608,668	159	12,030,000	116
1962	8,249	142	28,849	131	1,684,426	166	12,345,000	119
1963	8,463	146	30,119	137	1,770,371	175	12,672,000	122
1964	8,636	149	32,414	148	1,836,414	181	13,012,000	125
1965	8,810	152	34,810	158	1,957,836	193	13,365,000	129
1966	9,061	156	35,998	164	2,111,886	208	13,731,000	132
1967	9,258	160	38,403	175	2,241,477	221	14,111,000	136
1968	9,551	165	41,011	187	2,397,152	236	14,506,000	140
1969	9,853	170	43,638	199	2,552,807	252	14,917,000	144
1970	10,125	175	45,953	209	2,748,650	271	15,346,000	148
1971	10,551	182	50,193	228	2,936,905	290	15,776,000	152
1972	10,948	189	54,097	246	3,101,821	306	16,217,000	156
1973	11,427	197	58,319	265	3,312,283	327	16,671,000	161

SOURCE: *Bantu Education Journal*, XXI (December, 1974), 39.

grades. In these cases a single teacher instructs morning and afternoon classes, sometimes allowing them to overlap in one huge session for an hour or so at midday. Each class receives less attention than it would in a regular program. Some schools follow the platoon system, in which buildings are used in the morning by one group of students and their teachers and in the afternoon by a second group. Teacher training programs are not providing sufficient new teachers to close this gap, and many unqualified persons occupy staff positions. In Bophuthatswana in 1970, 831 of 3,907 teachers in public schools did not possess minimum qualifications. In 1975 Bophuthatswana and KwaZulu supported special programs to upgrade the abilities of underqualified teachers. But it has proven difficult to train qualified teachers at a rate sufficient to match the increase in the numbers of students in the lower and intermediate programs.

One of the great wastages acknowledged by all who study African primary educational systems is the very high rate of students leaving school. It is believed by many that those who depart before completing even the lower four grades reap little if any benefit from their education and represent a complete cost loss to the system. Whether this is so or not, statistics attest to the porosity of the school system. Table 5.2 traces the year-by-year progress of several entering classes through the system. The 1955 cohort numbered 283,000 in its first year, but shrank as it progressed. Only 72 percent of the group entered Substandard B, 69 percent Standard I, and 58 percent Standard II. Similar patterns held true for the classes of 1960, 1963, 1965, and 1967. The proportion of students advancing through the first four grades has not changed much, but from Standard III on subsequent classes show higher continuation rates. The pressure to provide additional teachers and schools is intensified by the growing number of entering students, reflecting population growth, and by the increased tendency for students to stay in school for longer periods.

It is difficult simply to explain high attrition rates. Many students help their parents with domestic and farming chores. As they get older, the income that they can earn is needed by their families. It is also costly to maintain children in school. Overcrowded conditions, underprepared and overworked teachers, and to some extent the nature of the courses, which tend to be academic and derivative of European materials rather than attuned to indigenous and rural life, are negative factors. Nonetheless, the educational system is a channel to better jobs and higher incomes and parents and students are willing to make considerable sacrifices to obtain an adequate education. At the end of Standard II an examination is held. Steady enrollment deterioration continues throughout the next four years, until the completion of the eight-year primary program. Here again there is a screening examination and only eight of every 100 students who enter primary school progress into secondary education. There is some evidence that the number

Table 5.2
Homelands and Republic:
Enrollment Progress of Selected Classes

Class	1955 Students	1955 Index	1960 Students	1960 Index	YEAR ENTERED 1963 Students	1963 Index	1965 Students	1965 Index	1967 Students	1967 Index
Substandard A	283,000	100	394,000	100	443,000	100	515,000	100	579,000	100
Substandard B	203,000	72	295,000	75	332,000	75	383,000	74	435,000	75
Standard I	196,000	69	268,000	68	301,000	68	346,000	67	397,000	69
Standard II[a]	164,000	58	218,000	55	239,000	54	276,000	54	324,000	56
Standard III	126,000	45	164,000	42	197,000	44	234,000	45	283,000	49
Standard IV	97,000	34	125,000	32	154,000	35	187,000	36	223,000	39
Standard V	79,000	28	104,000	26	132,000	30	160,000	31	195,000	34
Standard VI[a]	72,000	25	99,000	25	135,000	30	161,000	31	200,000	35
Form I	24,000	8	42,000	11	54,000	12	71,000	14		
Form II	18,000	6	35,000	8	47,000	11	63,000	12		
Form III	12,000	4	27,000	7	37,000	8				
Form IV	4,000	1	8,000	2	14,000	3				
Form V	2,000	1	5,000	1						

SOURCES: Republic of South Africa, Department of Bantu Education, *Annual Report for the Calendar Year, 1970* (Pretoria, 1971), 24–25; after 1970, April or May issues of the *Bantu Education Journal*.

[a]Examinations are held at the end of Standards II and VI to qualify students for advancement.

of Africans promoted has not always been determined exclusively by merit. To some extent, the Department of Bantu Education has suggested a proportion of passing marks, in effect setting a ceiling on the number of African students who can proceed. The chief reason for so doing is apparently the shortage of space. In Form V only 12 percent of those who entered Form I remained, and less than one out of every 100 initial entrants survived. Insofar as enough time has elapsed to tell, the more recent classes appear to be following the same general progression. There is, however, a tendency for a higher fraction of students to advance into secondary education and, as the size of the entering classes rises, this has a large multiplicative effect on secondary enrollments.

Gaining a relatively unfettered control (given a limitation on expenditures) over the curriculum and staffing of their schools has been one of the popularly appealing aspects of homeland autonomy. It has enabled the governments of Bophuthatswana and KwaZulu, following the example of the Transkei in 1963, to switch the languages of the first eight years of primary school instruction from the vernacular to English. The policy of Bantu education, instituted in 1953, required six years of mother-tongue instruction and then dual-medium education in secondary school, half the subjects being taught in English and half in Afrikaans. Yet this early compulsory instruction (consistent with the Afrikaner position with regard to their own education) in an indigenous language has been seen by blacks as a means of denying Africans equality of opportunity in the South African employment market. A mastery of Western languages and Western subjects is viewed as the key to personal and national advancement, and the earlier attempted the better.

The KwaZulu councillor for education and culture explained that Bantu Education "has caused perennial difficulties in communication between tutor and student at high school and university. A solution to this problem lies in the early familiarisation with the new medium as was the case prior to the advent to Bantu Education." KwaZulu passed legislation in October 1973 to provide for the teaching of all ordinary subjects only in English, not in Zulu, from Standard III through secondary school. Bophuthatswana decided in 1974 to follow the same course, though there the issue of medium of instruction is complicated by the presence in Bophuthatswana of many Africans from other ethnic groups. Some of these groups have insisted on the use of their own language medium, a posture that the Republican government would surely support. A Tswana opposition legislator has also pointed out that it is surely unwise for children to grow up in Bophuthatswana with no knowledge of Tswana. He therefore supported compulsory instruction in Tswana, a view supported by a Bophuthatswanan minister.[82]

82. For KwaZulu, see "Education Manifesto," 1973, mimeo., 4; for Bophuthatswana, *Mafeking Mail*, 25 Jan., 3 May 1974.

The problems of medium are not only those of the primary schools—where "mother-tongue instruction" is the issue. Under Bantu Education, high school education is equally in both of the original official languages—English and Afrikaans. Tswana children, and indeed citizens of the homeland, are thus placed not in a bilingual but in a trilingual environment, all official documents being printed in English, Afrikaans, and the relevant homeland language, and the same three languages are taught both as subjects and used as media in school. Inevitably parents and educators have complained, pointing out that in white, Asian, and coloured schools the "fifty-fifty" rule between English and Afrikaans for high school instruction is not followed.

In educational policy, as with regard to political and economic questions, homeland leaders are attempting to extend their power and act as spokesmen of urban blacks. If Zulu in Soweto are citizens of KwaZulu, surely its government should have a say in the education of urban black children? KwaZulu has pressed its claim for a common medium of instruction for all Zulu, wherever they may be. Urban blacks, at meeting after meeting have, usually without reference to the homeland governments, pressed for the early introduction of English in their school systems. But the central government has stuck to its decision that from 1975 mother-tongue instruction in the cities would be used to Standard V, a concession from its earlier insistence on Standard VI. Thereafter, in the white areas, the choice of medium would be made by the secretary of Bantu education.

This issue is by no means resolved and the complexities of educational administration are bound to increase. If Buthelezi, who has been more insistent than Mangope, should obtain a major concession regarding medium of instruction it will demonstrate the extent to which the logic of separate development and repeated public pressure by homeland leaders can enlarge the reach of homeland rule. At the summit meeting with homeland leaders in March 1974, Vorster ordered an inquiry prior to discussion at the next meeting. In January 1975, at the second summit, there was a confrontation on the fifty-fifty issue, with Buthelezi demanding a timetable, and Botha arguing that the matter "could not be rushed." "I denied that I wanted the matter 'steamrollered' but that schedule for fixing it up needs to be set down," said Buthelezi later.[83]

Apart from the debate over the languages to be used in instruction, the homeland governments have had to deal with the provision of education to their burgeoning populations. Student enrollments are rising in the primary, secondary, and technical-vocational schools of both homelands, as shown in Table 5.3. In Bophuthatswana, lower primary enrollment rose by 9.8

83. Buthelezi, "Report Back," 15.

Table 5.3
Student Enrollment in Primary, Secondary, and
and Technical-Vocational Programs, 1972–1974

| | *A. Bophuthatswana* | | | |
Program	1972	1973	1974	Change (%) 1972–1974
Lower Primary (SSA—Standard IV)	177,086	186,117	194,400	9.8
Higher Primary (Standards III–VI)	93,712	102,710	109,127	16.4
Forms I–III	17,459	20,410	24,137	38.2
Forms IV–V	1,597	1,936	2,423	51.7
Technical Secondary[a]	— —	— —	— —	— —
Teacher Training	1,773	2,140	2,304	29.9
Trade and Vocational Training	460	471	543	18.0
Advanced Technical Training[a]	— —	— —	— —	— —
Total Technical-Vocational	2,233	2,611	2,847[b]	27.5

[a]No students reported.
[b]An additional 330 students are listed as "unclassified."

| | *B. KwaZulu* | | | |
Program	1972	1973	1974	Change (%) 1972–1974
Local Primary (SSA Standard II)	318,710	342,256	377,526	18.5
Higher Primary (Standard III VI)	124,077	137,588	151,878	22.4
Forms I–III	24,094	28,001	31,730	31.7
Forms IV V	2,401	2,801	3,565	48.5
Technical Secondary	100	135	145	45.0
Teacher Training	1,319	1,511	1,652	25.2
Trade and Vocational	958	1,117	1,253	30.8
Advanced Technical Training	65	69	79	21.5
Total Technical-Vocational	2,442	2,832	3,129	28.1

SOURCES: BENBO, *Bophuthatswana, Economic Revue, 1975* (Pretoria, 1976), 48; *idem, KwaZulu, Economic Revue, 1975* (Pretoria, 1976), 56; *Bantu Education Journal,* XIX (April, 1973), 20–21; XX (August, 1974), 20–21; XXI (August, 1975), 20–21.

percent between 1972 and 1974, and the number of higher primary students grew by 16.4 percent. Primary education expanded by even larger percentages in KwaZulu. The tendency for students to remain in school longer, and the growing pressures of larger primary classes, have substantially raised the number of students in secondary education classes. Forms I to III and IV to V show gains of 32 to 52 percent in the two-year interval. Growth in technical and vocational education has also been substantial. It should be noted, however, that only about 1 percent of the students in the two homelands in 1974 was enrolled in Forms IV to V, teacher training or technical-vocational programs.

Increasing enrollments have necessitated the augmentation of schools and teachers. In Bophuthatswana, the number of primary schools rose from 589 in 1970 to 682 in 1974, and in KwaZulu the increase was from 1,345 in 1972 to 1,448 in 1974. In 1974 there were 80 secondary and teacher training schools in Bophuthatswana, compared to 51 in 1970, and 110 in KwaZulu, compared to 87 in 1972. The numbers of teachers have risen only commensurately. Pupil–teacher ratios, a good measure of the quality of education, have remained very high in both homelands. At the primary level in Bophuthatswana, for example, there were 64 students per teacher in 1973 versus 66 in 1970. During the same period, secondary and teacher training instructors have had to cope with an average of thirty to thirty-two pupils per teacher.[84]

Although universal literacy, and at least a basic grasp of enough arithmetic, health, and "social survival knowledge" to function in South Africa's complex modern society are the immediate goals of homeland education, the needs of the Republic and homelands for more sophisticated skills are pressing. It is difficult to obtain a clear overview of the existing secondary and other advanced training programs and determine their economic importance for the two homelands. Tswana and Zulu may be trained elsewhere and those who are trained within the homelands often move onto the national labor market.

Teachers are prepared at seven schools in Bophuthatswana. There is a small number of girls learning dressmaking or preparing to be preschool assistant teachers. KwaZulu has four teacher training schools: at Amanzimtoti, Madadeni, Eshowe, and Appelbosch, and a fifth is being built.

Advanced skill training is also provided by the homelands. In Bophuthatswana ten institutions offer trade and technical instruction; there are six such schools in KwaZulu. Technical and trade courses cover such subjects as applied mechanics, building construction, technical drawing, carpentry, masonry, welding, electrical wiring, automobile repair, and plumbing.

84. BENBO, *Bophuthatswana Economic Revue, 1975* (Pretoria, 1976), 47–9; *idem., KwaZulu Economic Revue, 1975* (Pretoria, 1976), 54–57.

Additionally, colleges at Taung in Bophuthatswana and Empangeni in KwaZulu graduate agricultural and veterinary service officers. The Bantu Investment Corporation provides business schooling at Temba, near Babelegi, in Bophuthatswana. Preemployment training for factory workers is offered at Babelegi and at Isithebe, a growth point in KwaZulu. Here, and in border industrial zones adjacent to the homeland, the Department of Bantu Education provides guidance to private industrialists who perform the actual instruction and are granted subsidies to cover their expenses. In some cases the department builds and equips industrial educational centers to supply graduates to clusters of nearby businessmen who share the operating costs. All of these various courses of training are in great demand, and there is certainly no evidence that sufficient facilities are being provided by the homelands, the Republic, or private concerns. The dispersal and small scale of most schemes is not conducive to quality instruction or low costs per graduate. The proliferation of many small manpower training projects by the uncoordinated white developmental bureaucracies in the homelands and urban areas cannot meet the manpower needs of South Africa or the homelands.

Mangope and Buthelezi recognize the necessity of the expansion of the universities. In 1974, of 111,000 university students in South Africa, fewer than 8,000 were black.[85] Neither Mangope (who has had a son at Turfloop) nor Buthelezi has any affection for the homeland universities, established under the Extension of University Education Act of 1959 and administered by the Department of Bantu Education. They are explicitly excluded from the purview of the homeland governments by the Bantu Taxation Act of 1971.

The university system has experienced rapid growth and a broadening of programs. The universities of Zululand at Ngoya and the North at Turfloop, where Tswana and others may attend, were established in the 1960s. Africans may also take correspondence courses from the University of South Africa. A few attend the Natal Medical School with Asians and coloureds. A few blacks attend white universities for courses of study not available in the homeland institutions. Between 1960 and 1974, the student populations rose sharply from 80 to 1,509 at Turfloop and from 41 to 1,003 at Zululand. The usual range of liberal arts and science subjects is provided, and there are some professional programs in law and forms of engineering and practical science. Table 5.4 lists the numbers of graduates by degree.

Given the universities' regional identifications, there is more diversity in the composition of the student bodies than might be expected. In 1973, only 172 (17.6 percent) of the 979 students at Zululand came from KwaZulu. The

85. *Rand Daily Mail,* 4 Feb. 1975.

Table 5.4
Numbers of Graduates
From the University of the North
and the University of Zululand

| | A. University of the North | | | | |
	1971	1972	1973	1974	1975
Dip. (S.W.)	3	3	—	1	1
Dip. (Commerce)	—	1	1	—	—
Dip. (Nursing Ed.)	—	—	6	8	14
Dip. (Nursing Admin.)	—	—	8	5	18
S.A. Teach. Dip.	52	36	—	—	—
Second. Teach. Dip.	—	—	53	32	36
P.S.L. Ex.	—	—	—	1	—
B.A.	36	46	38	56	82
B.A. Soc. Sci.	9	18	24	31	—
B.A. Soc. Work	—	—	—	—	23
B. Law	2	5	6	7	9
B. Commerce	—	3	4	3	5
B. Admin.	—	3	3	2	5
B.A. Theology	—	—	1	5	2
B. Theology	—	—	—	—	1
B.S.	5	4	7	5	18
B.S. Pharmacy	2	4	1	4	4
B. Pharmacy	—	—	—	—	3
Univ. Ed. Dip.	14	31	23	37	26
Univ. Ed. Dip. (non-grad)	5	7	—	5	4
Hon. B.A.	3	7	5	5	9
Hon. B.A. Soc. Sci.	—	—	—	2	—
Hon. B.S.	1	1	1	2	1
B. Ed.	2	3	7	5	7
M.A.	—	1	1	—	2
M. Ed.	1	—	1	—	—
LL.B.	—	—	—	1	1
D. Litt.	—	—	—	1	—
D. Ed.	—	—	—	1	—

Table 5.4 (Continued)

					B. University of Zululand								
	1963	1964	1965	1966	1967	1968	1969	1970	1971	1972	1973	1974	1975
B.A.	—	5	3	8	13	17	22	15	29	47	39	39	65
B.A.(S.W.)	2	2	5	10	5	8	10	3	5	9	16	20	27
B.Sc.	—	1	2	2	1	2	3	4	1	4	5	3	14
Dip.Com.Subj.	—	6	—	3	7	4	—	—	—	—	1	1	—
B.Adm.	—	—	—	—	—	—	—	—	—	—	—	1	2
B.Ed.	—	—	—	—	—	—	—	—	—	—	2	7	2
B.Bibl.	—	—	—	—	—	—	—	—	—	—	1	1	4
L.L.B.	—	—	—	—	—	—	—	—	—	—	—	—	2
P.S.L.Ex.	—	—	—	—	—	—	—	1	2	4	7	17	32
Att.Adm.	—	—	—	—	—	—	—	—	1	—	—	—	1
B.Com.	—	—	—	—	—	—	—	—	2	5	3	2	3
Hons.B.Com.	—	—	—	—	—	—	—	—	—	—	1	1	—
B.Juris.	—	—	—	—	—	—	—	1	—	4	—	10	8
Hons.B.A.	—	—	1	2	2	1	3	2	4	2	7	7	14
Hons.B.A.(S.W.)	—	2	—	1	1	2	4	—	1	2	—	1	2
L.Dip.Lib.	—	—	—	—	—	—	—	—	1	—	3	—	3
S.T.D.	—	28	11	14	7	27	23	39	34	71	73	67	65
J.E.D.	—	—	1	1	4	7	8	12	8	11	17	23	15
Dip.(S.W.)	—	—	5	4	4	2	8	11	—	7	7	9	5
Hons.B.Sc.	—	—	—	—	—	—	—	1	—	—	—	1	1
M.A.	—	—	—	—	—	—	—	—	—	—	—	—	2

SOURCE: Printed graduation programs of the University of the North; letter to Butler from the registrar, University of Zululand, 3 July 1975.

urban areas of Natal and the Transvaal accounted for a strongly preponderant three-quarters of the enrollment, and although many were Zulu, others were not. All the other homelands were represented, and there were students drawn from Namibia (Southwest Africa), Malawi, and Rhodesia. Similarly, while students from Lebowa are the main homeland component at the North, the other homelands, the Republic, and foreign nations sent students in sufficient quantity to produce a truly cosmopolitan student body. Of the 1,274 students, 142 (11 percent) were from Bophuthatswana.[86] Unlike primary and secondary education, which are oriented in the direction of reinforcing black linguistic and cultural differences, higher education is considerably more integrative of black communities. The homeland universities are the only places in southern Africa where relatively well-educated young Africans from all political entities are brought together.

Students show a preference for specialization in arts and education rather than science, mathematics, and commerce-administration. In 1973, 62 percent of the students at Zululand were in arts or education; 11 percent were in commerce-administration, and 8 percent were in science. At Turfloop 56 percent were in arts or education, 10 percent in commerce-administration, and 22 percent in science.[87]

The emigration of many university teachers, the reluctance of non-South Africans to take positions in the Republic, and the proliferation of white universities have badly strained the supply of academic talent available in South Africa. Even in these circumstances the staffs of the North and Zululand have remained predominantly white since their inception. The University of the North began with 5 African lecturers of a total of 26; in the early 1970s there were 28 Africans on a staff of 98. At Zululand, initially 3 of 18 teachers were African, the numbers changing in 1974 to 15 of 88. In 1974 it was reported that 6 of 94 professors at Fort Hare, Zululand, and the North were black; 15 of 142 senior lecturers and 53 of 139 lecturers were black. There may have been a modest increase in black staff at the junior level.

Although the quality of faculty at the black institutions is widely criticized, a more serious problem is their small scale and their isolation from each other, from other institutions of higher learning in South Africa, and from the intellectual community. The etiquette of apartheid is observed in relations between black and white staff, and between white staff and administrators and students. Such attitudes are incompatible with the spirit of university education and the logic of homeland development. Under such strained circumstances, it is not surprising that, despite the risks of suspension and arrest involved, students at the African universities have engaged in numerous

86. *Bantu Education Journal*, XVI (Sept., 1974), 28.
87. *Ibid.*

protests during the last several years. Authoritarian paternalism, social apartheid, and the lack of black faculty and administrators contribute to friction and an atmosphere of mistrust and hostility.

Unrest and poor morale at the University of the North in 1974 and 1975 became so serious that the South African Government appointed Justice J. H. Snyman as a one-man investigative commission. His report, issued in early 1976, reported that black students and faculty were discontented, especially about social apartheid, discrimination in salaries (especially the "inconvenience allowance" paid to white staff), limited black participation in decision-making, and continued white dominance of the faculty. Snyman recommended more autonomy, equalization of salaries and promotional opportunities, and greater black control. He further recommended that postgraduate students be allowed to attend white universities. These recommendations were emphasized in the Jackson report of 1976, the nominal brief of which had been the Africanization of the university but which ranged far wider and underlined the necessity of whites assuming a subordinate role in the education of Africans.[88] Their comparatively cosmopolitan students, the erudition of their black students and faculty, and their rapid growth in size are likely, however, even if the Snyman proposals are accepted by the Republic, to continue to make the African universities focal points for the expression of black dissent and hopes for change in South Africa.

One major problem is that adequate Ph.D. training for Africans is scarce in South Africa.[89] This shortage of higher-level schooling not only retards the Africanization of college faculties, but makes it impossible to secure sufficient trained staff and sophisticated expert advisors for the homeland governments and their leaders. Chiefs Mangope and Buthelezi have very little intellectual talent — economists, public administrators, management experts, engineers, or agricultural technicians — from whom they can seek assistance when they negotiate with or make appeals to the Republic's bureaucracy. The expertise of the Republic's agencies may be one of their principal means of dominating homeland developmental decision-making in the early phases of self-government.

The shortage of facilities affects not only the production of Ph.Ds to staff research and teaching institutions, but the professions like medicine, where on-the-job training is not nearly as feasible as it is in accountancy and law. Recently, expanded provision was made through an outgrowth of Mangope's attempt to found a university. In 1972, seeing little likelihood of the University of the North adequately serving the needs of Bophuthatswana, Mangope opened a fund to try to raise money for his own college. This

88. *Star Weekly,* 14 Feb. 1976; for the Jackson Report, see *ibid.,* 28 Feb. 1976.
89. See also above, 47–48.

became unnecessary, however, when the central government decided to open a university in GaRankuwa, a major Tswana township outside Pretoria. The new university will, aided by the faculties of Pretoria and Witwatersrand, open in 1978 and provide medical training.[90]

Several changes of policy are implied in the structure of the new university. Both English and Afrikaans universities are to be associated in curricular planning and in representation on the Council, the governing body of the university. Hitherto English universities have played little part in homeland development. The governments of the homelands will be given representation on the Council. Furthermore, the new university is to be a statutory institution, a device which may ensure considerably greater autonomy than that enjoyed by the existing homeland universities. However, the government is still insisting on segregating students according to race: at the end of 1975 it was announced that the Natal Medical School, which had accepted coloured, Asian, and African students, would be closed to Africans once they had a medical school of their own.[91]

The question of control of homeland universities has long been an issue. Until the announcement of the new medical school and university in Bophuthatswana, the Zulu were marginally better placed than the Tswana because of the existence of the University of Zululand. But the government of KwaZulu has not influenced the running of its university. Leaders of KwaZulu have complained that the university's Council has no Zulu members, and that its black advisory council has no power. KwaZulu would obviously want to revamp the educational approach of this university. But legislation passed by the Republic's Parliament in 1973 reiterated that government's intention to retain control over the universities. At the same time, in another enactment, Parliament permitted African universities to open branches or tertiary campuses. It extended to them the right to lend or borrow money and made it possible for the councils of the universities to assign functions to committees with "full power of action."[92] This act permits the siting of branches of universities in urban areas, like Soweto, or in the heart of a homeland. It does not provide, however, for the exercise of control by homeland governments over the universities in their own areas. It remains to be seen whether the Snyman recommendations will persuade the central government to improve relations between the universities and the homeland governments, and as the Jackson report recommended, allow the universities to develop close ties with the communities they are designed to serve.

90. *Mafeking Mail,* 3 May 1974; *Star Weekly,* 10 May 1975, 3 Jan. 1976.
91. *Star Weekly,* 27 Dec. 1975.
92. *House of Assembly Debates* (12 Feb. 1973), cols. 454–455.

Mangope, Buthelezi, and Separate Development

This examination of selected issues highlights the similarity of the views of Mangope and Buthelezi. Implicit in every stand they take is a disagreement with the premises of separate development. On the issue of power, both leaders want a redistribution in favor of their own people and of Africans generally. Both want a redistribution of resources and opportunity, whether it be land, jobs, education, or the general rights of their citizens in the South African cities. Both argue for consultation *before* decisions are made affecting their people, rather than the familiar South African pattern of deciding first and then simply informing Africans of changes in policy, or refusals to alter policy. If an overall label had to be affixed to their approach it would be liberal, not socialist. They are the inheritors of the traditions of the African National Congress—of an inclusionist liberalism with deep roots in South Africa. They want to minimize racial difference, enhance equality, and obtain more equitable sharing of national income and resources.

There are differences, too. There is a consistent anxiety to preserve Tswana identity in the actions of Bophuthatswana's leaders, which can be seen in their stands on federalism and on the medium of education. Mangope has argued that the arousing of Tswana nationalist feeling is a positive achievement of separate development, a point-of-view Buthelezi is unlikely to share. Mangope is in many respects closer to Matanzima than he is to Buthelezi in willingly using the language of ethnic nationalism. Buthelezi, a leader of the largest African group, understandably puts his appeal in the most general African terms. Furthermore, a major portion of the Zulu are not separated from him by an international boundary, i.e., if he were to think in ethnic terms his major potential allies are inside, not outside, South Africa. Moreover, he is the leader of one of the most homogeneous of the homeland populations, only about 2 percent of the population being Africans from other ethnic groups. Bophuthatswana, however, has a non-Tswana African population of about 284,000, roughly 32 percent of its total homeland population. Mangope therefore faces an entirely different political problem. His potential allies are the Tswana of Botswana. But until there are substantial concessions to Bophuthatswana, concessions that differentially favor it over KwaZulu, Mangope will have more to gain from common action with other homeland leaders than he will from attempting to go it alone.

6

National Income
and Public Finance

The economies of Bophuthatswana and KwaZulu are extensions or subsectors of that of the Republic and are not self-contained. Their economic dependence takes several forms. The lack of opportunities in the homelands compels many workers to seek employment in the white areas of the Republic. The resultant system of transitional migrant and commuter labor provides the bulk of the income by which homeland citizens survive; production within the homelands typically constitutes less than one-quarter of total area income. Wage rates for jobs held by Africans in the Republic are thus a major determinant of homeland economic welfare.

This dependence of the private sector is paralleled by the reliance of the homeland governments upon the financial support of the central government. Lacking a tax base of affluent, productive citizens, and barred from taxing white businesses or mines within their territories, the homeland governments receive most of their revenues directly from the Republic. For agricultural, industrial, and infrastructure development, the homelands depend upon the Republic for investment capital, management, and entrepreneurship. The Bantu Investment and Mining corporations have been given the major part of the responsibility for providing the industrial, commercial, and extractive enterprise necessary to make the homelands economically more self-reliant. These white-dominated agencies have become the major sources of capital and the locus of most decisions about developmental priorities.

Sources of Income and Structure of Output

The pattern of underdevelopment in Bophuthatswana and KwaZulu is in most respects that shared by the world's poorer countries and regions. Income per capita and labor productivity are low; economic growth is sporadic and dependent upon external factors. Rapid population growth causes a deterioration of the man–land and food production–population ratios. The supply of mature labor exceeds the economy's employment capacity and there is a mounting overbalance of persons in nonproductive, dependent age ranges (especially below age fifteen). Agriculture is the most important economic activity, but is for the most part customary and noncommercial. In Bophuthatswana, where the rainfall is light and there are no dependable rivers, the dominant rural occupation is cattle herding mixed with small-scale farming. In KwaZulu, water is more plentiful and in many areas farming is more important than husbandry. In both homelands, agricultural technology is backward and static, fertilizer and other modern inputs are rarely used, and extension services are limited.

Industrialization in Bophuthatswana and KwaZulu has hardly begun and its distribution is uneven. Unlike many newly independent nations, neither homeland has inherited a colonial industrial, plantation, or mining sector that could constitute the core of an industrial base. The sponsorship and management necessary to generate large-scale factory enterprise have not been forthcoming from either internal or external sources. Facilities to mobilize savings and provide agricultural and industrial credit, such as rural cooperatives, private banks, and specialized development finance corporations, are almost totally absent. Electricity consumption per person is very low, and vast areas of the two homelands remain without any power except that provided by men and animals. Transport facilities are primitive except in those few areas near white cities that are served by trains and buses. There is little piped drinking water and sanitation, and health facilities are rudimentary.

In an underdeveloped economy, the most important measures of economic welfare and growth are the national income accounts that measure annual production and earnings. The best calculations of national income in Bophuthatswana and KwaZulu are those released by the statistical sections of BENBO, the research and planning unit of the Bantu Investment Corporation.[1] Using the available population, national income, and homeland product statistics, it is possible to derive some approximate indices of per capita output and income.

Several limitations must be considered in assessing these "fairly rough" estimates. Subsistence income is essentially ignored; some farm, domestic, handicraft, and traditional personal service production is not adequately included. Since many workers are absent much of the time, the population

1. Scattered data are found in: J. A. Lombard and P. J. van der Merwe, "Central Problems of the Economic Development of the Bantu Homelands," *Finance and Trade Review*, X (1972), 1-46, tables 2 and 10; J. J. Stadler, "Demografiese en Ekonomiese Kenmerke van die Suid-Afrikaanse Bantoetuislande," *Agrekon*, IV (1970), 22-28; J. A. Lombard, "The Economic Philosophy of Homeland Development," in Rhoodie, *South African Dialogue*, 168-181; fuller series are found in BENBO's *Economic Revues* for 1975 of the two homelands (Pretoria, 1976). See also J. A. Lombard, *et al.*, *Focus on Key Economic Issues, 9, The Homelands* (Pretoria, 1974).

pyramid, or age and sex distribution, of the homelands is skewed toward females and young and old male dependents. Internal production is therefore depressed beneath that of populations of comparable size. Further, it is difficult to determine exactly how much income is earned and remitted by absentee workers: by commuters, migrants, and *de jure* homeland citizens living in white areas. An undetermined number of people work and earn illegally in white cities, either as commuters or as longer term migrants. There is no attention to the distribution of income, and averages can do little to suggest how many persons are found at the extremes of poverty and wealth.[2]

The most recent available income statistics are for 1973, with roughly comparable estimates for 1970 and 1960. These are presented in table 6.1 and include the major income aggregates such as internal earnings, absentee labor income, and total income of the *de facto* and *de jure* populations. The first column contains estimates of income earned by homeland residents: residents of Bophuthatswana earned R38.0 million and residents of KwaZulu earned R79.7 million in 1973. (An appropriate exchange rate for 1970 and 1973 is R1 = $1.40; for 1976, R1 = $1.15.) By way of contrast, the gross domestic product of the Republic in 1972 was over R15.3 billion, to which both homelands contributed less than 1 percent, far less than their area and population would imply. The total income of each of the homelands is smaller than that of an American town or medium-sized business firm. Computations based on the 1970 income figures and gross domestic product totals (from table 6.2) indicate that about 54 percent of area output in Bophuthatswana and 83 percent in KwaZulu are retained as income by homeland Africans, the remainder presumably going to whites and others as wages and salaries or business income.

Income earned inside the homelands is strikingly small compared to outside commuter and migrant incomes. Using the data in table 6.1, for the Tswana, internal income, commuter income, and migrant income amount, respectively, to 23, 58, and 19 percent of earnings; for the Zulu, the respective shares are 22, 36, and 41 percent. In the former case, commuter income earned in Pretoria, Rustenburg, and other white areas immediately south of the homeland is the major component, although for KwaZulu migrant income dominates. The average income earned from internal sources in 1973 was about R40 in Bophuthatswana and R35 in KwaZulu, but was only R28 and R26 respectively in 1970. These exceptionally low per capita output

---

2. Lombard, van der Merwe, and Stadler mention most of these reservations in their various publications. The net effect of the omissions and qualifications is difficult to assess. The underrepresentation of subsistence income reduces the homeland output figures below what they might be, but, on the other hand, estimates of the portion of absentee worker income that actually returns to the homelands are merely rough guesses and could be too high or too low.

Table 6.1

Gross National Income and Per Capita Income: Bophuthatswana
and KwaZulu, 1960, 1970, 1973

	Gross National Income (million rands)						Per Capita Income (rands)			Income of Permanently Absent Tswana or Zulu (million rands)
	Income Earned in Homeland	Commuter Income	Migrant Income	Total (1)–(3)	Income of Non-Blacks in Homeland	Gross National Income (4)+(5)	Income Earned in Homeland	De facto Inhabitants	De facto Inhabitants and Migrants	
	(1)	(2)	(3)	(4)	(5)	(6)	(7)	(8)	(9)	(10)
BOPHUTHATSWANA										
1960	11.8	—[a]	15.0	26.8	1.5	28.3	29.8	29.8	57.8	60.1
1970	24.4	58.0	19.5	101.9	2.4	104.3	28.2	95.3	112.5	158.7
1973	38.0	94.5	30.5	163.4	—[a]	—[a]	40.2	140.2	165.2	230.1
KWAZULU										
1960	34.2	—[a]	40.7	74.9	3.7	78.6	28.4	28.4	54.0	143.6
1970	54.7	80.0	94.1	228.8	5.2	234.0	26.0	64.1	100.9	254.0
1973	79.7	130.5	149.0	359.2	6.5	365.6	34.7	91.5	145.0	368.3

SOURCES: BENBO, *Bophuthatswana, Economic Revue, 1975* (Pretoria, 1976), 32; idem, *KwaZulu, Economic Revue, 1975* (Pretoria, 1976), 36.

[a]Figures are not available.

figures reflect the lack of productive employment opportunities, the absence of much of the work force, and, to a lesser extent, underestimation of subsistence production.

These low levels of productivity, and the fact that over three-quarters of Tswana and Zulu income comes from absentee labor, make abundantly evident the dependence of the homelands on the economy of the Republic. Because they are the baselines from which reconstruction of the homeland economies must begin, they are also dramatic measures of the immense gap that must be closed before productivity levels in the homelands can compare to those outside them. The race between population growth and diminishing returns in homeland agriculture (and minimal returns in industry) was lost a generation or more ago, leaving most workers no option but to seek employment in the Republic. In simple terms, the homelands would have to become four to five times more productive merely to reabsorb their *de facto* work forces at constant levels of living. To close the gap with the living standards in the Republic, or with those in middle-level developing nations, or to reabsorb a fraction of the now permanently absent Tswana or Zulu, would require much greater effort.

These broad aggregate conjectures, which do not allow for the increasing difficulty of sustaining worker productivity as more people are employed in a homeland, make it plain that an exceedingly well-financed and well-designed strategy will be required to overcome existing underdevelopment and provide satisfactory employment for a significant fraction of absentee workers.

The income of Tswana permanently absent from their homeland was R230.1 million in 1973; Zulu living in the Republic earned R368.3 million. If these aggregate incomes are added to the total incomes of the homeland Tswana and Zulu (column 4 of table 6.1), then total Tswana income was R393.5 million and total Zulu income was R727.5 million for 1973. But these global totals have no real meaning for the homelands, except in defining the total income of the *de jure* population and establishing the broadest definition of the homeland's personal tax base. Little income from permanently absent Tswana and Zulu is sent to the homelands, although some is doubtlessly returned to kin. Likewise migrants probably must spend most of their incomes on housing, food, and necessities, leaving little to send or take back.

Lombard, Stadler, and van der Merwe assume that all commuter income, one-fifth of migrant income, and one-twentieth of the earnings of those *de jure* citizens permanently living in white areas are remitted to the homelands. The addition of these amounts to income earned in the homeland yields an aggregate total called area national income. This is a measure of the total income generated within and flowing into the homeland economies. In 1973 area national income in Bophuthatswana was R150.1 million, and in Kwa-Zulu it was R258.4 million. Using estimates of 1973 populations, this means that per capita area incomes were R151 and R112, respectively. For 1970 comparable figures were R109 for Bophuthatswana and R79 for KwaZulu. These income estimates lie between the average income of the *de facto* inhabitants (column 8 of table 6.1) and an average income measure that includes full migrant incomes (column 9 of table 6.1).[3]

Despite the importance of external sources of income, internal economic development will depend upon the capacity of the homeland governments and Republic developmental institutions such as the Bantu Investment and Mining corporations to accelerate structural changes in homeland output. Generally speaking, although agriculture must grow absolutely and become more commercial, the relative shares of industry, mining, transportation and communication, and the public sector will have to expand relative to the farming sector. BENBO has recently made available data describing the sectoral origins of gross domestic product in Bophuthatswana and KwaZulu. These augment fragmentary information published by Lombard, Stadler, and van der Merwe.[4] From fiscal 1960/61 to fiscal 1971/72 the two homeland regional economies apparently experienced structural modernization in a moderate, uneven manner (see table 6.2). Of necessity the data depend upon rough estimates, but the estimates are probably no more conjectural than those used for many less-developed areas of the world.

The more important changes in the structure of Bophuthatswana's economic activity are the decline of agriculture, the sharp rise in the contribution of mining, the moderate industrial gains, and the shift away from traditional personal services. Because of the expansion of the value of total output (item 13), all sectors with the exception of agriculture show some absolute growth, but those with higher shares at the end of the period have been growing relatively faster. The stagnation of agriculture and its small share of output reflect the poor prospects for intensive farming in most of the homeland, the failure and small size of government programs, and the inability of indigenous farming and herding to commercialize and become more productive without substantial improvement in the availability of modern inputs, technology and extension advice, credit, infrastructure, and marketing outlets. The government sector (items 7 and 8) grew rapidly in the late 1960s and early 1970s, although this growth was disguised by the overshadowing rise of mining. Likewise, the growth point at Babelegi, the

3. Cf. Lombard and van der Merwe, "Central Problems," 35. Population growth rates from 1970 to 1973 are taken from 1951 to 1970 averages, *ibid.*, 33.

4. See chapter 6, note 1. Fuller series are published in BENBO, *Bophuthatswana, Economic Revue, 1975* (Pretoria, 1976), 30, and *KwaZulu, Economic Revue, 1975* (Pretoria, 1976), 34. See also Lombard, *Key Economic Issues*, figure 8.

Table 6.2
Structure of Output, 1960/61–1971/72:
Percentage of GDP Arising From Major Economic Sectors

Sectors	A. Bophuthatswana		Years		
	1960/61	1965/66	1969/70	1970/71	1971/72
1. Agriculture, hunting, forestry, fishing	30.9	14.0	15.7	7.3	8.5
2. Mining and quarrying	13.2	15.0	27.0	39.7	43.0
3. Manufacturing, electricity, gas, water, construction	4.4	4.5	6.4	7.4	4.0
4. Commerce, catering, accommodations	4.7	5.7	5.3	4.2	3.5
5. Transport and communication	4.4	5.9	5.4	5.2	3.5
6. Finance, real estate, business services	1.4	2.4	2.7	2.7	2.4
7. Public administration	5.0	14.6	9.9	10.0	9.1
8. Education	12.4	13.7	10.6	10.5	10.3
9. Health services	2.8	5.1	3.7	3.6	3.4
10. Other marketable services	0.2	0.4	0.2	0.2	0.2
11. Subsistence services	20.6	18.8	13.0	9.1	7.1
12. Total services (7–11)	41.0	52.5	37.4	33.5	30.1
13. Total gross domestic product	R14,892	R19,010	R30,862	R45,395	R59,903

Sectors	B. KwaZulu		Years		
	1960/61	1965/66	1969/70	1970/71	1971/72
1. Agriculture, hunting, forestry, fishing	44.4	27.9	32.1	27.5	30.6
2. Mining and quarrying	6.4	7.4	0.2	0.5	0.5
3. Manufacturing, electricity, gas, water, construction	5.6	5.9	5.5	5.3	6.1
4. Commerce, catering, accommodations	4.5	5.8	6.8	6.7	6.4
5. Transport and communication	2.7	4.3	4.1	5.5	4.9
6. Finance, real estate, business services	1.3	2.4	2.6	2.6	2.4
7. Public administration	5.3	10.7	11.4	15.8	14.5
8. Education	8.1	9.4	11.8	11.0	10.5
9. Health services	3.1	7.2	9.0	10.0	10.6
10. Other marketable servics	0.2	0.3	0.4	0.4	0.5
11. Subsistence services	18.3	18.7	16.1	14.7	13.0
12. Total services (7–11)	35.1	46.3	48.7	51.9	49.1
13. Total gross domestic product	R38,997	R44,146	R58,002	R65,298	R76,111

SOURCES: Computed from data in BENBO, *Bophuthatswana, Economic Revue, 1975* (Pretoria, 1976), 30; *idem, KwaZulu, Economic Revue, 1975* (Pretoria, 1976); J. A. Lombard *et al., Focus on Key Economic Issues,* 9, *The Homelands* (Pretoria, 1974), figure 8.

construction of a shopping center at Temba township in the homeland and new shops and beer gardens have been responsible for the growth reflected in the figures for industry, construction, and commerce.

The unique role of mining in Bophuthatswana deserves further comment. The value of the homeland's mineral output rose from R4.2 million in fiscal 1968/69 to R25.8 million in fiscal 1971/72. This increase accounted for 61 percent of the growth in the homeland. If this element is factored out, then the gross domestic product in fiscal 1971/72 would have been only about R38 million instead of R60 million. It is known that few Tswana work in the mines of their homeland, that the mines employ many white workers and are, of course, controlled by white-owned firms, and that the Tswana government does not participate directly in mineral earnings. The total income earned by Africans in Bophuthatswana was probably about R31 million in fiscal 1971/72,[5] which is only slightly more than half the gross domestic product. Although estimates have been omitted from the appropriate place in the income table (column 5, table 6.1), it is reasonable to suppose that much of the R29 million difference represented wages, salaries, and capital income paid by the white mining corporations. The data thus establish that the most dynamic area of Bophuthatswana's economy has had an extremely limited impact upon African incomes in the homeland. Further, under the present institutional arrangements growth in this sector should not be viewed as contributing in a major way to the development of the homeland.

The economic profile of KwaZulu is more representative of the homelands in general than is that of Bophuthatswana. Agriculture is the foremost activity. Modern sectors — industry and construction, transport and communication, and commerce and finance — have grown absolutely and proportionately, but remain relatively inconsequential. Public administration and education have expanded with rising spending on public services in the homelands. Mining is trivial. The reasons for the loss of over R4 million per year in mining output after 1968 are not clear; it appears either that an operation was terminated or that a boundary change removed a mineral deposit. However, a discovery of a major deposit of high grade anthracite was announced in 1975. Approximately 43 percent of KwaZulu's output in fiscal 1971/72 was generated by the subsistence sector; 57 percent arose in the private and public commercial sectors. This pattern bears out the continuing importance of traditional activities in KwaZulu, the extensive role of the homeland and the Republican governments in providing income and employment, and the inertia of private industry and commercial agriculture.[6]

5. R31 million is an interpolation between the figures for income given in column 1, table 6.1. For figures on mineral production, see BENBO, *Bophuthatswana, Economic Revue, 1975*, 30.

6. BENBO, *KwaZulu, Economic Revue, 1975*, 34.

In Bophuthatswana, subsistence production provided only 13 percent of the total; the private sector, dominated by big mining operations, was responsible for 61 percent.[7]

Welfare and Growth

The chief measure of living standards in a nation or region is per capita income, although it is necessary to recognize that averages mask the realities of the distribution of individual incomes over high, middle, and low ranges. Also average yearly per capita income measures of welfare must be supplemented by using other economic and social indicators in order to obtain a rounded profile of the overall standard of living. Although calculations of homeland output and incomes are still only rough approximations, in 1973 the average per capita income earned inside the two homelands was R40 for the Tswana and R35 for the Zulu, or $56 and $49, respectively (see table 6.1). If these were complete estimates, they would rank among the lowest, if not as the lowest, in the underdeveloped world. But when commuter income is considered, the per capita yearly income of *de facto* residents rises to R140 ($196) for the Tswana and R92 ($129) for the Zulu. The higher figure for the former homeland is a consequence of its greater dependence on commuter as opposed to migrant workers. If all migrant income is added, then average incomes are R165 ($231) for Tswana and R145 ($203) for Zulu. Incomes for permanently absent *de jure* citizens are even higher. In response to a question in Parliament, the minister of Bantu administration and development said that the average per capita income of all Africans in South Africa was R166 in 1973.[8] Although the Tswana are something of an exception, the per capita income of *de facto* homeland residents is about two-thirds that of all Africans. In other words, there is a sharp difference — partially closed by unmeasured subsistence income — between income in the homelands and African incomes in the Republic.

The area national income concept described in the previous section is an aggregate consisting of all internal income, all commuter receipts, one-fifth of migrant income, and one-twentieth of the earnings of permanently absent workers. In 1973 average area income in Bophuthatswana was R150 ($210) compared to R112 ($157) in KwaZulu. If average area output is arbitrarily doubled to allow for unrecorded subsistence income, and if no subtraction is made for possible overestimation of the remittances of absentee workers, then in 1973 Bophuthatswana had an average per capita income of about

7. Idem, *Bophuthatswana, Economic Revue, 1975,* 30.
8. *Survey of Race Relations, 1974,* 235. Related information on poverty datum levels and wages is also provided. Most of this is geared to the urban African worker and his family's needs, however, and is only indirectly related to the question of homeland welfare.

R190 ($266); KwaZulu had roughly R147 ($206). Even these maximal, generously biased numbers are not large enough to lift the average standard of living for homeland Tswana and Zulu beyond the margin of poverty and into the world's middle income range of $300 to $500 yearly per person. The level of income in Bophuthatswana and KwaZulu is above that of the lowest stratum of international poverty—that of Bangladesh, India, Ethiopia, Haiti, and Indonesia—and below that of middle-range developing nations such as Mexico, Iran, Zambia, or Taiwan.[9] The extraordinarily low levels of average income earned in the homelands indicate how enormous is the task of raising productivity to global middle-range standards. Considered as potentially independent states, Bophuthatswana and KwaZulu are in the anomalous position of having income levels that approach the intermediate range, but output levels that are as low as any in the world.

The standard of living in an area is not adequately represented by per capita income alone. Other economic and social indicators must be considered to obtain a complete picture of welfare. The homeland territories are sometimes called "rural slums" or "rural ghettos," and most casual visitors and professional observers have commented unfavorably upon living conditions in them. Their reactions are doubtless heightened by the juxtaposition of homeland poverty and white opulence. White average yearly income is thirteen times as great as African average income in South Africa,[10] but homeland Africans are poorer than most and the middle and upper strata of white society lead a suburban existence that is affluent and physically comfortable by American or European standards. The gradient in living styles, readily visible by travelling the few miles between the white suburbs of Durban, Pretoria, and Johannesburg and the adjacent Tswana and Zulu homeland exurbs, is as steep as one can find anywhere in the world.

Social indicators confirm the disparity between homeland economic levels and those outside. Health and nutrition measures reveal differentials that are the product of decades of inattention and unconcern. In South Africa as a whole in 1973 there were 10.0 hospital beds per 1,000 whites, 5.6 per 1,000 urban blacks, and 3.5 per 1,000 homeland blacks. Of about 15,000 medical practitioners and specialists in South Africa, 300 were African, and only 45 whites and 9 Africans practiced in the homelands.[11] (Another statement, obviously based on a second definition of homeland practice, placed

9. This impression was derived not only from abstract numbers, but from the subjective method of driving through and observing living areas in many of the main blocks of Bophuthatswana and KwaZulu, on and off the main roads.

10. SPROCAS Economics Commission, *Power, Privilege and Property* (Johannesburg, 1972), appendices B and C, 115–117.

11. Cora E. Erasmus, Director of Strategic Planning, Department of Health, as quoted in Muriel Horrell, *The African Homelands of South Africa* (Johannesburg, 1973), 162.

the numbers at 471 white and 70 African doctors.)[12] The average number of beds per 1,000 people seems to have declined in Bophuthatswana from 7.0 in 1972 to 6.5 in 1973 and 6.2 in 1974 as a result of a diminishing number of beds available in government hospitals. For KwaZulu, there appear to have been 3.6 beds per 1,000 members of the population in 1972 and 4.1 per 1,000 in 1973. In 1973 there were reported to be 74 occupied medical posts and 1,757 occupied nursing posts in Bophuthatswana; comparable data for KwaZulu are 191 and 4,256.[13] People living in the homelands either receive no Western medical treatment when they are ill, relying instead on home remedies or indigenous medical practice, or they must travel some distance, perhaps with sick infants and children, to towns. There are three white dentists practicing in the homelands and only one African dentist, trained overseas, in all of South Africa.[14] Infant mortality rates in the homelands are very high, but precise records are not kept. For all Africans, infant mortality has been estimated at 140 per 1,000 live births, compared to 22 per 1,000 births for whites and 40 per 1,000 births for Asians.[15] African male life expectancy is about fifty-two years, contrasted with sixty and sixty-five years for Asians and whites, respectively.[16]

Malnutrition is common, particularly among persons who are not living within family groups: men away from home, children who have been left with relatives while their parents work in white areas, and women and children trying to survive upon irregular or nonexistent remittances from migrant fathers. Homeland residents suffer from a number of diseases directly or indirectly related to an inadequate, unbalanced diet. High rates of kwashiorkor, marasmus, pellagra, and vitamin deficiency illnesses have been reported.[17] In addition, tuberculosis is endemic; eye diseases are a major

12. *Survey of Race Relations, 1974*, 383, quoting an answer of the deputy minister of Bantu administration and development to a question in the Legislative Assembly.
13. BENBO, *KwaZulu, Economic Revue*, 62; *idem, Bophuthatswana Economic Revue*, 54.
14. *Survey of Race Relations, 1974*, 384, quoting the minister of Bantu education.
15. J. L. Sadie, "The Costs of Population Growth in South Africa," *South African Journal of Economics*, XL (1972), 112.
16. *Idem., Projections of the South African Population* (Johannesburg, 1974), appendix tables.
17. SPROCAS, *Power, Privilege and Poverty*, 24–25; M. L. Neser, "Can We Eradicate Malnutrition in South Africa?" *South African Medical Journal*, XXXIX (1965), 1161; P. J. Pretorius and H. Novis, "Nutritional Marasmus in Bantu Infants in the Pretoria Area," *ibid.*, 237–238, 501–505; F. W. Quass, "The Nutrition of Preschool and Primary School Children," *ibid.*, 1137; M. E. Edginton, J. Hodkinson, and H. C. Seftel, "Disease Patterns in a South African Rural Bantu Population," *ibid.*, XLVI (1972), 974; J. V. O. Reid, "Malnutrition," in Peter Randall (ed.), *Some Implications of Inequality* (Johannesburg, 1971), 38; J. G. A. Davel, "The Incidence of Malnutrition among Bantu Children," *South African Medical Journal*, XXXIX (1965), 1148; Alexander R. P. Walker, "Biological and Disease Patterns in South African Interracial Populations as Modified by Rise in Privilege," *ibid.*, XLVI (1972), 1128. See also above, 20–21.

affliction.[18] African children are on average underweight and shorter than normal.[19] Although it is theoretically possible for people to feed themselves adequately even with very low levels of income, the patterns of production and consumption that have developed in the homelands are not conducive to good diet. Traditional agriculture and pastoralism have declined, but the loss of customary foodstuffs has not been offset by sufficient quantities of nutritious foods. Low levels of purchasing power, coupled with the lack of nutritional education, the lure of advertising and quick food counters in urban centers, and the shortage of good cafeterias and restaurants serving blacks, all contribute to a very unsatisfactory dietary picture.

The greatest inequality that homeland and other Africans confront in South Africa is not that of income or health. White South Africans benefit from the array of public services associated with a modern state, although they do lag behind residents of Western welfare states in the availability of many social services. From municipal governments, whites receive clean, paved streets, piped water, sewage disposal systems, and power. The provincial and national governments provide old age, disability, and war pensions, maintenance grants for needy families, and institutions to care for orphans, the mentally ill, and the aged. Africans receive most of these services, but at segregated and markedly lower levels of financing, care, and availability. Homeland towns and rural locations offer few urban amenities and services.

In addition to all of these economic and welfare inequalities are the disorganization of family lives caused by the migratory labor system, the many devices of petty and grand apartheid with their attendant indignities and inequities, and the constraints upon political expression and personal mobility. Poor housing, inadequate police protection, and the use of the police and the courts to enforce legal segregation further diminish African living standards.

The Republic's efforts to deal with these welfare problems are tied to the expansion of the functions of the homeland governments and increases in their funding. The central government has gradually taken over health care from provincial and private authorities. In 1965 the Department of Bantu Administration and Development assumed responsibility for capital expenditures for hospitals, major items of medical equipment, and maintenance of existing medical facilities. In 1970 control over health services and hospitals was assumed, and in 1973 a gradual takeover of mission hospitals was begun.

18. *Survey of Race Relations, 1972, 1973,* and *1974,* chapters on "Health."
19. P. M. Leary and J. E. S. Lewis, "Some Observations on the State of Nutrition of Infants and Toddlers in Sekhukhuniland," *South African Medical Journal,* XLVI (1972), 1157; B. S. Richardson, "Mortality Rates in Preschool Children," *ibid.,* XLII (1963), 964; F. M. Leary and D. Obst, "The Use of Percentile Charts in the Nutritional Assessment of Children from Primitive Communities," *ibid.,* XLII (1969), 1165–1168; *Rand Daily Mail,* 11 Nov. 1969.

New facilities are being added.[20] Spending on health services for homeland Tswana, including government, mission, and provincial hospitals, and clinics, rose from R5.2 million in fiscal 1970/71 to R10.6 million in fiscal 1974/75. Similarly expenditures for the Zulu approximately doubled during the same period from R11 to R21 million.[21]

Presumably, as health departments are created, responsibility for hospitals and clinics will gradually be transferred to the homeland governments from the agencies of the Republic. One proposal calls for a number of linked clinics and hospitals to provide health care to homeland districts. Some emphasis is being placed on nutritional education in the schools, and there is a plan to provide skimmed milk powder to local authorities in the homelands. Training of doctors and other medical personnel has for some time been undertaken at the Natal Medical School, at black colleges, and in technical schools. A new medical school, to be opened at GaRankuwa near Pretoria in 1978, will become the major training school for Africans. The Bantu Trust and the Bantu Investment Corporation are devoting substantial sums to creating townships and providing them with housing, businesses, theaters, and sports facilities.

Because national output, income, and population data on the homelands, as well as information on related measures of development and welfare, are sparse and incomplete, there is no way of precisely determining the rate at which the homeland economies have grown in per capita terms. Given the evidence available, and relying upon the impressionistic estimates of those in and out of government who are familiar with the homelands, the average rate of real output expansion per capita in the homelands was in the neighborhood of 1 percent per year between 1960 and 1975.[22] The homelands vary among themselves in performance, and there were considerable fluctuations from year to year attributable to the weather. Recession in the South African

20.. Horrell, *African Homelands,* 160–161.

21. BENBO, *Bophuthatswana, Economic Revue,* 54; *idem, KwaZulu, Economic Revue,* 62.

22. This conclusion is based on a compound rate of output growth of around 7.0 to 8.0 percent (see table 6.3), less inflation of about 3.0 to 3.5 percent and population growth of about 3.0 percent. The inflation rate is taken as roughly equivalent to the change in consumer prices in South Africa since there is no price deflator for homeland output. It is unlikely that the average change in per capita real output was much greater than 1.0 percent, and it may well have been nil, at least in most areas. There is a good deal of discretion involved in formulating the accounts, and information about crop output, a major component of homeland output, is highly unreliable. It requires a certain amount of optimism to believe that output in the public sector, commerce and trading, industry, and (outside Bophuthatswana) mining has risen in real terms by the 4.5 percent per year necessary to offset population growth of about 3.0 to 3.5 percent. On the other hand, those familiar with the homelands, in and out of the government, are reluctant to say that nothing at all has happened in the past fifteen years, and especially since 1970.

economy, which reduces purchases from the homelands and also restrains the amount of public funds that the Republic is willing to commit to home- land finance, can also depress the actual output of these small, peripheral regions temporarily below any growth trend line. During the early 1970s and afterwards, there appears to have been some acceleration in growth, attrib- utable to increased public sector spending, the building of homeland growth points, construction of infrastructure and housing, and, in Bophuthatswana, mining.

Table 6.3 summarizes the available statistics on growth in homeland output. There are three general patterns. First, as data for fiscal 1967/68 and fiscal 1968/69 indicate, growth has not been smooth, largely due to agricultural instability. Second, some acceleration in growth rates occurred at the end of the 1960s. Last, the statistics for all the homelands, and for Bophuthatswana and KwaZulu in particular, do show growth rates, uncor- rected for inflation and population growth, in the range of 6 to 9 percent, or of about 12 percent for Bophuthatswana if its enclave mining operations are included. On balance, even with the mining sector omitted, Bophutha- tswana has done somewhat better than KwaZulu. After allowing for higher rates of inflation, about 5 to 7 percent, there were still sharp jumps in output

Table 6.3
Growth of Gross Domestic Production
in the Homelands
(1960/61 = 100)

Year	Bophuthatswana GDP	Bophuthatswana GDP Less Mining	KwaZulu GDP	All Homelands GDP
1959/60	—	—	—	88
1960/61	100	100	100	100
1964/65	—	—	—	107
1965/66	128	141	113	124
1966/67	165	165	137	149
1967/68	193	194	126	139
1968/69	164	157	124	141
1969/70	207	174	149	171
1970/71	305	212	167	—
1971/72	402	264	195	—

SOURCES: Computed from data in BENBO, *Bophutha- tswana, Economic Revue, 1975* (Pretoria, 1976), 30; *idem, KwaZulu, Economic Revue, 1975* (Pretoria, 1976); J. A. Lombard et al., *Focus on Key Economic Issues, 9, The Homelands* (Pretoria, 1974), figure 8.

in both homelands between fiscal 1970/71 and fiscal 1971/72. In the mid-1970s continued public sector spending, especially on construction, education, and industrial development, has probably elevated real per capita output growth rates somewhere into the 7 to 10 percent range. Of course, whether this growth can be sustained, whether it has occurred in the sectors that the Tswana or Zulu might wish, and the extent to which the benefits of this growth have been distributed across the homeland populations remain questions to be considered.

The rise in real average yearly income levels in the homelands has probably exceeded long-run output growth of 1 percent per year, as the real incomes of commuter, migrant, and permanently absent workers have been rising in recent years.[23] Considerable controversy exists about the most appropriate measure of change in African real incomes in the Republic and of the gains of other groups; thus it is difficult to choose a single estimate. Because there is no accurate information about the remittance habits of absentee workers, it is also very difficult to say what the impact of rising black wages in the Republic has been on the homelands. Commuter income gains have directly influenced homeland incomes, but migrant and permanently absent workers may or may not transmit wage gains to the homelands.

The three income measures reported in Table 6.1 suggest that there has been modest growth in homeland average incomes, much of which is due to increased earnings of absentee labor. Average yearly per capita income from internal sources rose from R29.8 to R40.2, or 34 percent, in Bophuthatswana between 1960 and 1973, and from R28.4 to R34.7, or 22 percent, in KwaZulu during the same period. With a 3 percent annual rate of inflation, these apparent gains actually represent modest declines in real per capita income. In contrast, there was material improvement in real incomes when outside earnings are included, again using estimates: the average incomes of residents and migrants combined appear to have risen by about 4 percent in real terms after 1960, and the incomes of *de facto* inhabitants may have grown slightly faster. These estimates, based on the homeland income accounts compiled for BENBO, are somewhat higher than those made for the whole black population of South Africa by other authorities. Steenekamp estimates that the average growth of real income of all South African blacks was about 3.18 percent between 1964 and 1970. On the other hand, there is some evidence that black wages and incomes rose faster than this—and

23. Incomes and wages of the various population groups are constantly monitored and estimated by various organizations and reported in the annual editions of *A Survey of Race Relations in South Africa* published by the South African Institute of Race Relations. See *Survey of Race Relations, 1973*, 197ff, 206; also *ibid., 1974*, 231ff.

somewhat faster than white wages and incomes—in the early 1970s.[24] The very rapid inflation of the mid-1970s (14 percent from mid-1974 through mid-1975), which particularly affected food and essential consumer items, probably eroded some of these total and relative black income gains.

The following conclusions appear justified on the basis of the imperfect data available. By all measures, average yearly per capita incomes of homeland Tswana are significantly above those of homeland Zulu. The income gains of commuters and migrants have been responsible for raising average levels of living in Bophuthatswana and KwaZulu by a maximum of 3 to 4 percent per year. Because of the stagnation of the internal economy, incomes in the two homelands have become ever more dependent during the last fifteen years upon earnings that "trickle down" from the Republic's migrant labor system. Since these remittances would at best allow homeland incomes to keep pace with those of other blacks, it is unlikely that homeland residents have improved their position relative to other blacks. There has probably been some slippage. The remittance streams to the homelands, even when supplemented by rising public sector spending, have been insufficient to ensure that these laggard regions grow rapidly enough to keep pace with the growth of the central economy.

The Absentee Labor System
and the Income Multiplier

Against this backdrop of internal underdevelopment and relative regional stagnation, it is evident that the genesis of income-creating forces lies outside the homelands in the private and public sectors of the Republic. The overwhelming importance of these external links distinguishes the homelands from the remainder of the world's less developed nations, excepting Lesotho. Few other independent or potentially independent countries lie in such close proximity to a rapidly modernizing industrial economy. Where other small economic units have at least subsistence levels of output, and rely upon exports of goods and services to finance imports, the homelands have sub-subsistence output levels and rely upon exports of labor. Moreover, the homelands (except the Transkei) are fragmented and more open to external economic influences than other small states. Nowhere else is the degree of monetary, fiscal, and employment dependence apt to remain as great after political independence.

In the theory of economic growth, the investment multiplier plays a vital role. Basically, the multiplier relationship recognizes that an addition to

24. *Ibid., 1974,* 235-236.

expenditure in the form of investment has a cumulative impact on incomes as it passes from hand to hand: from investor to wage-earner, from wage-earner to shopkeeper, from shopkeeper to employee, and so on.[25] This notion has prompted an analysis of homeland underdevelopment called the "leakages" model. The model seeks to explain why growth in the South African economy does not automatically spill over into the homeland regional economies. It does not explicitly analyze the institutional, structural, and resource barriers to development, but lays stress upon the income flows that are a product of these conditions. This idea has wide currency in planning and academic circles in South Africa and constitutes part of the current conventional wisdom that underlies the government's analysis of homeland underdevelopment.[26] The chief fear is that public spending and private investment in the homelands will "leak" back immediately into the white economy, which would itself then experience the multiplied effects on income, consumption, savings, and employment rather than the homelands.

Homeland economies are linked in the macroeconomic sphere to the South African economy as shown in Figure 6.1. One block represents Bophuthatswana, KwaZulu, or any homeland; the other represents the economy of the Republic. The flow chart shows the major connections between the two units, but omits some internal circulations. The major flows are shown as solid lines and weak, underdeveloped linkages are shown as dashed lines. The chief real outflow or export from the African economic regions is labor: commuters, migrants, and permanently absent workers. These persons spend a large part of their earnings for goods in white and Asian stores and for services ("local purchases"). A portion is diverted to taxes, the estimated value of which is supposed to be converted automatically through the developmental agencies of the Republican government into expenditures inside the homelands.

25. The standard form of the investment multiplier is $\Delta Y = k \cdot \Delta I$, where an initial change investment, ΔI, has a multiplied effect, k, on income, Y. If each person withholds 1/5 of his receipts (as "savings") from the income stream, then $k = 5$. Where s is the proportion of an increment to income that will be saved, $k = 1/s$. Any injection of money into an economy has a similarly magnified result (neglecting the government and trade factors).

26. The Tomlinson Commission recognized the problem of deflections of the homeland income stream, but apparently did not give the matter formal treatment. See *Summary of the Report*, 150–151, and elsewhere. Lombard had made extensive analytical use of the national income flow concept. See, for illustrations, Lombard and van der Merwe, "Central Problems," 13; J. A. Lombard, "Political and Administrative Principles of Homeland Development," *Bantu*, XVIII (Feb. 1971), 28; *idem.*, "Background to Planning the Development of Bantu Homelands in South Africa," presented at a Conference on Accelerated Development in Southern Africa, Johannesburg, 1972. More concrete is G. D. K. Fölscher, "The Economic and Fiscal Relationships of the Transkei *vis-à-vis* the Rest of the Republic as Determinants of its Economic Development," *South African Journal of Economics*, XXXV (1967), 203–218.

Figure 6.1
The Flows of Labor, Money, and Goods Between Homelands and the Republic

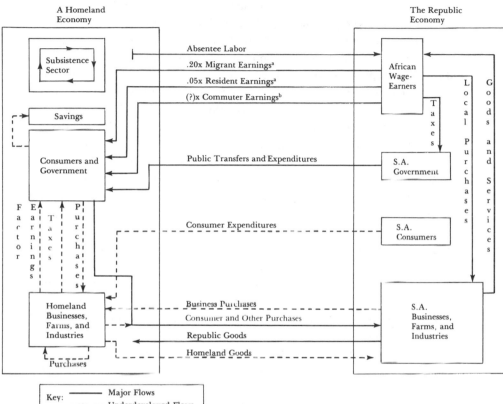

[a]These proportions have been suggested by Lombard and van der Merwe and appear reasonable. See, "Central Problems of the Economic Development of the Bantu Homelands," *Finance and Trade Review*, X (1972), II.

[b]Regular commuters probably spent one-quarter to one third of their incomes for transport and meals, and most shop in white or Indian stores near bus and train depots before returning home.

Commuters, migrants, and residents with some ties to a homeland take home or remit a fraction of their earnings, and these amounts constitute the most important component of homeland income. To these public sector transfers to the homeland governments and citizens (e.g., pensions) must be added. Consumers and businesses in the Republic may make purchases from homeland producers ("consumer expenditures" and "business purchases"), but they are small. These six items comprise the money inflows of the homeland from the Republic. Most funds go to homeland consumers or to a homeland government. Some are directed at homeland businesses, farms, and industries. As the remainder of the pathways make clear, these monetary movements have almost no secondary multiplicative or cumulative effects because they "leak" away immediately to non-African businesses and industries as "consumption expenditures." Only about 2 percent of this income is saved. As the dashed lines show, some consumption and public funds may go to African farms, shops, and industry, but the proportion is very low. Similarly, homeland businesses and industries may generate some monetary income that remains in the homeland as factor incomes or payments to local farms or firms, but there will be substantial leakages from their payrolls back to the Republic. Virtually all of their capital expenditure will be made outside the homeland. Local enterprises may pay some taxes to a homeland government. Most tax receipts come from local citizens and are then disbursed as teachers' or civil servants' salaries or are paid to contractors who meet local payrolls (these flows are not shown on the chart).

The pattern of circulation depicted on this chart has few dynamic effects inside a homeland like Bophuthatswana or KwaZulu. The absentee labor system and the dependence of the homeland populations on outside purchases, to the detriment of local farmers and businessmen, dominate the scene. The flow of goods out of the homeland is paltry compared to the reverse flow of goods from the Republic, leaving the regional economies with sizeable trade deficits that can only be covered by absentee labor earnings and fiscal supplements from the Republic. The circulation of funds does not stimulate local enterprise and employment. The absentee labor mechanism has become a rigidly institutionalized system rooted in the labor needs of the white economy and the money needs of Africans. The legislative and administrative details of the system, its origins, its influence on black and white society, and their interrelationships are well known. The labor pattern and the income flows associated with it have been little affected by the recent developmental efforts of the Republic, nor will greater homeland political independence lead to any sudden shifts.[27] It is probably true that the more

27. In general, all small, underdeveloped nations or regions, not isolated by distance or financial and trade barriers from larger, dynamic centers, experience similar problems. See Michael Ward, "Economic Independence for Lesotho?" *Journal*

rapid the growth of the Republic's economy is and the greater urban black and migrant participation in those gains are, the more present tendencies will be thrown into relief. With commensurate internal economic development, however, the dependence of the homelands on the Republic's economy will be somewhat changed in form, although not reduced. Greater goods exports from the homelands may be expected, and the composition of absentee labor may conceivably shift from wage-earners resident in the Republic to commuters, following the shift of black labor-intensive industries to border industry sites near the homelands.

Although it generates needed income for many homeland families, the absentee labor system has a number of negative effects on the homelands' potential for development. The male members of the labor force are withdrawn for long periods from participation in local economic activities, creating a concavity in the age distribution of the resident population. The laborers' oscillations between their homes and a variety of work places do not encourage the acquisition and retention of useful skills. There is little possibility of meshing early education, on-the-job training, and work experience to create valuable human resources. The fragmentary urban skills accumulated by absentee workers are not usually applicable to tasks in the home area. Consumption habits and the superficial traits of urban life, rather than economically useful knowledge, are far more likely to be brought back.

If a fraction of the absentee workers were required to remain permanently at home, total output in the homeland would rise, but average income would fall. The existence of relatively high earnings on the outside constitutes a barrier to enlisting manpower in internal development, unless the returns from participating in a local occupation rise in one step to a level competitive with earnings outside. In concrete terms, a worker who can obtain 100 wage units outside his homeland will not be drawn to employment in local agriculture or industry if it yields a net income of, say, only 50 or 75 units. Economic theory suggests that in a free labor market returns at the margin to labor in the homelands should equal earnings from absentee work. But the market is not free and too much labor is available in the homelands already. To raise internal agricultural or industrial productivity to equality with outside earnings in one step, on a large enough scale to reabsorb a

---

of Modern African Studies, V (1967), 363ff. The most recent major study of absentee labor in South Africa is Francis Wilson, Migrant Labour in South Africa (Johannesburg, 1972). The most interesting parts of his book are those derived from the author's personal investigations of the system. These impressions provide a sense of immediacy lacking in more abstract writings. Other recent general sources include: M. Ernest Sabbagh, "Some Geographical Characteristics of a Plural Society: Apartheid in South Africa," Geographical Review, LVIII (1968), 1–28; John C. Williams, "Lesotho: Economic Implications of Migrant Labour," South African Journal of Economics, XXXIX (1971), 149–178.

noticeable volume of labor, would require immense expenditures and substantial structural changes in both the homelands and the Republic. For those who are mobile the income advantages of external work constitute an opportunity cost barrier to the success of development projects aimed at providing them alternatives at home. Agricultural extension workers, for instance, feel they are limited to counselling a few men, most of them old, and women who tend gardens and small maize patches while their husbands work in the central economy. Extension workers and others who seek to increase homeland employment are correct in realizing that headway can be achieved only by creating jobs that offer incomes that are competitive, or nearly so, with those obtainable in the Republic.

The Homeland Public Sector

The largest single component of monetized area output in the homelands as a group is the public sector. Agriculture would be the most important economic activity if subsistence and commercial production were added together. But among monetized economic activities the homeland governments overshadow the private sector. Bophuthatswana's basic economic structure is somewhat anomalous because of its poor agricultural base and high mineral output. In fiscal 1971/72 the subsistence sector accounted for only 15 percent of output, compared to 24 percent for the public and 61 percent for the private sectors. In KwaZulu in fiscal 1971/72 about 24 percent of output was generated in the private market sector and 43 percent in the subsistence sector.[28] The public sector is also responsible for virtually all of the capital formation in the homelands, although the agency system does bring some white investment in the growth points. Most of this spending comes from the Bantu Trust, but the homeland governments are increasingly engaging in expenditures for housing, fencing, wells, roads, schools, utilities, and other fixed capital items. Provincial governments and departments of the central government also make some investments, presumably in housing and infrastructure.

The expenditures of the homelands are contained in their annual budgets. These budgets show the growth in spending by the homelands, and their composition affords some insight into the relative emphasis on different activities. In summary form, the budgets of Bophuthatswana and KwaZulu distinguish internal and external sources of funds and show expenditures according to departments as allocated by the legislative assemblies. These initial allocations and revenue estimates are sometimes changed or supplemented during the financial year, but without distorting the general pattern.

28. BENBO, *Bophuthatswana, Economic Revue, 1975,* 30; *idem, KwaZulu, Economic Revue, 1975,* 34.

The homelands obtain revenue from two sources: 1) taxes, fees, and licences directly under their control, collectively referred to in the estimates as Part I; 2) sums voted by the Parliament of the Republic, called Part II revenues. Until fiscal 1975/76, the Republic's contribution was composed of: (i) A sum based on the cost of services at the time of transfer to the homeland government, less revenue from certain services accruing at the time to the homelands, and less the salaries and allowances of seconded white personnel. This sum is referred to as the "statutory grant." (ii) A grant, determined annually and drawn from the Consolidated Fund, referred to as the "additional grant." In addition, the Department of Bantu Administration and Development pays a supplementary amount representing general overhead expenses, such as the salaries of white personnel on loan. The amount is small, amounting in fiscal 1974/75 to 9.2 percent of total revenue for Bophuthatswana and 6.1 percent for KwaZulu.

In late 1974 Vorster announced a new formula for "providing funds" for homeland governments that would furnish "a more accurate reflection of the degree to which their expenditure was financed from sources which were due to them." These suggestions in part met demands by homeland leaders that their fiscal footing be made more secure and also made it clearer to whites that payments to the homelands were transfers of funds to which blacks had legitimate claims, not burdensome handouts. Vorster was careful to point out that although the formula did not directly affect the amount of money available to homelands, it would place "homeland governments in a much better position to project revenues ahead and plan their expenditure programmes." The change involves a transfer of some indirect taxes, such as customs, excise, and sales taxes on goods consumed by blacks. Further grants would be made from taxes paid by companies or branches of companies in the homelands (and possibly in the border industrial areas), whether controlled by blacks or not.[29]

The Bantu Laws Amendment Act of 1975 embodied these modifications. The statutory grant was changed to a 31 March 1974 base for all the homelands, in order to reflect changes in the costs of functions that had been handed over earlier and to permit all of the homelands, some of which had acquired functions earlier on a lower cost basis, to be treated equally. This amount will continue to be supplemented by the costs of any new programs subsequently transferred to the homeland governments. Except for African-controlled companies, the revenues of which are already subject to homeland taxation, homelands will also be credited with taxes paid by companies operating in their areas. In addition, allowance will be made for customs, excise, and sales duties derived from the area of the homeland. Payments to white

29. Vorster to Federated Chamber of Industries, 2 Oct. 1974, *Star Weekly,* 19 Oct. 1974; *Comment and Opinion* (Pretoria), 14 Oct. 1974.

personnel will no longer be separated from the statutory grant. The effect of these changes will be to raise the regular or normal amounts paid to each homeland while reducing the discretionary additional grant. In fiscal 1975/76, the annual grant to the homelands was R163.6 million, and the supplementary grant totalled R86.5 million, together equalling R250 million. In addition, the revenue vote for Bantu administration provided R49 million for health services and R14 million for the salaries of seconded whites. Significantly, from the Loan Account the Bantu Trust received R116.4 million, up from R90.4 million the previous year, for developmental projects. Much of this money will be channelled through the investment and mining corporations.[30]

The new allocation may help to reduce the dependency of the homelands. One approximate global estimate asserts that the homelands' share of customs and excise taxes comes to about R100 million annually, and that mining taxes and royalties will bring a further R100 million, the two sums together being roughly equal to the R199 million voted for all the homelands in fiscal 1973/74. However, the new law does not empower a homeland government to tax South African companies operating within its borders; South Africa will continue to tax such companies and remit revenue to the homelands. Mineral royalties will presumably still be paid over by companies to the tribal and regional authorities that have received them in the past and to the Bantu Trust. The new law may conceivably benefit Bophuthatswana if mining profits are treated as industrial earnings. There is considerable mining there, and potential for more.[31] Mangope now can at least employ a line of argument not previously available to him.

The sources of revenue for Bophuthatswana and KwaZulu (for the years for which they are available) are shown in table 6.4. In both instances there are clear changes in the relative importance of the different categories of funds. From fiscal 1972/73 to fiscal 1974/75 Bophuthatswana's statutory grant remained more or less constant, then in fiscal 1975/76, under the older accounting practices, the transfer of a new Department of Health brought with it added revenue equivalent to that which the Republic had been spending at the time of the transfer. Similarly, for KwaZulu, the statutory grant remained around R20 million from fiscal 1972/73 to fiscal 1975/76. Although the statutory grants remained nearly constant, the level of grants from Parliament and revenues from internal sources rose. The additional grant to Bophuthatswana increased six-fold and that to KwaZulu twenty-fold. Internal revenues have almost doubled in Bophuthatswana since fiscal 1972/73 and have climbed by nearly 70 percent in KwaZulu during the same period. The proportionate importance of these homeland receipts and taxes

30. *Survey of Race Relations, 1975,* 121–125.
31. *Star Weekly,* 19 Oct. 1974.

has not risen however, because of the more rapid growth of the supplementary appropriation. The statutory grants declined relatively as well. The effects of the fiscal reforms can be seen in the separate calculations for fiscal 1975/76. It is probable, however, that the statutory amounts will once again diminish in weight — although not so precipitously as before — because the new excise and profit contributions will not be elastic enough over time to provide sufficient new revenues to permit homeland budgets to grow as rapidly as they have been growing, and as they will need to grow in the future.

The homelands will continue to receive much of their revenue from the Republic for at least the next two decades. Only a major shift in policy that would allow the homeland governments the fiscal autonomy to tax white businesses and mines, and would also allow them to collect income taxes from their absentee populations, could create a situation in which fiscal independence would prove feasible. The discretionary amount remains important even after the recent reforms, and there is no guarantee that an independently-minded homeland would not be subject to the sanction of budget cutting, including part or all of the statutory amount.

Rather surprisingly, the rapid growth of spending on the homelands — matched only by increases in defense spending — has not been challenged by white public opinion or politicians. The government has been successful in defending the amounts as necessary for internal security and for the alleviation of the pressures of black migration toward white cities. The spending levels can also be justified as ways of meeting foreign criticism of racial segregation and as humanitarian necessities. Although the homelands will have to rely upon funds that are subject to decisions beyond their control, it is unlikely that such support will be withdrawn capriciously. Nonetheless, dependence on the Republic for over 80 percent of revenues is a major factor constraining the political and economic independence of the homelands.

Since the autonomy of the homelands will depend vitally upon the capacity of their governments to finance themselves from internal sources, their present tax bases merit examination. Table 6.5 shows the sources of revenue under the control of Bophuthatswana and KwaZulu in two recent years. In both homelands the general personal tax is the preponderant source of income. The respective homeland assemblies have imposed new per capita taxes, R2.50 in the case of the Tswana and R3.00 for the Zulu; the assemblies will depend upon the Republic to collect these amounts from permanently absent persons. The increases appear to have added several million rand to the homeland revenue accounts, and the share of taxes in total revenue has been rising. The other important revenue item is township rental income. The remaining income consists of licensing fees and income from small charges for public services rendered by government

Table 6.4
Homeland Sources of Revenue

A. Bophuthatswana, 1969/70–1975/76

	1969/70		1970/71		1971/72		1972/73	
	Rands	%	Rands	%N	Rands	%	Rands	%
1. From the Republic								
(a) Statutory grant	a						8,244,000	50
(b) Additional grant voted annually by Parliament	a						4,099,000	25
Subtotal From Republic	6,957,000	78	11,900,500	86	11,804,000[b]	85	12,343,000	75
2. Own Sources	1,925,804	22	1,949,021	14	1,540,000	15	4,020,000	25
Total	8,882,804	100	13,849,521	100	13,344,000	100	16,363,000	100
Change Over Previous Year			+4,966,717	+56	-505,521	-4	+3,043,200	+23

SOURCES: For fiscal 1969/70: Republic of South Africa, *Report of the Controller and Auditor-General on the Accounts of the Tswana Territorial Authority and the Lower Authorities in Its Area for the Period 1 December 1968 to 31 March 1970* (Pretoria, n.d.), 9, 25.

For fiscal 1970/71: Republic of South Africa, *Report of the Controller and Auditor-General on the Accounts of the Tswana Legislative Assembly in Respect of the Former Tswana Territorial Authority and of the Lower Authorities in Its Area for the Financial Year 1970/71* (Pretoria, n.d.), 13, 45.

For 1971/72: Preliminary official estimates reported in Muriel Horrell et al., *A Survey of Race Relations in South Africa, 1971* (Johannesburg, 1972), 119.

For fiscal 1972/73, 1973/74, 1974/75 and 1975/76: Republic of South Africa, Bophuthatswana, *Estimate of the Expenditure to be Defrayed from the Revenue Fund of Bophuthatswana*, for the years ending 31 March 1973, 1974, 1975, 1976.

For 1975/76 (new): *Survey of Race Relations, 1975*, 123.

[a]No distinction was made between the statutory grant and the additional grant before the coming into operation of the Bantu Homelands Constitution Act, 1971.

[b]Grant from South African Bantu Trust Fund to be paid into the Treasury of the Tswana Legislative Assembly.

[c]The virtual doubling of the statutory grant is due to the creation of the Department of Health.

[d]Includes a sum of R690,000 "for the development of government headquarters" under Section 6(2)(d) of the Bantu Homelands Citizenship Act.

B. KwaZulu, 1972/73–1975/76

	1972/73		1973/74		1974/75		1975/76	
	Rands	%	Rands	%	Rands	%	Rands	%
1. From the Republic								
(a) Statutory grant	19,681,000	61	20,073,000	44	19,767,000	30	18,148,000	21
(b) Additional grant voted annually by Parliament	2,429,000	7.5	13,703,000	30	32,079,000	48.5	51,562,000	60
Subtotal From Republic	22,110,000	68.5	33,776,000	74	51,846,000	78.5	69,710,000	81
2. Own Sources	10,199,200	31.5	11,679,000	26	14,252,300	21.5	16,883,000	19
Total	32,209,200	100	45,455,000	100	66,098,000	100	86,593,000	100
Change Over Previous Year			+13,245,800	+41	+20,643,300	+45	+20,495,000	+31

SOURCES: Republic of South Africa, KwaZulu, *Estimate of the Expenditure to be Defrayed From the Revenue Fund of the KwaZulu Government*, for the years ending 31 March, 1973, 1974, 1975, 1976.

For 1975/76 (new): Muriel Horrell et al., *A Survey of Race Relations, 1975* (Johannesburg, 1976), 123.

NOTE: A territorial authority had not been established in KwaZulu, so there are no figures prior to the coming into operation of the Bantu Homelands Constitution Act, 1971.

1973/74		1974/75		1975/76 (old)		1975/76 (new)	
Rands	%	Rands	%	Rands	%	Rands	%
8,177,000	41	7,464,000	24	13,054,000ᶜ	29	23,515,100	52
6,429,000	32	17,575,000	56	24,360,000ᵈ	54	13,898,900	31
14,606,000	73	25,039,000	80	37,414,000	83	37,414,000	83
5,396,000	27	6,160,000	20	7,809,500	17	7,809,500	17
20,002,000	100	31,199,000	100	45,223,500	100	45,223,500	100
+ 3,639,000	+ 22	+ 11,197,000	+ 56	+ 14,024,500	+ 45	+ 14,024,500	+ 45

1975/76 (new)	
Rands	%
40,936,700	47
28,773,800	33
69,710,000	80.5
16,883,000	19.5
86,593,000	100
20,495,000	+ 31

Table 6.5
Sources of Own Revenue: Bophuthatswana and
KwaZulu, 1973/74 and 1975/76

	Bophuthatswana				KwaZulu			
	1973/74		1975/76		1973/74		1975/76	
	Rands	%	Rands	%	Rands	%	Rands	%
Taxes and levies	2,257,900	42	4,334,500	56	5,777,000	49	10,830,000	64
Fines and forfeitures	10,000	0	100,000	1	75,000	1	800,000	0
Rents of government property	100,000	2	160,000	2	130,000	1	155,000	1
Townships	1,250,000	23	2,000,000	26	3,200,000	27	3,500,000	21
Interest	50,000	1	100,000	1	100,000	1	300,000	2
Bottle stores and beer depôts	— —	0	10,000	0	90,000	1	— —	0
Clinics	50,000	1	75,000	1	70,000	1	110,000	1
Boarding hostels	290,000	5	250,000	3	245,000	2	320,000	2
Other	1,388,600	26	780,000	10	1,992,000	17	1,660,000	10
TOTAL	5,396,000	100	7,809,500	100	11,697,000	100	16,883,000	100

SOURCES: Republic of South Africa, Bophuthatswana, *Estimate of Expenditure to Be Defrayed From the Revenue Fund of Bophuthatswana,* for the years ending 31 March 1975 and 31 March 1976. Republic of South Africa, KwaZulu, *Estimate of the Expenditure to Be Defrayed From the Revenue Fund of the KwaZulu Government,* for the years ending 31 March 1975 and 31 March 1976.

departments. In KwaZulu, forest revenues and income from sugar cane and fibre estates have amounted to over R1 million in recent years (included in "Other"). Since in both homelands over four-fifths of revenue comes from a fixed personal tax and from housing and hostel rentals, it is clear that raising revenue from these sources will be painful and politically unpopular. Given the already low incomes of many homeland citizens, tax or rental increases will have deleterious effects on welfare. Absentee workers and those in the homelands who do not feel any particular allegiance to the new political entities are not likely to greet new taxes—particularly when governmental services are so woefully inadequate in rural locations and in the burgeoning homeland cities—with any degree of enthusiasm. Probably the most that can be expected is that homeland internal revenues will rise rapidly enough to avoid even greater proportionate reliance upon the Republic's subventions.

Both homelands face practically insurmountable obstacles in increasing their autonomy by bringing a greater proportion of revenue under their control. Even if every man, woman, and child in Bophuthatswana were to pay the per capita tax, the yield would be only in the order of R4.25 million per year—only 9.4 percent of total revenue for fiscal 1975/76. Similarly, even if all the *de jure* population of KwaZulu were to pay the tax, it would raise something in the order of R12 million—13.9 percent of total revenue in fiscal 1975/76. In fact, the new tax in KwaZulu will raise about R1 million in fiscal 1975/76, about 33 percent of the net gain in Part I revenues. Similarly, Bophuthatswana's new tax will raise R1.2 million in fiscal 1975/76, 73 percent of the net gain coming in Part I revenue. Although these proportionate increases are impressive, revenue realized directly by the homelands fell in the case of Bophuthatswana from 25 percent in fiscal 1972/73 to 17 percent in fiscal 1975/76, and in the case of KwaZulu from 31 percent to 19 percent during the same period. Every delegation of function to the homelands and every increase in cost due to inflation only makes more difficult the gaining of greater control over revenue, and, therefore, greater freedom to initiate policies that would provide increased services, not merely maintain existing ones.

The fiscal 1974/75 budget totals and estimated populations show that Bophuthatswana spent R28 per resident and R16 per member of the *de jure* population; KwaZulu spent R27 per resident and R14 for each *de jure* citizen. The amounts are up by about four-fifths in nominal terms since 1970, perhaps by half allowing for inflation. In contrast, the Republic was spending R296 per white resident in 1970, or R53 for each person in the Republic. By 1975 these averages had risen considerably, but these lower figures suffice to indicate how far the homelands currently lag behind South Africa in public spending.

The funds that the homelands have at their disposal are disbursed by their several departments: seven in Bophuthatswana, six in the case of KwaZulu. Table 6.6 shows the allocation of funds among these departments. The addition of a Department of Health in Bophuthatswana in fiscal 1975/76 sharply reduced the share of the Department of the Interior, which had previously contained some health functions. With the bias in the pattern of spending toward the Departments of Works and Education, and the absence of a defense account, these budgets resemble those of states (provinces) or cities more closely than those of national units. As such, they delineate the regional character of the homeland governments.

The budgets of both homelands show how rapidly their functions and spending authority have expanded. Between fiscal 1972/73 and fiscal 1975/76 expenditures have almost exactly tripled—from R16 million to R50 million in Bophuthatswana and from R31 million to R93 million in KwaZulu. Bophuthatswana's rate of increase accelerated from 22 to 60 percent per year,

Table 6.6
Homeland Expenditures by Departments

| | A. Bophuthatswana, 1969/70–1975/76 | | | | | |
| | 1969/70 | | 1970/71 | | 1971/72 | |
Expenditures	Rand	%	Rand	%	Rand	%
Authority Affairs and Finance	418,200	5	445,367	3	550,400	4
Interior	2,269,188	28	2,237,380	16	2,632,200	20
Works	1,512,597	19	6,368,426	46	4,232,100	32
Education	2,842,027	36	3,758,657	27	4,720,700	35
Agriculture	761,686	10	791,508	6	1,002,400	8
Justice	166,028	2	156,373	1	182,000	1
Health and Social Welfare	— —	—	— —	—	— —	—
Total[a]	7,969,726	100	13,757,711	99	13,319,800	100
Change Over Previous Year			+5,787,985	+73%	-437,911	-3%

| | B. KwaZulu, 1972/73–1975/76 | | | | | |
| | 1972/73 | | 1973/74 | | 1974/75 | |
Expenditures	Rand	%	Rand	%	Rand	%
Authority Affairs and Finance	528,800	2	551,400	1	696,500	1
Community Affairs	6,678,400	21	8,674,500	19	13,799,700	21
Works	13,579,600	42	20,979,000	45	32,784,000	49
Education and Culture	7,868,500	25	10,733,800	24	12,087,500	18
Agriculture	2,759,600	9	4,475,600	10	6,037,100	9
Justice	563,800	2	722,700	2	877,500	1
Total[a]	31,978,700	101	46,137,000	101	66,282,300	99
Change Over Previous Years			+14,158,300	+44%	+20,145,300	+44%

SOURCES: Republic of South Africa, Bophuthatswana, *Estimate of the Expenditure to Be Defrayed from the Revenue Fund of Bophuthatswana During the Year Ending 31 March 1974* and for the years ending 31 March 1975, 31 March 1976; Republic of South Africa, KwaZulu, *Estimate of the Expenditure to Be Defrayed from the Revenue Fund of the KwaZulu Government During the Year Ending 31 March 1974.*

[a]Discrepancies in percentage totals are due to rounding errors.

1972/73		1973/75		1974/75		1975/76	
Rand	%	Rand	%	Rand	%	Rand	%
339,000	2	572,150	3	686,550	2	1,065,200	2
2,864,200	18	3,816,450	19	5,460,350	18	1,023,000	2
6,047,000	37	6,645,550	33	11,532,750	37	17,432,400	35
5,660,500	35	6,906,400	34	10,622,000	34	12,700,200	26
1,073,800	7	1,826,250	9	2,180,250	7	3,072,200	6
261,150	2	364,650	2	420,150	1	707,000	1
— —	—	— —	—	— —	—	13,500,000	27
16,245,650	101	20,131,450	100	30,902,050	99	49,500,000	99
+ 2,925,850	+ 22%	+ 3,885,800	+ 24%	+ 10,770,600	+ 54%	+ 18,597,950	+ 60%

1975/76	
Rand	%
1,413,310	1
17,627,640	19
46,996,090	51
18,522,120	20
7,247,250	8
904,590	1
92,711,000	100
+ 26,429,000	+ 40%

while KwaZulu's expenditure went up by about 40 percent per year. The proportion of the budget spent by each department shows differences from one homeland to another, but there are broad similarities. Authority Affairs and Finance, Community Affairs, Interior and Justice are essentially administrative departments and have maintained steady proportions of the budgets. Surprisingly, Agriculture also shows a constant rather small share (about 9 percent in each case) of expanding budgets. The rise in expenditures on new agricultural activities and continued spending on physical planning have not given Agriculture an increased share. The two largest spending shares are those of Works and Education, together taking 61 percent of the budget in Bophuthatswana in fiscal 1975/76 and 71 percent of the budget in KwaZulu that year. In Bophuthatswana, Works maintained a constant high share and Education fell a little. In KwaZulu the share of Works rose by 9 percent between fiscal 1972/73 and fiscal 1975/76, while that of Education fell by 5 percent.

The heavy increase in expenditures of the Departments of Works was made up in part by the cost of the "establishment of townships," to quote the budget item. In Bophuthatswana the figures also show increases in expenditures on townships, but less of a preoccupation with them than in KwaZulu. From fiscal 1972/73 to fiscal 1973/74 expenditures on townships actually fell by 8 percent but rose by 29 percent from fiscal 1973/74 to fiscal 1974/75 and by a further 16 percent in fiscal 1975/76. Increases in expenditures on housing took a much smaller proportion of the total increase in the Works vote, only 22 percent in fiscal 1974/75 and 17 percent in fiscal 1975/76. In KwaZulu 47 percent of the increase in the Works vote between fiscal 1972/73 and fiscal 1974/75 went to townships; between fiscal 1973/74 and fiscal 1974/75, 69 percent; and between fiscal 1974/75 and fiscal 1975/76, 57 percent

It is possible that these expenditures raise an ideological issue. The establishment of townships in the homelands is a highly controversial issue, being related to the resettlement policy that is aimed at reducing the numbers of Africans in white farming areas and the cities, especially those not employed there. It has been policy, at least until very recently, to compel as large a proportion as possible of the African labor force to migrate and to provide housing and facilities for dependents and the unemployed primarily in the homelands. Also, "black spot" removals have returned Africans to Bophuthatswana and KwaZulu. It is not possible to establish which expenditures are based on these policies. Nor is it clear why expenditures on new townships are relatively so much more important in KwaZulu than in Bophuthatswana. What is patent is that a great deal of the expanded expenditures on Works is going into social capital in the form of townships with electricity, water, and sanitation, and into the expansion of hospitals and schools. Whether or not this is the most efficient way to provide housing and urban services for

African populations, a major portion of homeland budgets will continue to be committed in this fashion.

The needs of the homeland populations for education, housing, and other urban services remain great. There are grave deficiencies to be made up even if the homelands want merely to ensure that every resident obtains a rudimentary education and has an adequate place to live. Highways, streets, power, water, and schools need to be provided in most areas. The homelands are also responsible in part for agricultural and commercial development. They must contend with inflation and with the expansion of their populations due to natural growth and the influx of persons from white farms and "black spots." Under these pressures, the homeland governments have sought increased funding from Parliament and have also searched for additional internal sources of funds.

Other Expenditures on the Homelands

Homeland governments are not the only agencies involved in heavy expenditures affecting the lives of homeland citizens, nor are they in a position to control many aspects of developmental policy. The Bantu Trust, set up in 1936, is generally responsible for land acquisition and consolidation for a homeland as well as for a number of social services. The Bantu Investment Corporation was established in 1959 by the Bantu Trust to promote investment, especially by Africans, in the homelands. The Xhosa Development Corporation performs the same functions in the Ciskei and the Transkei. A separate development corporation for the Tswana is now being created. The Zulu and other groups are expected to obtain their own investment institutions in the near future. The Bantu Mining Corporation is responsible for overseeing the activities of white mining firms in the homelands and for developing African mining operations. Table 6.7 sets out estimates of expenditures for the homeland governments, the Bantu Trust, and the development corporations. These core expenditures amounted to over R221 million in fiscal 1972/73 and rose to R418 million in fiscal 1974/75. The homeland governments have accounted for about 60 percent of current expenditures, but the Bantu Trust has spent large sums on land planning, housing, and infrastructure. Prior to fiscal 1975/76, substantial Bantu Trust funds were also spent on social services, including payments to the Department of Health for clinical and medical services. The decline in the trust's spending in fiscal 1975/76 apparently reflects, at least in part, the transfer of these activities to the homelands.

The expenditures of the three development corporations have grown proportionately more rapidly than those of the homelands and of the trust, their share of the total having risen from 8 to 18 percent since fiscal 1972/73.

Table 6.7

Expenditures on Homeland Administration and Development, 1972/73–1975/76

Agency	1972/73		1973/74		1974/75		1975/76	
	Rand (000)	%	Rand (000)	%	Rand (000)	%	Rand (000)	%
Homeland Governments	125,524	57	176,759	63	238,859	57	337,019	64
The Bantu Trust	75,759	34	74,285	26	122,900	29	91,506	17
Bantu Investment Corporation	11,850	5	17,042	6	33,644	8	59,769	11
Xhosa Development Corporation	7,632	3	11,854	4	20,749	5	38,774	7
Bantu Mining Corporation	775	0	1,718	1	2,214	1	3,303	1
Total	221,540	99	281,658	100	418,366	100	530,371	100
Change			+ 60,116	+ 27%	+ 136,708	+ 49%	+ 112,005	+ 27%

SOURCE: BENBO, personal communications (xeroxed documents), 19 March 1976.

Most of the corporations' activities are aimed at creating income and jobs, and their rising share of the totals shows a shift in emphasis in the bureaucracy from routine governmental activity toward growth-inducing activities. But these organizations are not black-controlled and development decision-making has not on balance gravitated toward the homelands to the same degree as has the performance of routine administrative tasks. The Board of Directors of the new Tswana Development Corporation is, however, equally divided between homeland-appointed black and Republic-named white members, including officials of the Bantu Investment Corporation. This change resolves a controversy over the management of development banks and may bring together homeland governments, private economic interests, and the Investment Corporation.

To these expenditures in the homelands must be added part of the budget of the Department of Bantu Education. In fiscal 1972/73, R28 million was spent on African education in the Republic and in fiscal 1973/74, over R35 million, an increase of one-quarter.[32] Most funds were spent upon urban and rural black schools and their supporting systems, but some financed the homeland universities, and part covered examination, inspection, and advisory services in the homelands. The department spent in the neighborhood of R60 million in fiscal 1974/75, and, if one-fifth of this total can be assigned to the homelands, then about R10 million could be added to the core spending of the agencies listed in table 6.7. This would raise spending in fiscal 1974/75 to R430 million. In fiscal 1975/76, the Department of Bantu Education spent R10.4 million in the homelands, but this figure may not include general overhead expenses. Health absorbed R50.6 million, explicitly apart from the Bantu Trust accounts.[33] Added to the core disbursements, these amounts yield a comprehensive sum of R591 million.

Adding the relevant expenditures directly affecting the homelands made by other departments of the Republic, the fiscal 1974/75 total could be as high as R450 to 460 million, and that of fiscal 1975/76 could be in the range of R610 to 620 million.[34] If allowance is made, however, for expenditures connected with policies such as "black spot" removals that are of no clear benefit to Africans, the figure would be smaller, although how much smaller depends upon judgments on the merits of aspects of the homeland development program. Whether one uses the core spending figures, the overall totals, or some corrected interpretation of both, it is plain that spending in and on the homelands has climbed steeply since the late 1960s. The data are too fragmentary and not comparable enough, and the time span is too short,

32. *Survey of Race Relations, 1974*, 342.
33. BENBO, personal communication (xeroxed document), 19 March 1976.
34. An incomplete estimate of R13 million for South African departmental spending in the homelands is given in *Survey of Race Relations, 1975*, 125.

to allow computation of meaningful growth rates or to permit projections. Homeland government spending rose by over 168 percent from fiscal 1972/73 to fiscal 1975/76; the corporations' disbursements rose by 403 percent. Total core spending rose by 27 percent, 49 percent, and 27 percent in the three year-to-year intervals between fiscal 1972/73 and fiscal 1975/76, implying an average compound growth rate of about one-third. At the same time, South Africa's cost of living rose by about 10 to 12 percent per year. Using this figure as a rough guide, the real value of these funds grew by only about 20 to 22 percent per year. African population growth of 3.5 percent would reduce this growth to about 18 percent on a per capita basis. Real increases in teachers' salaries or the pay of homeland civil servants, or the transfer of new functions to the homelands, would further shrink the available incremental funds. Nonetheless, even with these allowances, it is obvious that the trend of spending on the homelands is strongly upwards.

The homeland governments have not issued debt instruments or received foreign loans. Under the Second Bantu Laws Amendment Act of 1974, the minister of Bantu administration and development is empowered to guarantee the interest and principal of homeland debts. The question of foreign aid has been explicitly raised by Chiefs Mangope and Buthelezi following overseas trips to the United States and Europe. The South African government has approved the idea of external aid in principle, but still insists that it must enter the homelands through the Republic's channels. It is difficult to imagine exactly how external assistance would fit into existing financial practices and the developmental projects proposed by the white agencies. Aid grants from outside could lead to a reduction in the effort of the Republic by an equivalent amount. If foreign sources are able to transfer funds to the homelands, the preferred form would be grants, since the simple and inelastic tax systems of the homelands are unlikely to provide a basis for the interest payments and principal amortization required by loans. Mangope and Buthelezi may fare better by cultivating their own tax resources and affecting the Republic's allocative process rather than by pursuing the chimera of foreign grants. By campaigning for external funds, however, black leaders may induce the Republic to raise its own levels of expenditures for the homelands.

7

The Administration of
Economic Development

The implementation of South Africa's policy of homeland development is entrusted to a large and growing bureaucracy. Except in the homeland governments, and then not at the senior level, this bureaucracy is white. Broad policy guidelines emanate from the prime minister and his cabinet and are subject to approval and review by Parliament, but actual operations are performed by the administrators of departments of the central government, the semipublic developmental corporations, and the fledgling homeland governments. This bureaucracy implements the vital decisions that determine the directions in which the homeland economies move. It is this policy-setting mechanism and its derivative bureaucracy that the homelands must influence in order to have an impact on the economic welfare of their populations.

The gradual emergence of a separate bureaucracy charged with dealing with African problems has left the governance of blacks to specialized white bureaucrats concerned with such matters as investment, infrastructure, education, health, housing, influx control, and justice. The central white political and administrative system has long been insulated from contact with blacks, except when there have been breakdowns in management and control. The press, voluntary humanitarian agencies, and the parliamentary opposition provide some monitoring of policies affecting blacks, but for the most part the day-to-day operations of the white bureaucrats who deal with blacks lie outside the perception of whites.

Although increasing concern with the effectiveness and credibility of the homeland policy has to some extent eroded the invisibility of the African-oriented bureaucracy, it nonetheless remains a self-contained subsystem, with great latitude to operate as it chooses. For blacks, the white bureaucratic apparatus has become a cradle-to-grave presence. Labor officials, the police, and now the planning administrators are omnipresent. The establishment of the homeland governments with their own partially Africanized bureaucracies has, however, produced two discontinuities. Whites who are involved in new developmental programs in the field are trying to expand homeland economic options in agriculture, industry, commerce, and education. Their actions now contrast with the older white bureaucracy, which aimed merely to police and control the black population. A second change is that the embryonic homeland political system provides a partial mechanism through which black goals and grievances can be articulated.

The bureaucratic apparatus charged with implementing homeland development thus exhibits a two-way differentiation. There is a cleavage between the earlier control function and the newer developmental orientation. This cleavage was seen in the wave of post-1948 legislation, in the new functions taken on by old departments, and in the establishment of new change-oriented agencies. Another division in the bureaucracies overseeing homeland development has arisen with the devolving of responsibilities to homeland governments. These divisions encourage interagency conflict and rivalry. They add to the cost and reduce the efficiency of the homeland development program.

Evolution of the Bureaucracy

By the late nineteenth century, the security of white farms and settlements had been attained by the force of arms that established permanent white hegemony in South Africa. White access to additional land and to the newly discovered mineral wealth was also assured. Many Africans remained in or near white areas because there were too many to push aside. Their labor was also valued.

Once interests in land and minerals had been protected, a system of executive rule was developed. Areas of potential friction between blacks and whites were closely administered, but otherwise Africans were permitted to go their own ways and retain their own social patterns — at least in theory. As economic relations became more complex, it was decided to limit African access through the market system to land, jobs, and urban housing. The Union government followed its precursors and African colonial practice in allowing white officials wide latitude in dealing with Africans and in denying Africans protection against arbitrary state behavior. From 1910 to 1948 the executive structure that surrounded the open spaces of African life rapidly became more elaborate and restrictive, eventually creating what the authors of the Tomlinson Commission Report called a "state within a state."[1]

A predominant strand in the historical development of the imposition of white government on homeland Africans was paternalism. White society and black society, and individual whites and blacks, were conceived as having parent-child, leader-follower, superior-inferior relationships. Cultural supremacy is organic to European thought, especially as it has developed in

1. See *Summary of the Report,* 67.

South Africa, and it is difficult to separate and weigh its racial, cultural, militaristic, technical, and religious contents. Whatever its origins, however, paternalism is not merely an abstract value; it is the rock upon which African administrative and homeland development have been constructed. A key derivative principle is "trusteeship" or "guardianship," which provides a justification for the intervention of white organizations that make decisions about the use of resources for development in African areas. The trusteeship principle permeates the development and mining corporations.

> The Government of the RSA is intensely aware of the special problems which are created by an historical heritage which has placed the White nation in a position of trusteeship over various underdeveloped Bantu people. . . . In an artificially integrated unified state, the Bantu would, as a result of their enormous backlog in comparison with the Whites (in terms of economic, technical and political-administrative development), be doomed to become a backward proletariat.[2]

When it came to power in 1948 the Nationalist government recognized the need to develop an affirmative dimension in white policy toward South Africa's black population. The government recognized that little knowledge was available about the reserves and decided that the mapping of a comprehensive program of economic development had to be placed in technically skilled hands. An investigative commission was appointed and assigned two tasks: first, to ascertain the state of economic and social conditions in the African areas; and, second, to suggest measures for their development. The Tomlinson Commission, as it was known after the selection of F. R. Tomlinson as its chairman, worked methodically for four years, from 1950 to 1954, before submitting its report.[3] Much of its time was spent visiting reserves and gathering information. No remotely comparable study has been conducted since, leaving a hiatus of more than twenty years in reporting of any quality

2. Bantu Investment Corporation, *Homelands: The Role of the Corporations* (Pretoria. 1973), 10.

3. The commission was appointed in November 1950 and its full report was actually completed and submitted in late 1954. It was bound in eighteen volumes containing fifty-one chapters and 3,755 pages, 598 tables, and an atlas of 66 maps. In addition, sixty-nine volumes of original data were bound and filed with the government.

Several papers and documents commenting on the report appeared soon after its issuance. The government's *White Paper on the Development of the Bantu Areas* was published in May 1956. It indicated specifically which portions of the committee's program the government was prepared to accept and which it rejected. The South African Institute of Race Relations published its own summary of the report, D. Hobart Houghton (ed.), *The Tomlinson Report: A Summary of the Findings and Recommendations in the Tomlinson Commission Report,* (Johannesburg, 1956). An excellent early evaluation of the report is Sheila T. van der Horst, "A Plan for the Union's Backward Areas: Some Economic Aspects of the Tomlinson Commission's Report, A Review Article," *South African Journal of Economics,* XXIV (1956), 89-112.

on the physical features, infrastructures, and economies of the African areas. Baseline data compiled for the report have not been kept up to date, and only in the 1970s were efforts begun to generate statistics that measure change in the homelands.

The Tomlinson Report attempted to build a bridge between the ideological rhetoric of apartheid and the need for positive action to deal with economic conditions in the reserves. The report had to satisfy the separationist principles enunciated by the Nationalist leadership and simultaneously devise a program to raise incomes and employment in small, divided territories that shared remarkably deficient infrastructures, appalling demographic tendencies, and backward-looking agricultural methods. The commission worked during a period in which Europe's decolonization of Asia and Africa was accelerating, the rhetoric of national planning that was then current providing part of the inspiration for the government's approach to homeland development.[4] The commission's development plan was not perfect, but it did lay out programs that, had they been implemented at once, had a good chance of making a positive impact. It was not the commission's fault that its plan was in part rejected, that the remainder was not funded according to the commission's estimates, and that the developmental administration charged with implementing the parts acceptable to the government was incapable of carrying out the necessary measures.

The Tomlinson Report is still a working blueprint for economic development, although its influence has diminished in the past few years as new strategies have been promulgated. Its facts, idioms, and recommended procedures remain part of the parlance of white developmental bureaucrats. In the context of the 1950s and 1960s the report's aim was to effect a major change in the structure and performance of the white bureaucracy governing the African areas. A recognized prerequisite to putting into action the specific programs set out in the plan was to activate the African affairs bureaucracy and to add to it such new organizations as might be required to make economic development a feasible enterprise. That the process of overcoming

4. There are a number of parallels between the Commission's report and the plans that emerged in the first blush of independence from the governments of the former colonies. There was a strong bias in favor of state-led development, guided by development agencies and reinforced by development banks. Also, the economic program is backed up by a plea for nationalistic fervor and the promise of a new day. In economic method, too, there are striking similarities. Reflecting the state of the art of developmental planning at the time, there is concern with the problem of intersectoral balance during the transition from a largely agricultural economy to one with increasing employment in industry and services. The chief difference between the report and the plan of a new country is that the impetus was to come from outside rather than from within. A final parallel is that the program was in part rejected or ignored, in part captured, manipulated, and distorted by the existing bureaucracy in its own interests, and in part the program failed when applied in the field.

inertia was to take twenty years suggests that the government did not act with the urgency recommended in the report and that the attitudes of the bureaucracy were not readily malleable.

The report noted that reorganization of the Department of Native Affairs had taken place to a considerable extent in the period between 1948 and 1954 as new functions had been assigned to it by legislation. The post of under-secretary in charge of development (agriculture, engineering, and lands) was added in 1949, and there was a further reorganization in 1955 when responsibility for African education was removed from the four provincial authorities. The commissioners asserted that much more reform was needed if officials were to perform their tasks effectively. In one of the most powerful parts of the report, they pointed out that technicians in agriculture, reclamation, and construction had become the first line of contact with Africans. Unlike the old native affairs officers, these specialists knew little or nothing of African languages or customs. They rarely received any cross-cultural training. Africans were not told why certain steps were being taken and there was no feedback to the bureaucracy. The commission recommended in strong language that the administration become "African-oriented" and that language and cultural training be provided for officials of the department. Finally, the report suggested that a means be provided for the direct enlistment of Africans in the administrative process:

> It is only by systematic exercise of functions that the Bantu can be led along the way to self-activity. Only by actual practice of development, can they become its bearers. The time has arrived when, if anyone is to sit in the sun and restfully watch the world go by, it should be the official rather than the Bantu.[5]

The period from 1948 to about 1968 was a time of transition. The dominant ideology evolved from segregation to segregation-with-development and there was considerable change in the administrative framework governing the homelands. The Department of Native Affairs acquired new functions in the field and experienced internal diversification, rapid growth in size, and, in 1959, the loss of control over African education. By the late 1960s the process of institutional diversification and expansion had progressed to the point where the developmental orientation had become at least as important as the peace-keeping function. Growth had been accretionary, as new posts, offices, and organizations had been added. Simultaneously the white bureaucracy assumed greater authority and shed activities to the homeland governments; both were possible because more was being attempted at all levels. By 1970 the new organizations had all been formed, many homeland governments had been established, and a commitment to eventual "independence" had been hinted. Yet there had been no unified enunciation of policy beyond the Tomlinson Report, and the three-fold

5. *Summary of the Report,* 177.

bureaucracy managing homeland economic affairs was able to react to the more pressing problems only in a piecemeal fashion.

The Modern Structure

In attempting quickly to gain coordinated control over economic trends in the homelands in the 1970s, South Africa has adopted a strategy of "development from above" in which local involvement and preferences are less significant in setting goals and determining methods than decisions taken at the top of the developmental administration. The success of the program will therefore be determined by two factors: 1) the operating efficiency of the administrative structure and 2) the assumptions that it makes about the needs and responses of the people whom it is supposed to help. Even substantial increases in the amount of money being spent may make little difference if the bureaucracy is operating at cross purposes or wasting money promoting programs that are based on faulty premises.

In addition to the homeland governments and the African-oriented central institutions, actions of the other Republican departments also affect the homelands. Table 7.1 lists the major agencies and their functional involvement in homeland development. There are six homeland departments (seven in Bophuthatswana). They share the seven functions listed across the top of the table but normally each undertakes only two or three. All departments have routine administrative and service duties not included under any of the functional categories. In a homeland, the Department of Agriculture is involved in agricultural development and, through the restructuring of rural locations, in population resettlement. Since the Department of Authority Affairs includes the local authorities that have numerous responsibilities, it appears to be more important than it really is.

The white-directed, African-oriented institutions are the critical ones at this stage since the homeland governments are weak. The Departments of Bantu Administration and Development and Bantu Education jointly cover all functional areas, although their role has become increasingly advisory and concerned with coordination rather than operations. The Bantu Trust, as part of the Department of Bantu Administration and Development, is particularly important in land acquisition and township development; it also funnels capital into the investment corporations. The major developmental impetus in agriculture, industry, commerce, and infrastructure is guided by the Bantu Investment Corporation, the Xhosa Development Corporation, and, in a specialized way, the Bantu Mining Corporation.

Almost all white governmental departments make decisions that affect African welfare and homeland development. Those listed in the table are directly involved and have responsibilities that cannot be shifted to one of the African-oriented institutions. Industrial development and location, the construction of roads, rail lines, and ports, and the development of communications are controlled by white agencies. The homeland governments have little involvement in industrial planning or in labor utilization. They share responsibility for manpower training with African-oriented and Republican institutions.

Numerous agencies of each type are involved in each development function. These functional categories are very broad and there is a good deal of specialization within them. Nonetheless, responsibilities overlap. Where there is insufficient coordination to reconcile conflicts, avoid duplication, and put forward a coherent, consistent approach, homeland planning tends to be confused and ineffective. An illustration is agriculture, the most important homeland sector. Its development is handled by seven of the twenty-five agencies listed in table 7.1. Six organizations are involved in education and manpower training. Fifteen share responsibility for industry, commerce, and infrastructure. There are coordinating bodies at various levels that try to maintain policy consistency and keep everyone headed in the same direction. The prime minister, his cabinet, and ministerial level committees are important in determining priorities. The Board for the Decentralisation of Industry, which is made up of ministers and high-level civil servants, coordinates the program of industrial decentralization. On the African-oriented agency side, the minister of Bantu administration and development, his secretaries for development, administration, and education, and the Bantu Affairs Commission, with its economic and agricultural subcommittees composed of interested citizens and experts, have a coordinating responsibility. BENBO, the planning and research unit of the Bantu Investment Corporation has acquired mediating responsibilities as advisor to the Bantu Affairs Commission and the minister of Bantu administration and development. Sometimes there are cross-agency meetings of persons concerned with education, manpower, agriculture, or other facets of development administration. The importance and growth of the Bantu Investment Corporation and the increasing expertise of BENBO are propelling these two agencies to the forefront of decision-making, and they are the key monitors of effectiveness and progress. The splitting off of separate development banks with equal representation on their boards for homeland blacks amounts to a redistribution of power to the homeland regions.

Despite these various consulting and coordinating bodies, it cannot be said that there is at present a well-worked out, consistent plan for developing the homelands. In agriculture, for example, the aims and methods of the homeland agricultural departments, the Bantu Investment Corporation's agricultural branch, and the agricultural divisions of the Department of Bantu Administration and Development are not identical. Similarly, there is no

Table 7.1
The Modern Bureaucracy: Structure and Functions

Institutions	Development Functions						
	Agriculture	Industry, Commerce and Infrastructure	Education and Training	Population Settlement	Labor Affairs	Health and Welfare	Land Consolidation
A. *Homeland Government Departments*							
1. Agriculture	X			X			
2. Authority Affairs and Finance; regional, tribal authorities	X	X	X	X		X	X
3. Community Affairs; labor bureaux				X	X	X	
4. Education and Culture			X				
5. Justice							
6. Works		X	X	X			
7. Health[a]						X	
B. *White-Directed, African-Oriented Institutions*							
1. Bantu Administration and Development	X	X		X	X	X	X
2. Bantu Education			X				
3. Bantu Investment Corporation: XDC,[b] BENBO[c]	X	X	X				
4. Bantu Mining Corporation		X					
5. S.A. Bantu Trust				X		X	X
C. *Republican Institutions*[d]							
1. Agriculture[e]	X						X
2. Industry; Decentralization Board		X					
3. Labour[f]		X	X		X		

Item				
4. Mines		X		
5. Planning; Growth Points Committee		X		
6. Tourism		X		
7. Transport; National Transport Commission		X		
8. Water Affairs	X			
9. Posts and Telegraphs; Railways and Harbours; S.A. Airways		X		
10. Provincial and Local Authorities			X	X
11. Industrial Development Corporation		X	X	X
12. S.A. Broadcasting Corporation		X		
13. Agricultural Marketing Boards	X			

SOURCE: Based on a similar table constructed by J. A. Lombard and P. J. van der Merwe, "Central Problems of the Economic Development of Bantu Homelands," *Finance and Trade Review*, X (1972), 42–45.

[a] The Transkei has had a Department of Health for some time and the other homelands are beginning to establish such departments, sometimes named Health and Social Welfare.

[b] Xhosa Development Corporation.

[c] Afrikaans acronym for Bureau for Economic Research re Bantu Development; coordinating and research division of the Bantu Investment Corporation.

[d] Only the Republican departments having a significant, immediate connection with homeland development are included.

[e] Includes Agricultural Credit and Land Tenure, Agricultural Economics and Marketing, and Agricultural Technical services.

[f] Includes Bantu Building Workers Advisory Board, Central Bantu Labour Board, Industrial Tribunal, National Apprenticeship Board, and Wage Board.

all-South African program for the development of African human resources. Most of the newer agencies and the newer departments and personnel of the older institutions have a greater activist orientation than their predecessors. There thus is tension between the newer and older parts of the bureaucracy. This ambivalence presents a bewildering and unsettling impression to black officials, businessmen, and farmers and can scarcely inspire their confidence.

Another conflict is that the older agencies are public institutions, dispersing public funds. They measure their results by such indicators as the increase in the number of schools and pupils, acres mapped and planned, or houses built. The newer agencies are profit-making semiautonomous corporations and must generate a surplus of revenue over expenditure. This dichotomy of service and profit motivation adds to the diversity of the homeland administrative agencies. It means, for example, that projects that are acceptable to a public agency on the basis of their social costs and benefits may not be acceptable to a semiprivate body responsive to market-measured profits.

As homeland development is structured there is little feedback from blacks to the administration agencies. Figure 7.1 suggests the nature of the problem. The three groups of agencies set out in table 7.1 are shown separately in summary form. Quite apart from the fact that few Africans are accustomed to receiving services from government, and to complaining if they do not get them, the structure of government does not yet provide for effective indigenous involvement. The first group of agencies, the homeland governments, has limited constitutional powers, and still dispenses only a restricted range of public services. With a large proportion of able-bodied men absent at any one time, these governments do not yet face demanding and articulate electorates. The third group of agencies in table 7.1, the predominantly white-oriented Republic institutions, have some impact on a homeland. Several examples — the Industrial Development Corporation, and the Departments of Mines, Labour, and Transport — are shown. In this part of the bureaucracy the flow is entirely downward to the African population; there is no return flow in the form of electoral and interest group politics. Even in the second group of agencies in table 7.1, the African-oriented agencies set up by the Republic, there is little movement of information and complaint from the African population to the bureaucracy. Some scattered face-to-face impressions of discontent, acceptance, or neutrality may be conveyed, but such encounters are subject to the risks of misinterpretation, of biased sampling, and of people seeing what they choose to see.

The development corporations have white boards of directors who are isolated from both the black and white political process. They can act without prior contact with the Department of Bantu Administration and Development or the Department of Bantu Education, although all are linked through BENBO and the Bantu Affairs Commission and its subcommittees.

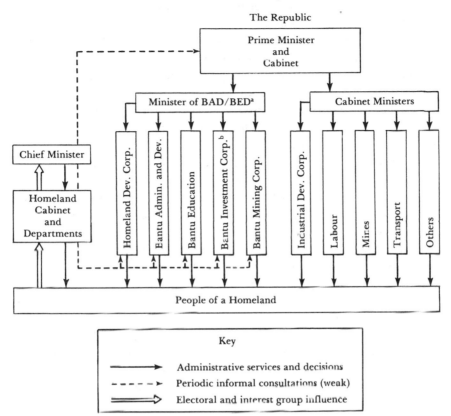

Figure 7.1
Public Administration and the People of a Homeland

The Republic

Prime Minister
and
Cabinet

Minister of BAD/BED[a]

Cabinet Ministers

Chief Minister

Homeland
Cabinet
and
Departments

Homeland Dev. Corp.

Bantu Admin. and Dev.

Bantu Education

Bantu Investment Corp.[b]

Bantu Mining Corp.

Industrial Dev. Corp.

Labour

Mines

Transport

Others

People of a Homeland

Key

Administrative services and decisions

Periodic informal consultations (weak)

Electoral and interest group influence

[a]The minister of Bantu administration and development is also minister of Bantu education.
[b]The Bantu Investment Corporation is a parent body that is losing functions to investment corporations as they are set up in each homeland.

Immediate interaction between the bureaucracy and the people of a home-land is limited to the homeland government departments and ministers. The development corporations for each homeland will apparently receive guid-ance from both the homeland governments and the white agencies through their boards, and in a routine way from the staffs of the Bantu Investment Corporation and the homeland departments.

The effectiveness of at least some parts of the development bureaucracy is limited not only by a lack of internal coordination, and by limited black input, but also by the persistence of obsolete explanations for African under-development. A primary reason for the backwardness of the homelands is said to be the lack of African motivation. This is a recurrent theme in dis-cussions with white officials ranging from homeland field staff to officers of the developmental agencies. In the Bantu Investment Corporation there is a special concern for the lack of black business drive and entrepreneurship. The task of the white agencies is conceived to be the motivation of African farmers, workers, and businessmen. Some suggest that a long process of education and leadership by example will be needed. The presumed thrifti-ness and drive of the white man are cited, and it is asked how long it will take to instill similar values in Africans. Others argue that coercion—higher taxes on livestock to encourage herd turnover, or high rents on land to ensure more economic use—will be needed.

These attitudes are a throwback to the ideology of colonial administration in Africa and Asia in the early twentieth century.[6] There are echoes of Boeke's interpretation of Indonesian dualism, in which he contrasted a Western and an Eastern mentality, arguing that Eastern peoples did not have the economic spirit of the West.[7] But these doctrines are out of date. If sustained, they will delay the removal of the technological input and the institutional constraints that have limited black aspirations and achievements.

The sensitivities of black politicians and administrators can be of great help in designing a structure within which economic activities can be stimu-lated. The constrictive legal and social framework imposed by South Africa has depressed black attainments far below what they would otherwise be. The most homeland policy can do is to reopen some channels for black development. Unless the older attitudes are abandoned and the African role enlarged, development work will tend to be ineffective, costly, and directed into dead ends, with frustrating results and increased ill-will on all sides.

6. See, for example, W. J. Barber, *The Economy of British Central Africa* (Oxford, 1961), chs. 1-4; R. E. Baldwin, *Economic Development and Export Growth* (Berkeley, 1966), chs. 5 and 6.

7. J. H. Boeke, *Economics and Economic Policy of Dual Societies* (New York, 1953).

Functional Budgeting and Homeland Development

Apart from the peculiar difficulties presented by South Africa's heritage of racial domination, there is a universal conflict in the public administration of economic development between the maintenance of control and change-oriented or consciously disruptive functions of the bureaucracy. As less developed nations have secured independence they have confronted the problems of shifting the emphasis of administration from tasks such as maintaining law and order, collecting taxes, and providing limited services for the colonial business and export sector, toward newer responsibilities including the creation of an active planning system, the sponsorship of public sector enterprises, and the provision of employment and social services. This redirection of effort induces a number of bureaucratic jealousies and strains and poses problems of psychological and behavioral adjustment for governmental cadres. The difficulty of the transition is often exacerbated by the severe shortage of talented administrators in an underdeveloped country: usually there is no quantity of new blood available to replace old line personnel.

In South Africa, one conflict between change-oriented and traditional bureaucracies has involved budgeting methods. In the absence of formal national or regional planning, some alternative mechanism for coordinating public sector activities was needed. Change-oriented experts successfully advocated the use of the budgeting process as a means of activating, implementing, controlling, and evaluating homeland developmental programs. Whatever their merits for internal accounting purposes, the old-style line-item budgets of the Department of Bantu Administration and Development, the Bantu Trust, the Department of Bantu Education, and the homeland governments provided little insight into the nature of homeland development programs and their effectiveness. It was difficult to identify the priorities of agencies and assess their annual progress toward the attainment of their targets.

The proposed solution to this problem is a planning-programming-budgeting (PPB) system.[8] Since 1969 BENBO has attempted to develop a PPB program suited to the guidance of homeland development. BENBO is in a unique position to carry out such a program because it is the only organization, including the homeland governments, that oversees the great majority

8. One of the leading advocates of this system has been J. A. Lombard, chairman of the economic subcommittee of the Bantu Affairs Commission. His articles on programming homeland development include: "Political and Administrative Principles of Homeland Development," *Bantu*, XVIII (Feb., 1971), 24–31; "Problems of Regional Economic Programming in the Development of the Bantu Homelands," *South African Journal of Economics.* XXXIX (1971), 383–401.

of homeland developmental activities. After several years of preparation and experimentation, the homeland budgets for Bophuthatswana and KwaZulu recently assumed two forms, the standard one and the new PPB format. The extent to which the new procedures have displaced the older financial control system has so far been constrained by widespread unfamiliarity with the method, purpose and terminology of the PPB system and some resistance to its use. Most ministers, departmental secretaries, and their staffs in the homelands budget and think in the old style, and then translate the results into the PPB system adopted by BENBO.

The Allocation of
Public Resources for Development

In the absence of planning documents, the homeland functional budgets afford the best insight into the manner in which resources are being devoted to development. The functional budgets, as they are being implemented in Bophuthatswana, KwaZulu, and the other homelands, identify seven objectives in terms of which the departments of the homelands, the development corporations, and other institutions can evaluate their progress during each accounting year. Table 7.2 identifies these objectives and shows how in the budget of Bophuthatswana the greatest emphasis has been on the development of human potential and on population resettlement. The provision of social services and physical infrastructural construction are important secondary activities. Land planning and conservation, and employment and income creation, are of comparatively minor significance. The transfer of health functions elevates the share of social services and reduces the shares of the other departments. In KwaZulu, where the settlement of the population consumes one-third of the budget, the development of human potential is of lesser importance than in Bophuthatswana. In both homelands there has been a moderate relative shift toward planning and administration and, since fiscal 1972/73, a step-up in physical infrastructure building. The absolute figures show gains in every category, so a stable or declining proportion does not necessarily imply a shrinkage of resources devoted to a particular objective. The dominant overall impression is that both governments are concerned primarily with the provision of services to the homeland populations rather than with activities that yield immediate income, employment, or other developmental benefits.

The budgeting and planning technique becomes more powerful as it is applied at the departmental level. The functional budgets for Bophuthatswana and KwaZulu are detailed, thick volumes that are several hundred pages long. They leave little uncertainty about how funds have been allocated across the seven budgetary objectives by the homeland departments and (with

Table 7.2

Homeland Government Spending by Planning Objective:
Bophuthatswana and KwaZulu, 1972/73–1975/76
(1,000 rands and percent)

Objective	Bophuthatswana				KwaZulu			
	Year				Year			
	1972/73	1973/74	1974/75	1975/76	1972/73	1973/74	1974/75	1975/76
Land planning and conservation	244 (1.5)	292 (1.4)	292 (0.9)	850 (1.7)	414 (1.3)	604 (1.3)	1,003 (1.5)	1,771 (1.9)
Population settlement	4,132 (25.4)	3,600 (17.9)	5,678 (18.4)	6,527 (13.2)	10,962 (34.2)	14,027 (30.4)	21,879 (33.0)	29,796 (32.1)
Employment creation and income generation	926 (5.7)	1,300 (6.5)	1,619 (5.2)	2,125 (4.3)	2,628 (8.2)	3,906 (8.6)	5,221 (8.6)	5,633 (6.1)
Development of human potential	6,043 (37.3)	7,124 (35.4)	10,983 (35.5)	13,578 (27.4)	8,488 (25.5)	11,609 (25.2)	13,561 (20.5)	21,765 (23.5)
Provision of social services	2,505 (15.9)	3,192 (15.9)	4,553 (14.7)	16,296 (32.9)	6,188 (19.4)	7,568 (16.4)	12,533 (18.9)	16,643 (18.0)
General administration	894 (5.5)	1,700 (8.4)	3,084 (10.0)	4,164 (8.4)	1,395 (4.4)	3,099 (6.6)	5,638 (8.5)	8,361 (9.0)
Infrastructure	1,502 (9.2)	2,923 (14.5)	4,693 (15.2)	5,960 (12.0)	1,904 (6.0)	5,323 (11.5)	6,447 (9.7)	8,742 (9.4)
Total	16,246 (100.0)	20,131 (100.0)	30,902 (99.9)[a]	49,500 (100.0)	31,979 (100.0)	46,136 (100.0)	66,232 (100.0)	92,711 (100.0)

SOURCES: BENBO, Bophuthatswana, Economic Revue, 1975 (Pretoria, 1975), 58, 60; idem, KwaZulu, Economic Revue, 1975 (Pretoria, 1976), 70. Some percentages were calculated from original data. For 1974/75 to 1975/76, BENBO, personal communications (xeroxed materials) 19 March 1976. There are a few minor discrepancies between the 1974/75 data in the first two sources and the last, which are those used.

NOTE: Spending by Bantu Investment and Mining corporations and other agencies is not included.

[a] Rounding error.

related documents) by the other development agencies. They thus provide an effective means by which decision makers can supervise, assess, and redirect the flows of public resources into the homelands.

The planning budgets represent a considerable advance over the previous financial control methods. Nonetheless, they do not provide a complete solution to the problem of planning in the homelands. The seven objectives are not explicitly ordered, and there is no evident reason for determining how additional R1,000s of revenue should be allocated. There is a conflict between the social needs of the homeland populations—housing, education, health, and sanitation—and the desire of the Republic to maximize the rate at which internal employment is created.

The present budgeting framework also fails to establish a relationship between financial disbursements and the achievement of physical targets. It is difficult to ascertain whether increased outlays on a subprogram are matched by more substantial physical achievements in the forms of more or better houses, higher crop yields, or more trained automobile mechanics. There would also appear to be considerable scope for the application of cost-benefit project analysis. Although several subprograms may contribute to employment generation, there is no basis for determining the comparative costs of creating an additional job. These are likely to vary widely between, say, a sisal farm and a growth point like Isithebe. Similarly, in education, should additional funds be devoted to primary education, secondary education, or teacher training? These decisions are not purely economic, but a clear understanding of the benefit-cost ratios associated with each program would be of considerable benefit to homeland politicians and the developmental planners. In a broader perspective, it may even be that investigation into the alternative costs of housing, employment, or some types of schooling in the homelands as a whole, compared to border areas or the core industrial areas, could substantially affect the direction of large portions of homeland development efforts.

The clearest picture of the structure of homeland government departmental activities may be obtained from the outlines contained in table 7.3. The table divides departmental outlays by function and shows how functional expenditures are spread over the six or seven departments of the governments. In the Tswana and Zulu homelands, for example, the Departments of Chief Minister and Finance and of Justice provide general administrative services, with the minor exception of the R100 devoted by the former to employment creation and income generation in each of the fiscal years 1974/75 and 1975/76. Educational spending falls under the heading of human resources. (In Bophuthatswana the Department of Health and Social Welfare finds its R13.5 million allocation under provision of social services.) Interior, Works, and Agriculture range more widely over the functional categories.

Increases in some of the items provide some indication of year-to-year priorities. In Bophuthatswana spending by the Department of Agriculture on land planning and infrastructure nearly tripled in fiscal 1975/76, implying a greater commitment to attempts to stabilize grazing, build fences, and accelerate physical planning. A six-fold rise in the Department of Works' spending on employment and income creation is probably attributable to the attempt to involve more local workers in construction. The division of funds into current and capital expenditures under the various objective headings tells something about the balance between routine expenses, mostly salaries, and capital improvements in the form of new equipment or construction. Population settlement and infrastructure give the greatest impetus to direct physical capital formation by the public sector. The share of capital expenditures in total spending shifted from 21.9 percent to 36.1 percent between fiscal 1974/75 and fiscal 1975/76. It should be noted, however, that little of this capital formation contributes in a direct fashion to the augmentation of output in subsequent periods. Finally, measures of the percentage increase of spending on each objective show some deemphasis of population settlement, a slowdown in development of human potential, a swing toward employment and income creation, and a rapid expansion in expenditures on social services.

The functional responsibilities of KwaZulu's governmental departments are essentially identical with those of Bophuthatswana. There are, however, important differences between them. KwaZulu's population is double that of Bophuthatswana, its total expenditure according to the budgeting in fiscal 1975/76 was R93 million compared to Bophuthatswana's R49 million. The concern with population settlement is greater in KwaZulu, requiring 32 percent of total expenditures in fiscal 1975/76 compared to 13 percent in Bophuthatswana. This emphasis is partially responsible for the higher overall rate of public sector capital formation in KwaZulu as opposed to Bophuthatswana (41 percent compared to 36 percent) since expenditures on population settlement are biased in this direction. In KwaZulu there has been no corresponding increase in expenditures on social services because the homeland government has yet to assume responsibility for them. In the percentage distribution across the seven functional categories, KwaZulu shows no spectacular reallocations. In terms of changes in fiscal 1975/76 there have been declines in the rate of increase in population settlement (though the proportion remains high), employment creation, and social services, but large increases in development of human potential and land planning. Neither homeland has had major successes in employment creation.

Adoption of the new budgets, with the greater control they imply, has important consequences for the formulation of spending and developmental policies in the homelands and their ability as governments to move toward

Table 7.3
A Functional Classification of the 1973/74, 1974/75, and 1975/76
Homeland Budgets of Expenditure According to Objective and Department
(thousand rands)

A. Bophuthatswana

Objective	Land Planning and Conservation			Population Settlement			Employment Creation and Income Generation		
Department	1973/74	1974/75	1975/76	1973/74	1974/75	1975/76	1973/74	1974/75	1975/76
1. Chief Minister and Finance	..	-	-	..	-	-	..	1	1
2. Interior	..	4	-	..	129	363	..	2	-
3. Works	..	2	-	..	5,499	6,164	..	102	605
4. Education	..	-	-	..	-	-	..	-	-
5. Agriculture & Forestry	..	286	850	..	50	-	..	1,514	1,519
6. Justice	..	-	-	..	-	-	..	-	-
7. Health and Social Welfare	-	-	-	-	-	-	-	-	-
Total	292	292	850	3,600	5,678	6,527	1,300	1,619	2,125
Current Expenditure (%)	..	58.9	79.6	..	40.2	45.2	..	93.9	59.4
Capital Expenditure (%)	..	41.1	20.4	..	59.8	54.8	..	6.1	40.6
% of Annual Total	1,5	1.0	1.8	17.9	18.4	13.2	6.5	5.2	4.3
% of Increase Over Previous Year		+191.1			+57.7	+15.0		+24.5	+31.3

SOURCES: Compiled by BENBO from Republic of South Africa, Bophuthatswana, *Estimate of the Expenditure to be defrayed from the Revenue Fund of Bophuthatswana During the Year Ending 31 March 1974* for the year ending 31 March 1975, and 31 March 1976.

NOTE: . . = not available; - = nil.

B. KwaZulu

Objective	Land Planning and Conservation			Population Settlement			Employment Creation and Income Generation		
Department	1973/74	1974/75	1975/76	1973/74	1974/75	1975/76	1973/74	1974/75	1975/76
1. Authority Affairs and Finance	- -ᵃ	- -	- -	- -	- -	- -	84	57	- -
2. Community Affairs	- -	- -	- -	262	416	370	- -	- -	- -
3. Works	- -	- -	- -	13,765	21,463	29,426	345	130	169
4. Education	- -	- -	- -	- -	- -	- -	- -	- -	- -
5. Agriculture and Forestry	604	1,003	1,771	- -	- -	- -	3,527	5,034	5,464
6. Justice	- -	- -	- -	- -	- -	- -	- -	- -	- -
Total	604	1,003	1,771	14,027	21,879	29,796	3,956	5,221	5,633
Current Expenditure (%)	31.8	67.1	60.9	23.0	18.0	17.0	82.0	81.7	81.4
Capital Expenditure (%)	68.2	32.9	39.1	77.0	82.0	83.0	18.0	18.3	18.6
% of Annual Total	1.3	1.5	1.9	30.4	33.1	32.1	8.6	7.8	6.1
% of Increase Over Previous Year		+66.1	+76.6		+56.0	+36.2		+32.0	+7.0

SOURCES: Compiled by the authors from Republic of South Africa, KwaZulu, *Estimate of the Expenditure to be Defrayed from the Revenue Fund of the KwaZulu Government for the Year Ending 31 March 1975* and for the year ending 31 March 1976.

ᵃThe authors are unable to draw a distinction between "not available" and "nil" as was done by BENBO for Bophuthatswana.

A. Bophuthatswana

Development of Human Potential			Provision of Social Services			General Administration			Infrastructure		
1973/74	1974/75	1975/76	1973/74	1974/75	1975/76	1973/74	1974/75	1975/76	1973/74	1974/75	1975/76
..	–	–	..	–	–	..	686	1,065	..	–	–
..	14	24	..	4,553	–	..	758	636	..	–	–
..	365	864	..	–	2,796	..	1,202	1,746	..	4,363	5,257
..	10,604	12,690	..	–	–	..	18	10	..	–	–
..	–	–	..	–	–	..	–	–	..	330	703
..	–	–	..	–	–	..	420	707	..	–	–
–	–	–	–	–	13,500	–	–	–	–	–	–
7,124	10,983	13,578	3,192	4,553	16,296	1,700	3,084	4,164	2,923	4,693	5,960
..	90.3	87.5	..	100.0	52.2	..	90.3	74.3	..	62.1	54.3
..	9.7	12.5	..	–	47.8	..	9.7	25.7	..	37.9	45.7
35.4	35.5	27.4	15.9	14.7	32.9	8.4	10.0	8.4	14.5	15.2	12.0
+54.2	+23.6		+42.6	+257.9		+81.4	+35.0		+60.0	+27.0	

B. KwaZulu

Development of Human Potential			Provision of Social Services			General Administration			Infrastructure		
1973/74	1974/75	1975/76	1973/74	1974/75	1975/76	1973/74	1974/75	1975/76	1973/74	1974/75	1975/76
— —	— —	— —	— —	— —	— —	467	639	1,413	— —	— —	— —
51	— —	120	7,533	12,182	15,688	828	1,202	1,450	— —	— —	— —
828	1,492	3,144	35	351	955	1,027	2.901	4,560	4,979	6,447	8,742
10,730	12,069	18,501	— —	— —	— —	4	18	21	— —	— —	— —
— —	— —	— —	— —	— —	— —	— —	— —	12	345	— —	— —
— —	— —	— —	— —	— —	— —	723	878	905	— —	— —	— —
11,609	13,561	21,765	7,568	12,533	16,643	3,049	5,638	8,361	5,324	6,447	8,742
92.0	87.3	84.5	99.5	97.0	94.1	96.2	68.9	59.5	58.0	64.8	53.7
8.0	12.7	15.5	0.5	3.0	5.9	3.8	31.1	40.5	42.0	35.2	46.3
25.2	20.5	23.5	16.4	18.9	18.0	6.6	8.5	9.0	11.5	9.7	9.4
	+16.8	+60.5		+60.61	+32.8		+84.9	+48.3		+21.1	+35.6

[cont.]

A. Bophuthatswana

Department	1973/74	Total 1974/75	1975/76
1. Chief Minister and Finance	471	687	1,066
2. Interior	3,817	5,460	1,023
3. Works	6,645	11,513	17,432
4. Education	6,906	10,622	12,700
5. Agriculture & Forestry	1,826	2,240	3,072
6. Justice	466	420	707
7. Health and Social Welfare	–	–	13,500
Total	20,131	30,942	49,500
Current Expenditure (%)	–	78.1	63.9
Capital Expenditure (%)	..	21.9	36.1
% of Annual Total	100.0	100.0	100.0
% of Increase Over Previous Year	-	+ 53.7	+ 60.2

B. KwaZulu

Department	1973/74	Total 1974/75	1975/76
1. Authority Affairs and Finance	551	696	1,413
2. Community Affairs	8,674	13,799	17,628
3. Works	20,979	32,784	46,996
4. Education	10,734	12,087	18,522
5. Agriculture and Forestry	4,476	6,037	7,247
6. Justice	723	878	905
Total	46,136	66,282	92,711
Current Expenditure (%)	67.0	61.8	58.7
Capital Expenditure (%)	33.0	38.2	41.3
% of Annual Total	100.0	100.0	100.0
% of Increase Over Previous Year		+ 43.76	+ 39.9

greater autonomy in decision-making. These budgeting changes represent a gain for the more technically progressive and change-oriented elements of the white bureaucracy. But greater control makes it possible for the agencies of the Republic to pursue their own set of objectives more efficiently. In the absence of any, or only very limited ("consultative") black participation in the planning and budgeting process, white preferences, cloaked in the technical garb of the PPB system, may dictate the targets to be pursued.

There are several potential conflicts between the Republic and the homelands over the ranking of developmental priorities. For the Republic the expansion of homeland employment is the number one priority. This aim is of less immediate importance for the homelands, where more education, housing, and urban amenities, and the expansion and unification of homeland territories are of paramount interest. If Africans want jobs, they are not necessarily interested in having them located in the homelands. Indeed, for most single persons or married couples willing to be separated there are better job opportunities in the white areas. There is thus a considerable discrepancy between what people in the homelands want, insofar as their wishes can now be read, and what the white bureaucracy in conjunction with the homeland governments is able to provide. The current diffuse quality of articulated black aims, and especially the wish to pursue courses of action with low short-run employment and income effects (like education, housing, and land purchases), alarm white planners, who see these choices as wasteful or "too political." They regard their own preferences as technically chosen — not "political" — and are hesitant because of the incipient conflict over the objectives of homeland administration to allow substantially greater black participation in the decision-making process.

If the homelands are to assume more political control over economic functions, black objectives must be given increasing influence in planning. Ministers and staff in the homeland governments will need to become fluent in the language of PPB in order to understand what their departments are doing and to affect the choice of budgetary direction. Homeland leaders must be enabled to deliver the "goods" — new schools, roads, bridges, cattle pens, sugar or mining concessions, commercial permits, and so on — to their allies, supporters, and constituents and generally to use economic benefits to maintain and broaden their bases of support. This is what political independence is all about.

Lastly, the PPB system requires a relatively high degree of economic and management expertise to master and use effectively. It is currently not fully intelligible to African cabinet members or to the white secretaries who administer the governmental departments of Bophuthatswana and KwaZulu. There are no Africans trained in its use, and no training program is underway in the black colleges, on white campuses, in the government, or outside the country. In consequence, a planning expertise gap is widening between the white developmental agencies and the personnel of the homeland governments. As this gap grows, it will become increasingly difficult to transfer the real budgeting and decision-making responsibility to the unprepared homelands. There exists a fundamental conflict between the enhancement of the planning and control capabilities of the newer white developmental agencies and the desired movement toward political and economic autonomy for the homelands.

8

The Economic Development
of the Homelands

South Africa's modern economic history began with the mineral discoveries of the mid-nineteenth century. The exploitation of diamonds, gold, and other minerals offered substantial employment outside agriculture to whites and blacks for the first time. New transport networks linked port cities to growing inland centers, and blacks were drawn to the towns to work in mining, commerce, and industry, and on white-owned farms. However, this new economic growth produced a pattern of infrastructural development, population settlement, and location of employment that for the most part bypassed the African reserves. The economies of the reserves became dependent on the white-dominated core economy and increasingly lagged behind the rest of South Africa. Predominantly pastoral and agricultural, the reserves offered only a drastically restricted range of opportunities for economic security and achievement for their peoples. In explicitly dedicating its policies to the development of these backward areas, the Republic is undertaking an immensely complex task of economic reconstruction as well as trying to alter an historic pattern sustained by a variety of powerful interests.

Agriculture

The forces that have shaped the growth of agriculture in the Republic over the last century have had little positive effect upon the traditional subsistence economy of the homelands. As South African society became more urban and industrial, the demand for food and raw materials grew. Tariffs protected the home market and export subsidies opened the way for larger overseas sales of maize, sugar, wine, wool, and dairy goods. Sources of credit were provided by the Land and Agricultural Bank of South Africa, created in 1912, and by the Cooperatives Act of 1922. The extension of railways and roads brought isolated farmsteads into closer contact with city markets, sources of supplies, and technical and price information. As a result the productivity and profitability of agriculture in the white areas was increased and farming became a commercial undertaking.[1] In the African reserves, however, these changes had little impact because blacks were barred from participating in most of the government's programs and because the systems of land and labor use in the homeland agriculture were geared, not to money gain, but to the subsistence production of food—to be supplemented by wage income when necessary—and the attainment of a measure of security in the form of a family plot and a few head of livestock grazing on common pasture.

As in other parts of the economy, Africans responded to the constrained opportunities that were open and contributed to South Africa's agricultural growth as laborers, tenants, foremen, and managers, and, before being barred in 1913 from land ownership and working "on halves," Africans were successful sharecroppers and owners.[2] Today about 30 percent of the African population lives and works on white farms, and this exposure, added to the background of decades of participation in a modernizing South African agriculture, makes the stagnation—actually the retrogression—of the homeland's primary sector all the more striking. A number of farms in white areas are occupied and run by blacks for white absentee owners. The backwardness of homeland agriculture must therefore be explained by the unique structure of that sector, not by an inherent unresponsiveness or disinterest on the part of Africans.

A major reason for the agricultural underdevelopment of the homelands is the long-standing neglect of the needs of black farmers by the Union and Republican governments, a neglect that contrasts sharply with the zealous attention devoted to white South African farmers. After 1910 there were enough problems arising from the changing structure of white agriculture, and in the related rapid exodus of poor whites to the cities, to occupy the Union government and turn its attention away from the politically impotent reserves. Yet, many of these stresses were felt as keenly, or more keenly, in the reserves. Growing populations and redundant farm families, overgrazing and improper burning of pasturage, recurrent droughts, raging epidemics of rinderpest and other diseases, wide swings in prices, and the vicissitudes of war and depression afflicted South African farmers of all colors. Agricultural education and extension services were slow in developing, at first even in white areas, and poor cropping practices abused the soil and its cover. Erosion became a national affliction. The stabilization of tenure in 1913 and the measures taken over the next several decades to ensure a supply of cheap black labor to white farms, in combination with measures to provide better

1. For a description of agricultural development in South Africa after 1866, see Francis Wilson, "Farming, 1866-1966" in Monica Wilson and Leonard Thompson (eds.), *Oxford History of South Africa* (Oxford, 1971), II, 104-171.
2. Colin Bundy, "The Emergence and Decline of a South African Peasantry," *African Affairs*, LXXI (1972) 269-288.

technologies, prices, and open marketing channels, pushed white agriculture down an uneven road to progress. Farmers in the reserves were left to their own devices to try to live as best they could with a set of agrarian conditions inappropriate to growth. Ever larger numbers of men and their livestock had to be absorbed on steadily shrinking and depleting allotments of farmland and pasturage.

By 1929 the Union government had become alarmed enough about the deteriorating agricultural conditions in the African reserves to establish a Native Agricultural and Lands Branch within the Department of Native Affairs. Having an extremely limited budget and an equally narrow range of responsibilities, this branch focused its activities on soil conservation and the stabilization of grazing. After the South African Native Trust was formed in 1936, most of the agricultural branch's attention was directed to the newly acquired white farmlands, with the hope that these tracts could be preserved until resources for development became available.[3] Some very limited extension work was essayed, including herd culling, stock dipping, and inoculation. Quality breeding stock was provided. There were scattered demonstration projects and sales of subsidized implements. After the interruption of World War II, conservation efforts were renewed, but progress throughout the 1950s and 1960s was slow since the program was confined largely to trying to increase the proportion of land brought under strict land-use management. Ideally at least, this "physical planning" was intended to limit herd sizes, set up a rotational grazing plan, and allocate house and garden plots to the residents of rural locations.

The state of agriculture and animal husbandry in the reserves was not affected to any great degree by these programs, patently insufficient as they were in relation to the magnitude of the task. They were also unimaginative and unattuned to African economic and social conditions. In the managed or planned areas, people had to move to new housing, change the sites of their fields, and practice unfamiliar rotational grazing on fenced pasturage. There was no particular gain to an individual from doing any of these things — indeed, there were private gains in violating the rules — and the program was never adequately explained to the majority of Africans. Resistance to relocation sometimes became violent, but most often took the form of open gates, cut fences, and disregard for herd size guidelines. Even if the program had been enthusiastically adopted, it would have done nothing to raise farm or pasturage productivity since no complementary extension

3. *Summary of Report*, 74–75. Since 1948 there has been an extensive renaming of institutions and legislation, principally by the substitution of "Bantu" for "Native." Thus the South African Native Trust is now the South African Bantu Trust, and the Native Agricultural and Lands Branch of the Department of Native Affairs is now the Agricultural and Development Branch of the Department of Bantu Administration and Development.

advice, credit, new technologies, or other measures were forthcoming. The Tomlinson Commission reported:

> [It] is clear that the existing land settlement policy in the betterment areas of the Reserves brings no alleviation of the agricultural poverty of the Bantu, and that it remains necessary for the family head and, possibly, for other members of the family as well, to sell their labour outside the Reserves in order to provide for the needs of the family.[4]

Output and Yields

By everyone's admission homeland crop yields and stock turnover rates remain low in the mid-1970s and renewed efforts to grow more food, develop commercial crops, and increase livestock productivity have had only spotty success. The homeland governments, the Bantu Investment Corporation, and the Agricultural and Development Branch of the Department of Bantu Administration and Development have not yet overcome the inertia of the agricultural sector.

Maize accounts for about 70 percent of the output of food grains, by weight, in Bophuthatswana, and about 80 percent in KwaZulu. In the former homeland, the remainder of production is divided between sorghum and dry or irrigated wheat. In the latter, sorghum is almost exclusively the alternative food grain. There are negligible amounts of cowpeas, beans, peanuts, potatoes, and millet grown.[5] Table 8.1 shows the trends of maize output, area, and average yields for Bophuthatswana, KwaZulu, and all the homelands. The quality of the data is poor, but differences among the homelands and over time are probably in the right directions even if the precise numerical values are subject to a margin of error.[6] It should be recognized, too, that averages are highly misleading. Often the best cultivators, and particularly those with access to water and better land, do much better

---

4. *Ibid.*, 77.

5. These proportions are calculated from data available in Republic of South Africa, Department of Bantu Administration and Development, *Annual Report, 1970*, 32, 99, and Republic of South Africa, Bophuthatswana, Department of Agriculture, *Annual Report, 1972*, 15–22. It is unlikely that there has been much change.

6. Agricultural statistics for herds and crops are assembled from the estimates of regional field personnel. Although some do this chore conscientiously, others are more casual, and all are busy with other duties. In the data there are unwarranted fluctuations in crop output or herd sizes from year to year, and some five-figure numbers do not change at all. Private studies have found considerable errors in official local crop, herd, and human population statistics, but they are too few to permit conjectures about general biases. The shortcomings of African herd and crop statistics are well known to the government, and rapid improvement in their quality is universally desired so that they can be used for planning and evaluation. Small-area sampling could be used to provide additional information and to correct for systematic biases in the aggregate data.

than average. Also, larger scale operations organized on the European model, and possibly managed by a government-paid white overseer, have high yields. Dry-cropped maize and sorghum are very susceptible to variations in rainfall. This factor further complicates the ascertainment of trends in yields.

The data suggest that from 1968 through 1972 Bophuthatswana devoted an increasing area to maize, eventually almost tripling cropping. Output rose by over five times, so that average yields almost doubled. There was a sharp fall off in plantings in 1973, apparently due to inadequate rainfall. In 1974 the area sown rebounded to 60 percent of the 1972 peak, but output was higher and yields were substantially above previous levels. A speculative explanation is that the larger government and private farms and the better small holder areas were drawn back into production and received enough fertilizer and other inputs to raise yields. More marginal areas had not recovered from the previous drought and were not replanted. Thus these gains were highly localized.

Only about 6 to 7 percent of the land area of Bophuthatswana is arable, but in KwaZulu a much larger share of the land can be used for perennial farming. In recent years, KwaZulu's cultivators have planted in maize an area four to ten times the size of the similarly planted area in Bophuthatswana. Most fields are quite small, some only garden plots, others amounting to a few acres. But the aggregate output of these household plots and small peasant holdings is a major determinant of nutritional and economic welfare in the homeland. Weather is more predictable than in Bophuthatswana, and the area planted in maize has fluctuated between 232,000 and 301,000 hectares. Output more than doubled between 1968 and 1972 and yields rose steadily, until the decline of 1973. Some notion of the benefits of irrigation can be obtained from the high yields obtained on watered lands, although it is also obvious how small a fraction (about 0.5 percent) of the arable area is presently irrigated. On white farms, depending on the area, maize yields are 1,600 to 2,300 kilograms per hectare, six to seven times average homeland yields.

The longer time series available for all the homelands shows some tendency for yields to rise, especially after 1965. The stabilizing and productivity-enhancing effects of irrigation are again readily apparent. Bophuthatswana's yields are higher than those of KwaZulu's, which are only about average for all homelands. This is not a sign of agricultural strength, but rather of the fact that intensive farming is practiced in those few areas where conditions are most favorable.

There has been considerable speculation about agricultural trends in the homelands. The Tomlinson Commission estimated that yields averaged about 264 kilograms per hectare in fiscal 1949/50, this amount being exceeded by

Table 8.1
Area, Output, and Yields of Maize in the Homelands

	A. Bophuthatswana, 1968–1974 Dryland			Irrigated Land		
Year	Area (hectares) (1)	Output (metric tons) (2)	Yield (kg./ha) (3)	Area (hectares) (4)	Output (metric tons) (5)	Yield (kg./ha) (6)
1968	23,545	5,699	242	648	420	648
1969	44,919	8,086	180	749	581	776
1970	45,674	14,236	312	946	559	591
1971	64,086	18,043	282	946	559	591
1972	66,376	30,696	462	801	301	376
1973	13,935	6,725	483	628	311	495
1974	38,811	34,474	888	--	--	--

B. KwaZulu, 1968–1973

Year	(1)	(2)	(3)	(4)	(5)	(6)
1968	232,983	45,971	197	733	906	1,236
1969	301,462	72,675	241	496	474	956
1970	256,036	67,167	262	690	870	1,261
1971	254,229	86,274	339	1,029	1,104	1,073
1972	248,838	93,859	377	1,640	1,526	930
1973	232,113	67,369	290	1,199	1,307	1,090

C. All Homelands, 1960–1973

Year	(1)	(2)	(3)	(4)	(5)	(6)
1960	1,309,583	246,591	188	4,417	2,898	535
1965	530,156	75,866	143	5,005	4,166	832
1966	471,825	91,751	194	4,002	2,311	577
1967	502,526	142,732	284	6,264	5,305	847
1968	659,063	134,785	205	4,936	3,826	775
1969	881,366	189,726	215	4,956	3,786	764
1970	882,404	213,977	242	6,131	3,368	549
1971	1,121,991	382,627	341	5,338	4,618	865
1972	1,134,900	402,136	354	8,188	7,722	943
1973	846,160	230,494	272	6,449	6,123	949

SOURCE: BENBO, personal communication (xeroxed materials), 19 March 1976. Compiled initially from data from the Department of Bantu Administration and homeland Departments of Agriculture.

NOTE: Private farms only, some very small totals for government farms not included. A cautionary note: these estimates are at best approximate and indicate only rough orders of magnitude and broad changes over time.

any margin only in 1971 and 1972 among the years covered by table 8.1.[7] Allowing for regional differences and the effects of the weather, it appears safe to conclude that yields fell unevenly until the mid-1960s.

Since that time there may have been some improvement. This improvement has come about, however, under favorable conditions such as are found on stabilized Bantu Trust farms, in irrigated garden schemes, and where a few African farmers have had close ties to homeland agricultural extension officers. In Bophuthatswana, for instance, one-third of the crop comes from the Ditsobotla district, south of Mafeking. In those areas yields are three to five times those of other districts.[8] These higher yields are encouraging because they indicate what is feasible given a solid resource base, modern inputs, and extension services. But since they also imply that most women who have household gardens, and many other small farmers, are probably not participating in the gains, they also measure the failure to universalize agricultural reforms. As is generally the case in underdeveloped areas, if all regions and farmers could attain the standards set by their most productive neighbors, the problem of realizing agricultural growth would be solved.

There are projects underway in both homelands to broaden the agricultural base by developing commercial crops. Following a recommendation of the Tomlinson Commission, fibre crops have been introduced. There are three small sisal projects in Bophuthatswana, covering about 1,200 hectares; the yield in 1972 was 212 tons of fibre, up from 130 tons in 1970. A canal irrigation project at Taung covers almost 1,600 hectares, and there are other irrigated areas in the Kuruman, Thaba 'Nchu, and Lehurutse districts.[9] Vegetables, lucerne, and root crops are produced for use and sale. Phorium tenax (flax) is grown in KwaZulu on 3,551 hectares. Coconuts, cashew nuts, coffee, and tea are in experimental stages. Irrigated areas are used for gardens of specialty crops. There are also plans to utilize small reservoirs as fish farms in KwaZulu; there is an established fish farm at the Klipvoor Dam near Mabopane and GaRankuwa in Bophuthatswana.

Since its agricultural division was formed in 1973, the Bantu Investment Corporation has begun to assume responsibility for large-scale projects, such as plantations, irrigation works, and trust farms, that require capital investment and management. Most of the new commercial crop projects have been transferred to the corporation from the agriculture departments of Bophuthatswana and KwaZulu. Also, the corporation has assumed control of the Taung

7. *Summary of the Report,* 84–85; also see J. A. Lombard and P. J. van der Merwe, "Central Problems of the Economic Development of the Bantu Homelands," *Finance and Trade Review,* X (1972), 37; Muriel Horrell, *The African Homelands of South Africa* (Johannesburg, 1973), 86.

8. Republic of South Africa, Bophuthatswana, Department of Agriculture, *Annual Report, 1972,* 16.

9. *Ibid.,* tables on irrigated land production.

irrigation project, where a feed lot will be established to use fodder production for cattle and to fatten cattle sold through a stock sale scheme. A similarly integrated plan is being established for KwaZulu, where the agricultural division of the corporation has taken over the long-established project now embracing the Tugela and Ferry estates, where cotton, citrus, vegetables, and fodder crops are grown experimentally. The plan is to establish market outlets in homeland townships for the produce of these farm plots. In KwaZulu, where there is considerable potential for more irrigation, there is hope that the Pongola River dam may eventually provide irrigation water.

The Bantu Investment Corporation wants to support relatively large-scale projects with outside management and adequate amounts of capital. If these projects become self-sustaining, they will be handed over, presumably on favorable terms, to Africans. In some cases, the larger units may be broken up into smaller parcels held by private owners who compose a cooperative. In others, control may pass to single owners or possibly to corporate ownership. No commitment has been made to any particular schedule or to any method of transfer. It is uncertain whether direct control of large farms and plantation-style units by white managers using hired African labor will permit the rapid transfer of skills and managerial ability.

The only cash crop that is currently important in either homeland is sugar cane in KwaZulu, although some cotton is planted in both. The Natal coast is a prime area for sugar cane, and parts of KwaZulu, the only remaining lands suitable for sugar cane expansion, could become very productive. High world prices have spurred an interest in expanding sugar cane acreages and improving yields. A quota system is in effect in the Republic and KwaZulu has been granted an allotment. This is divided and allocated to farmers by the KwaZulu government on the advice of white extension agents. Although allotments usually comprise only a few hectares, the returns to sugar cane farmers are lucrative and assured. The crop takes over a year to mature, however, and, in contrast to subsistence farming (or working in industry), a threshold amount of capital is needed to plant the crop, hire labor, buy fertilizer and other inputs, and support the farmer and his family while the crop matures. Understandably, all of KwaZulu's quota has not always been utilized, but the South African Sugar Association has helped initiate a credit and training program to assist small producers, and the homeland agricultural department is attempting to devote more effort to cane production. If large enough acreages can be granted to Zulu farmers, and if they are supplied with credit and extension guidance, they can earn individual incomes that are attractive compared to those earned in factory work.

In the six-year period, from fiscal 1968/69 to fiscal 1973/74, about 3,300 Zulu farmers supplied sugar cane to mills. Output has varied from about 275,000 to 420,000 tons, with no clear trend. The recent higher price for sugar has, however, almost doubled the earnings of Zulu farmers from R1.5 million in fiscal 1968/69 to R2.8 million in fiscal 1973/74.[10] Sugar cane output amounts to about 10 percent of the total value of KwaZulu's agricultural output, but is roughly half of industrial output (more than R5 million). It appears that relatively small expenditures on sugar cane can have a profound effect on KwaZulu's total domestic product.

Animal products and livestock sales are a major component of agricultural production. It is well known that cattle play an important role in African society, serving as a measure of wealth and status and as a means of extending marriage and kinship alliances. Less clear, however, are the effects of these traditional factors on present-day practices. It is arguable that veterinary, extension, and marketing shortcomings, contrasted with the persistence of tradition, are at least as important in explaining the underutilization of African herds. There is some evidence that initial expenditures on improving livestock quality and on bettering market facilities are yielding substantial gains. The statistics are subject to error, but the cattle population of the homelands probably reached a plateau several decades ago and has since fluctuated with weather and grazing conditions. Between 1968 and 1973 the number of cattle in Bophuthatswana was in the range of 345 thousand to 384 thousand; in KwaZulu, there were 1.2 to 1.3 million.[11] Much of Bophuthatswana is suited for at least light grazing, and cattle numbers there are in line with an estimated carrying capacity of about 400,000 head, allowing for other stock; KwaZulu, however, has double the number of cattle it should have. Again, averages may be misleading, since there are probably parts of both homelands that are more severely overstocked than others, and there may be tracts, even in KwaZulu, where levels are acceptable or even below capacity.[12]

Any increase in herd sizes would obviously be undesirable, but two reasonable aims of a stock development program are to improve animal quality and to increase the proportion of the herd marketed annually. Livestock experts believe that gradual modernization of homeland animal husbandry is taking place. Knowledge of the purposes of stock dipping and preventive inoculation is spreading, and less pressure is needed to secure compliance. They say that herd sizes are better controlled, that the value of quality breeding stock is appreciated, and that animal size and quality have improved. The African herdsman does take pride in good stock, and the few breeding bulls that are sold each year draw premium prices.

10. BENBO, *KwaZulu, Economic Revue, 1975* (Pretoria, 1976), 40.

11. *Ibid.*, 38; BENBO, *Bophuthatswana, Economic Revue, 1975* (Pretoria, 1976), 34.

12. Bantu Investment Corporation, *Homelands: the Role of the Corporations in the Republic of South Africa* (Pretoria, 1975), 2nd ed., 66.

In the last few years these older extension programs have been supplemented by better marketing and finishing facilities. The homeland government agriculture departments and the Bantu Investment Corporation have established new stock marketing projects in both homelands, at Taung in Bophuthatswana and at several sites in KwaZulu. There is an open competitive auction, sellers are offered at least a minimum price, and substandard stock are fattened before final sale. The initial response, boosted by rising world prices for beef in 1973 and 1974, was very positive and strongly suggests that fair prices, good marketing and finishing facilities, and continued attention to improved quality may encourage a more commercial approach to livestock management. The data show a very strong positive supply response to higher prices, belying the often heard maxim that Africans will not treat their cattle as economic goods.[13] Increased turnover rates—selling animals as they mature, and not carrying them to old age and death—could add millions of rand of almost costless income to the homelands. But much must still be done to improve the handling of cattle and to upgrade marketing before the potential economic value locked up in the herds of the homelands can be released.

Another aspect of livestock management where improvement is needed is dairying. The history of dairying in the homelands has been disappointing, as early efforts to form cooperatives languished in the 1950s.[14] The Bantu Investment Corporation estimates that 107 million litres of milk are required each year by the towns of the homelands, but only 613,000 litres—0.6 percent of the needs—are currently being produced in organized schemes. In 1974 a dairy unit of 320 cows was started in Bophuthatswana to service part of the needs of GaRankuwa; similar projects are planned for KwaZulu.[15] The corporation appears ready to make a commitment to large commercial dairies, which have good marketing potential and good backward linkages to suppliers of fodder crops.

There are over 800,000 sheep and goats in each homeland, and large numbers of pigs, horses, mules, donkeys, and chickens. Little is known of the economic worth of these animals, their importance in the African diet, and their role in the ecological system. Wool and skins are sold, and some sheep and goats are marketed or slaughtered privately.

The agricultural development of the homelands depends upon improving the output of food crops, commercial crops, and animal products. An overview of growth patterns in these areas from 1965 to 1973 is presented in

---

13. *Ibid.*, 75. Data available on increased sales since 1973 and 1974 from KwaZulu Department of Agriculture, Pietermaritzburg, discussions with officials in homeland governments, and the Bantu Investment Corporation.

14. H. Hamburger, "Animal Production in Developing Communities," *Proceedings of the South African Society for Animal Production* (1968), 29–40.

15. Bantu Investment Corporation, *Homelands*, 2nd edition, 73.

table 8.2. Once again the estimates must be regarded as tentative approximations, but they are a considerable improvement over the fragmentary statistics previously available. Although in the previous year the gain was only 27 percent, the value of agricultural output in Bophuthatswana had risen by 96.5 percent in 1973 over the 1965/67 base. In KwaZulu, the gain over the period was 54 percent, but again, through 1972, growth amounted only to 32 percent. The 1972 figures imply low compound growth rates and it would be necessary to correct these by an appropriate price index before reaching any conclusion about volume movements. The two key components in both homelands are animal products and food grains. Growth in food grains in Bophuthatswana has been negligible, and only the higher prices of 1973 and possibly increased sales due to poor rainfall and grazing buoyed the value of animal production above the flat trend of earlier years. The results in Kwa-Zulu are similar for livestock, but there does appear to have been modest growth in the value of food grain production. The utilization of forests for firewood and timber has declined.

The most obvious gains have come in the most recent few years and in specialized areas. The sisal projects, and stimulus to fodder and horticultural products provided at Taung, have elevated the value of these relatively minor items in Bophuthatswana. KwaZulu has benefited from higher prices for sugar, the main component of commercial crops, and there has evidently been some progress in horticulture.

Overall, there has not been any sort of decisive improvement in food grain farming or in livestock management in the two homelands. Most gains in these two critical areas have occurred unevenly and have been concentrated in few areas and — probably — among relatively few persons. There are signs of retrogression, too, where herds are too large for grazing lands to sustain, where fencing and conservation works are not maintained, and where more and more people try to eke out a subsistence existence in overcrowded rural locations. Success and failure often lie side by side. Tractors, trucks, and modern equipment are found in many rural areas. Several Tswana ranchers have built up herds of registered stock. In Natal, there is an emerging group of sugar cane growers making an acceptable living out of farming.

Where resources and personnel have been committed, as in sisal, phorium tenax, vegetable gardening, and stock sales, there have been some measurable gains — gains large enough to hold out some hope that with more resources and more personnel even more growth may be realized. The nagging question is whether the management of these pilot projects can be transferred to local people. Expenditures on agricultural development have been small, and the fact that measurable gains have resulted at all is noteworthy. It would therefore be surprising if cost-effectiveness studies did not show large returns to more expenditures. On balance, however, there simply has not been enough forward movement to make a real difference: cumulative growth has not been

Table 8.2
Homeland Agricultural and Forestry Production:
Bophuthatswana and KwaZulu, 1965–1973
(thousand rands)

			A. Bophuthatswana				
Year	Foodgrains (1)	Fodder Crops (2)	Commercial Crops (3)	Horti- culture (4)	Animal Production (5)	Forestry (6)	Total (7)
1965	226	166	15	312	3,085	158	3,962
1966	349	144	15	318	2,901	134	3,831
1967	1,587	244	3	511	2,933	98	5,376
1968	659	132	17	352	3,413	73	4,646
1969	804	111	27	434	3,406	56	4,838
1970	822	86	13	521	3,304	82	4,828
1971	928	71	19	592	2,925	104	4,639
1972	1,521	85	23	799	3,020	118	5,566
1973	810	389	63	621	6,619	122	8,624
%Change from 1965–1967 to 1973[a]	+ 12.4	+ 122.7	+ 472.7	+ 63.3	+ 122.6	–6.2	+ 96.5

			B. KwaZulu				
Year	Foodgrains (1)	Fodder Crops (2)	Commercial Crops (3)	Horti- culture (4)	Animal Production (5)	Forestry (6)	Total (7)
1965	1,468	1,047	951	1,529	8,914	389	14,298
1966	1,891	1,157	677	1,774	9,469	297	15,265
1967	2,730	848	1,467	1,933	10,174	276	17,428
1968	1,725	643	1,881	1,644	10,698	280	16,871
1969	2,995	949	1,648	2,490	10,149	209	18,440
1970	2,556	1,074	1,918	2,513	9,657	316	18,034
1971	3,228	1,124	1,981	3,573	10,260	394	20,560
1972	3,457	787	2,950	3,986	9,153	298	20,631
1973	3,615	1,259	3,008	3,423	12,602	255	24,162
% Change from 1965–1967 to 1973[a]	+ 78.1	+ 23.8	+ 191.6	+ 96.1	+ 32.4	–11.3	+ 54.3

SOURCE: BENBO, personal communication (xeroxed materials), 19 March 1976; partially available in *idem,
Bophuthatswana, Economic Revue, 1975* (Pretoria, 1976), 34; *idem, KwaZulu, Economic Revue, 1975* (Pretoria,
1976), 38.

[a] The increase in 1973 over the average value for 1965–1967, divided by that average value.

initiated in homeland agriculture. And if such growth depends on major inputs from outside, what will be the reaction of the white farming community to special prices, marketing arrangements, and subsidies? And how will the homeland urban markets be shared, and what of Soweto and the other African townships of South Africa?

Causes of Agricultural Underdevelopment

The agricultural problems of the homelands are not unique, although they do differ in some ways from those of other underdeveloped areas. Nor, if properly diagnosed and dealt with by applying a coherent set of policies, are they insoluble. The causes of low productivity and stagnation in homeland agriculture are obvious and numerous—indeed, the only real difficulty is to determine which should be given the greatest weight. They may be grouped under three headings: 1) inadequate modern inputs and poor infrastructure; 2) obstructive land tenure and labor practices; and 3) shortcomings in extension and policy.

The shortage of water in Bophuthatswana and the lack of control over water in both homelands keeps total production of food, other crops, and livestock down and reduces the productivity of land and labor. The western areas of Bophuthatswana average ten to fifteen inches of rain a year, and the Transvaal blocks receive only twenty to twenty-five inches. But nowhere in this homeland is rainfall reliable. Only 6 to 7 percent of the area is arable, and only about half of this is cultivated. Outside the eastern Molopo and Ditsobotla areas, and Thaba 'Nchu, there is little agricultural potential except in ranching. Small irrigation projects, such as one at Taung, may make possible a limited amount of intensive gardening or small-scale truck farming. But there is little ground water potential and few sites for riverine canals. In some areas it will not be easy even to keep people and livestock supplied all year with potable water, Since Bophuthatswana must compete with the cities, mines, and industries of the Pretoria-Johannesburg region for water, and with white farmers, it is improbable that its agricultural needs will be given high priority. The proportion of the work force that can be retained in herding and light farming is likely to be very small.

In KwaZulu the agricultural potential is great, but there may be a tendency to overestimate what can be done by way of providing incomes for numbers of workers that can compare with those offered in industry, government, or education. Rainfall averages thirty to fifty inches almost everywhere and the growing season is long. The northern part, between Swaziland and the coast, is not useful except for the grazing of livestock; most of the inland regions can sustain herding and intermittent cultivation, merging into mixed farming regions near the coast and on the interior plains. A major problem is the rolling, hilly terrain, which heavy rains scour when protective vegetation has been destroyed. Reclamation and runoff control can add substantially to the cost of sustaining stable farm operations. Apart from herding and farming, there are the essential water and land resources, and climatic conditions conducive to fruit and plantation crops. KwaZulu has the potential for the expansion of timber production. There is no environmental reason for KwaZulu's agriculture to remain as unproductive as it is, but considerable investment, adaptive ingenuity to bring in new crops and technologies, and good private and public resource management will be needed before agriculture can advance.

Information about the use of modern inputs is difficult to obtain. Some chemical fertilizer is applied in both homelands, mostly in the Ditsobotla maize and Taung irrigated areas in Bophuthatswana and in the sugar cane areas of KwaZulu. Some high yielding seeds are used, and crops and animals are protected from diseases with modern chemical products. Plowing is still more likely to be done with oxen than with owned or rented tractors. Some dairy and other cooperatives have been formed in both homelands, but few have survived. In 1973 provision was made for the creation of a Bophuthatswana Agricultural Board, with the power to establish district advisory committees. The homeland minister of agriculture may act on the recommendation of the board to extend credit and other forms of assistance to cooperatives. Bophuthatswana's fiscal 1975/76 budget set aside R369,000 for loans to agricultural cooperatives, up from R100,000 of the previous year. If the Bantu Investment Corporation also moves ahead with plans to provide certain kinds of credit, then at least a few farmers and stockmen may be able to obtain the financial assistance they need to survive and expand. On the whole, however, shortages of credit, modern inputs, and controllable water supplies remain major, immediate causes of low yields and poor farmer responsiveness.

At the core of the process of agricultural production is the organization of labor and land. In the homelands both of these major inputs are subject to social and political forces that make it impossible for them to move flexibly into (or out of) agriculture. Rural and urban land use is not determined by economic advantage, but by factors intrinsic to South African society and the homelands' place in that society. Similarly, labor use is affected by the absentee labor system and by the limitations on labor mobility imposed by influx control. Neither of the two main factors of production is allocated by its returns in the market system. In these circumstances, and given the dearth of modern inputs and market outlets, agriculture cannot be anything but a subsubsistence, noncommercial activity. There is neither incentive for the average person on the land to do things any differently, nor, if he wanted to, is there any way in which he could bring together in profitable production the land, labor, capital, and supplementary inputs needed. It is commonly recognized that Africans on the land are in some sense noneconomic, but this behavior is often wrongly attributed to motivational, psychological, or cultural factors beyond the immediate control of the government and its extension agents. That this diagnosis is outdated and wrong is gradually being understood, but neither the real reasons for the persistence of sub-subsistence practices nor the means of breaking them down are widely apprehended.

The use of labor in agriculture is subject to several constraints. In tradi-tional times there existed a division of work within the household between husbands and wives, boys and girls. Each family unit was to a large extent self-reliant, and its members were responsible for and skilled in a number of tasks. It is difficult to gauge to what degree the customary division of labor endures in Tswana or Zulu society and to what extent, if any, its lingering inhibitions affect attitudes to agricultural work. As the reports of Schapera and others make clear, modern influences, such as the plow and Christianity, and economic necessity, have altered attitudes toward the work roles of men and women.[16]

There is a good deal of variation by area in the degree to which customs have broken down, but such older social restrictions are now much less important than economic considerations. For most men the returns to full-time labor in agriculture are not commensurate with earnings outside. The labor pattern looks much the same as before, since women often handle agricultural tasks, but the root cause is not custom but economic calculation acting under political constraint. As long as influx laws keep women from moving to their husbands' place of work, much of the minor agriculture will remain in their hands. Homeland agriculture thus has a reciprocal or symbiotic relationship with the absentee labor system, economically and socially, the one being the obverse of the other. Families straddle both economic sectors, trying to build a partial subsistence base and security in house, land, and livestock on one side and to realize adequate cash income on the other. This is individually rational, but amounts to collective suicide insofar as developing a modern agricultural sector is concerned.

The absentee labor system and restrictions on the movement of workers and their families act in effect as a rural "depressor," overloading grazing and farm lands in the homelands with redundant labor that, given the shortage of other resources to work with, is casual and unproductive. A change in the system of labor would draw the excess population off the land, and, with new land tenure laws, make it easier and cheaper for government action to raise incomes for full-time farmers to parity with earnings from absentee work. Doing the reverse, further restraining the flow of African

16. Isaac Schapera, *The Tswana* (London, 1971), 27.

workers to the cities as population expands without creating enough non-agricultural jobs in the homelands, will force more women and men into subsubsistence agriculture and make raising average productivity impossibly expensive. Plots will become smaller — perhaps shrink to only a few hectares — and gains could come only with the addition of enough inputs — water, fertilizer, and credit — and sufficient training to create a Japanese-style agriculture in a part of the world where such intensive methods are alien.

Many experts believe that another fundamental barrier to the development of homeland agriculture is the system of land tenure. The present system is widely and erroneously regarded as a carefully preserved relic of earlier times. As with the division of labor, the modern pattern of allocating rights in land bears but a superficial resemblance to and incorporates vestiges of traditional practice. For the most part land is not allocated through the market but by chiefs and headmen working with the approval of the white authorities. White officials created the present tenure system, oversee the distribution of lands in many localities through the "physical planning" or "betterment" program, and have the power to force black individuals and groups to abandon homes and lands and move elsewhere.

To simplify, some lands are owned both by Africans with private property rights and by collectivities like churches or missions. Most land in Bophutha-tswana and KwaZulu is predominately held under what is usually known as traditional communal tenure, the most important feature of which is the prerogative of the chief to give rights to land which supposedly include a homesite, adequate fields for crops, and grazing rights in the common pasturage. Yet a continuation of the traditional ideal has become impossible with the growth of population, and fields are now mostly too small to support a family. Grazing rights are insufficient for everyone's stock. The main feature of the existing tenure system is its enormous elasticity in absorbing population, although unlike an Asian intensive agriculture based on small holdings, it does so only with diminishing returns and ecological damage. The system is made flexible by its very inchoateness: white commissioners and their deputies, and chiefs and headmen acting in their designated capacities as land donors, can accept, or at least tolerate, squatters, migrants from other parts of the homeland, or alien blacks drifting in from other homelands, white farms, or foreign countries. The rigidity of the Republic's influx controls, "black spot" removals, and homeland consolidation plans is matched and made workable by the fluidity of homeland tenure rights.

Although it is often said that the chief has the power to evict persons, most people in fact acquire hereditary rights of usufruct. Under the homeland concept, every African in South Africa is obligated to identify himself with a homeland constituency and vote as if he were from its area. As a citizen-"resident" it would appear that no person could be denied access by a chief

or by any white authority to a modicum of living space in his official homeland area, regardless of what a chief says. This is just one of the many unresolved contradictions and anomalies involved in the system of homeland
tenure rights. The government and local chiefs, who often collect "rents,"
also condone squatting—such as exists in the sprawling collection of shanty
towns north of Pretoria—although it has no legal basis.

Nominally, chiefs still control land distribution, but the titular chief of
all Africans is the president of the Republic, who is invested with discretionary
powers to alter African land occupation and use. Under the Republic's law
a black person or persons can be administratively evicted and told to live
elsewhere—this is the basis for "black spot" removals and resettlements.
This power will also be used to consolidate the homelands without African
approval.

For a time many tribes were indifferent to or resisted the planning of their
areas, but acquiescence is not required and local wishes can be overriden.
Control over land-use patterns—where people live, how much farm land they
have—ultimately rests with executive authorities who can act in uncon-
strained ways. No traditional or modern rights of blacks on the land are
strong enough to provide secure immunity from the executive powers held
by whites.

Because land rights are granted by legal and political authority, there is
no land market. Africans are not free to buy and sell land in white areas or
in homelands, except where there are rare privately held farms and in certain
townships where housing plots are available. Otherwise access to land is
obtained through inheritance rights or by obtaining additional grants from
tribal authorities. Agricultural extension agents think that this tenure system,
which attempts to provide each rural family with a full or partial subsistence
base, does not permit efficient farmers to add to their holdings, and in no
way discourages casual, ineffective land use. The traditional grant of access
to unlimited grazing likewise impedes attempts to improve herding methods.
The lack of private ownership makes it impossible for farmers to put up land
as security for loans. Although loans on crops alone could be feasible in
some cases, such as on sugar cane, where output and prices can be predicted,
credit-granting institutions, such as cooperative or agricultural banks, will
otherwise have difficulty making loans unsecured by mortgages on land.

A central problem in homeland agriculture is to break down the barriers
that now exist to the economic allocation of land and labor in production.
Land is distributed on the basis of social and political principles. Labor is
drawn off into the commercial economy, leaving agriculture as a predominately subsubsistence occupation for dependents and those temporarily
withdrawn from the absentee labor system. There is no capital or credit
market. There is simply no way for the enterprising farmer to acquire the

land and credit he needs, in union with his own and any hired labor, to make a commercial success of growing crops or raising livestock. Furthermore, as matters now stand, he will find it difficult to secure advice, modern inputs, technology, and access to product markets. The market system is not a panacea, but the creation of at least limited markets for land and capital is essential if farming in the homelands is to become economically oriented.

Suggestions for tenure reform have been numerous. The Tomlinson Commission called for the survey and allocation or sale of subsistence-sized plots to absorb the maximum amount of African labor in agriculture and for the creation of a land market. The creation of at least a limited land market is favored today by most extension workers. KwaZulu has appointed a commission to study land tenure. Bophuthatswana is interested in a similar review of land policy. It would be possible to put a ceiling on land holdings and to limit tenancy so that the stratification of rural society into a small class of large holders and a mass of unpropertied laborers would be avoided. Experiments with cooperative or corporate farming might not be out of the question.

Resistance to change in African tenure comes from the very highest levels of the South African government. The reasons usually given are the need to preserve the culture of Africans and a desire to maintain the positions of chiefs and *induna*. The first objection is transparently false, but the second demands some attention. In earlier days, the power of the local ruler allowed him to allocate rights to land, but the establishment of homeland governments has effectively modernized the administrative and political position of the chiefs by specifying their functions and by awarding many of them *ex officio* seats in the assemblies. It may no longer be necessary to impede agricultural progress to secure the chiefs' political position. In any event, compensation in the form of cash, bonds, or lifetime annuities could assure the chiefs' compliance. Tenure reforms would make it easier for homeland Africans to acquire township housing and business sites, subject to zoning laws or other types of regulation, and could accelerate urban as well as rural development.

Some observers fear that the commercialization of land would lead to radical changes in African life and create new burdens on the homeland and Republican governments. Presently, many of an African migrant worker's needs are met by his right to a homestead in the homelands. He would have a house, his family would raise at least a portion of its food needs, and he would have a place to go when sick or old. In theory he belongs somewhere, and kin and family give him comfort and support. If land rights can be disposed of, however, the Republican and homeland governments must cope with a mounting need for expensive social programs—social security, unemployment benefits, health care, housing, and poverty relief. Access to land in a designated homeland is one of the few unambiguous rights Africans enjoy, and unless job benefits and government social services can replace the security conferred by that right, a change in the tenure system might prove socially harmful.

Three agencies are involved in setting and implementing agricultural policy in the homelands: homeland government departments, the advisory services branch of the Department of Bantu Administration and Development, and the Bantu Investment Corporation. Because of the division of control over agricultural policy, it is not possible to describe and evaluate a single strategy of development. Homeland government departments continue to concern themselves with thinly spread extension work aimed at improving crops, gardens, and herds and with the erosion and grazing controls implicit in physical planning. The Department of Bantu Administration and Development advocates traditional policies including betterment. The Bantu Investment Corporation favors large-scale projects.

The extension work of homeland governments has not been very effective, despite the expenditure of much energy. Even the showpiece sisal and phorium tenax projects in Bophuthatswana and KwaZulu are for the most part unprofitable. In the irrigated areas, such as at Taung in Bophuthatswana or along the Tugela River in KwaZulu, allotments are tiny and often neglected despite the efforts of extension workers. African extension workers in rural districts find it difficult to convince people to adopt new seeds or techniques. The extension staffs of both homelands work in an atmosphere of defeat and frustration countered by individual concern and hard work. There is not enough money to do those things that promise gains, and barriers such as the lack of credit, the rigidity of the land system, and the absence of transport and marketing outlets, make real progress difficult. Large commercial projects mean nothing to Africans who cannot command the capital, land, and labor needed to establish similar enterprises. Nor can irrigated plots, no matter how fertile and profitable, signify progress in parts of the homelands where water is scarce.

Extension staff is spread unbelievably thin. Lipton reported that "while 90,000 rich, educated white farmers have 3,000 extension officers (plus enormous injections of easy credit, marketing facilities, and guaranteed prices) 600,000 black farmers have less than 1,000 extension officers: and these hopelessly overstretched men (and their small budgets) have been concentrated on the irrigation schemes." She adds, "the black peasant had not yet been given a chance."[17] Some of the senior white officers are well informed, but as Lipton also points out, others are seriously out of touch with advances in agriculture in Africa, Asia, and the rest of the world during the

17. Merle Lipton, "The South African Census and the Bantustan Policy,," *The World Today*, XXXVIII (1972), 266.

past few decades. One of the great advantages of détente between the Republic and the rest of Africa would be openings created for the staffs of the homeland departments—and of the development corporations, too, for that matter—to travel and visit countries where similar developmental problems are being attacked and sometimes solved.

The belief that Africans in agriculture will not react to high prices or to the opportunity to make profits is inaccurate, as the recent response to better stock prices shows and as isolated individuals of surpassing enterprise have proven. Unfortunately, belief in the unresponsiveness of the black farmers appears to be confirmed by the poor results of current extension policies and by the general sluggishness of homeland agriculture. Yet these are not the result of African conservatism, but rather a positive response to the income rewards of absentee labor, the inability to obtain and hold enough land, and the absence of controlled water supplies, capital, and markets. Until stable, certain economic opportunities are provided, Africans will not risk committing themselves to new practices.

One brighter spot is the output of African extension officers from the agricultural colleges at Taung, for Bophuthatswana, and Cwaka, for Kwa-Zulu. The graduates of these institutions are well trained (under strong paternalistic white supervision) and have positions virtually guaranteed for them in the homeland extension services.[18] The training programs appear well enough designed, although they may lack enough attention to the human and cultural sides of extension work. The quality of incoming student material has not always been high, and some young men doubtless regard the work as unappealing. Agreeable conditions in the colleges, larger stipends, and higher pay after graduation can ensure that these important institutions do not operate under capacity.

For over forty years resources have been poured into betterment schemes in order to stabilize and develop agriculture in the homelands. But the program has had no visible positive impact on production in the homelands. Moreover, because it has been widely circumvented, it is doubtful that it has really done much to prevent erosion or control the size of herds. It has had the dubious negative virtue of poisoning relations between agricultural field workers and local farm communities. The percentages of the homelands planned, and the miles of fence and grass strips annually laid down, have stood for many years as the leading benchmarks of progress in homeland agriculture.

18. H. W. L. Lilley reports that Cwaka graduates scored better on a test of farming knowledge than did older African extension officers in Natal and the Ciskei and white farm overseers; they were equalled only by a group of whites holding agricultural diplomas. "B.E.O. Knowledge and Understanding of Agriculture and Extension: A Comparative Study," unpub. paper (January, 1972), mimeo.

Physical planning involves the reorganization of existing land-use patterns into clearly demarcated residential, cropping, and fenced grazing areas.[19] There are high social costs to rural Africans of these physical rearrangements, but they are not considered in relation to the conservation benefits perceived by the planners.[20]

Lilley provides an account of the reaction of local Zulu to the planning and resettlement of a location near Port Shepstone. After little consultation it was proclaimed a betterment area in 1954 and, by the middle of 1960s, was divided into the prescribed three parts. One clan, the Ngeleka, was moved away from the homesites to which they had unusually strong emotional claims. People did not comprehend what was being done to them and felt cramped in the residential sites. Stories circulated of people who had lost land through the resettlement scheme. A small tax was imposed at about the same time for unrelated reasons, but was felt to be part of the program. Everything came by fiat from the government and was part of the same incomprehensible scheme.[21]

At the end of 1974 Bophuthatswana was 57 percent and KwaZulu 49.1 percent planned.[22] Yet there often is a considerable lag between the planning on paper of an area and its actual resettlement. More tribal authorities in Bophuthatswana are now said to desire planning than the Department of Bantu Administration and Development can oblige, while the Zulu are regarded as uncooperative. By the department's own standards, the progress of physical planning has been too slow, its explanation being the resistance by some peoples to the policy and a shortage of available funds. The subsistence plots sought by the Tomlinson Commission have been compromised by population pressure, and families have received only one-half, one-third, or even one-quarter of a recommended unit.

It is difficult to see why the betterment policy has been pursued for so long. An explanation may lie in the commitment made to the program long ago

19. Since physical planning is a spatial reorganization of houses and fields it is best understood in terms of maps. See J. S. Murray, "The Development of Agriculture in the Bantu Homelands," *Tegnikon* (March, 1967), 30–36; P. Smit, "Physical Planning in the Bantu Homelands of South Africa," *ibid.*, 5–17. Both Smit and Murray have been heavily involved in the direction of physical planning.

20. The attitude of the Tomlinson Commission was that "All of these stabilization measures can be undertaken without the approval of the inhabitants of the Reserves in question, since the necessary powers will have been obtained by legislation. . . . Planning for stabilization and the carrying out of such plans must, wherever possible, be undertaken with the consent and cooperation of the reserves concerned; but where protection of the soil demands it, stabilization must be carried out even without such consent." *Summary of the Report,* 118.

21. H. W. L. Lilley, "Characteristics and Motivational Orientation of the Amazimakwe Land-Occupiers of Location 4B," master's thesis (University of Pretoria, 1967).

22. *Survey of Race Relations, 1975,* 142.

by senior personnel who continue to head the agricultural branch of the department and who have passed the policy on to the relevant homeland departments. As the Tomlinson Commission emphasized, physical planning affords no solution to the problem of raising African farm productivity. It stated bluntly that the mere rearrangement of the spatial structure of an area had not up to that time and could not in the future make any lasting differences.[23]

The reasons are obvious. Physical planning entails a once-and-for-all change in production conditions; under the best circumstances, it would allow for slightly higher crop and herd productivity. But there is no fundamental change in the organization of the patterns of use of land and labor, and if much greater quantities of modern inputs together with credit and extension advice are not simultaneously added, sustained growth will not be initiated.

Agriculture must be the key sector in any attempt to develop the homelands as hospitable living areas and to create growing regions increasingly self-sufficient in food, raw materials, and jobs. Of all the homelands, Bophuthatswana probably has the lowest potential. KwaZulu is at the other end of the continuum. Its agricultural sector can probably support a significant number of full-time farmers and herdsmen as well as provide some cash income for dependents of absentee workers and part-time agriculturists. It would be wrong, however, to talk in static terms about the carrying capacity of the homelands and to try to estimate how many farm families earning subsistence incomes could be packed into them. The homeland economies are going to become urbanized at a very rapid pace and a larger share of their work force is going to move into industry and service jobs, regardless of whether they are located in white areas, in border industrial areas, or inside the homelands. Incomes in farming will have to rise in step with those in other sectors; even dependents and part-time workers will withdraw from agriculture as wages rise in the nonagricultural occupations. With development, a smaller share of area national income will come from homeland agriculture. The Tomlinson vision of a static, subsistence agricultural sector was utopian even in its time.

The bias in the Bantu Investment Corporation today is in the direction of larger farm units; this is probably also the dominant sentiment of the homeland governments' field staffs. It is very likely that homeland agriculture will come increasingly to resemble white agriculture, because it is the model known to white and black farmers and extension advisers. Black farms, because of population pressures, inflexible land tenures, and capital shortages, will probably remain smaller and will yield less output per unit of labor

23. *Summary of the Report,* 77.

input than white farms, but productivity per unit of land will gradually rise. In the next decade and a half, if the flow of inputs is allowed to grow, there should be rather large absolute increases in output, mostly because levels are currently so abysmally low. In the near term, an effort could be made to reach part-time farmers, many of whom are women or older men. This step would not generate the highly visible employment and income that the Republic wants, but the homeland governments could scarcely do anything that would do more to improve the quality of diet and the output of food.

Returns to investment in homeland agriculture, either in larger scale units or in the household sector, will be great if projects are carefully planned, in the technical sense, and if they are suited to local conditions and provide real incentives for black enterprise. There is no better way to meet those conditions than to rely as heavily as possible on the insights and opinions of the black farmers, extension staff, and technical experts, as they are trained, and on political leaders, all of whom will have to make the programs work.

Industry and Commerce

It has long been recognized that the development of the homelands cannot depend exclusively upon the agricultural sector. Even the Tomlinson Com mission's optimistically low homeland population projections exceeded by a wide margin its estimates of the employment absorptive capacity in agriculture. Further, in order to halt and if possible reverse the exodus of labor to white areas, the commission acknowledged that a large number of job opportunities would have to be created in mining, commerce, and industry in the homelands. But Verwoerd, then minister of native affairs, rejected the report's suggestion that white capital be allowed to invest in the homelands. Instead he preferred to see the creation of industrial centers on the homeland borders. This decision blocked industry from moving into the African areas for fifteen years.

South Africa's industries are heavily concentrated in four regions: Pretoria-Witwatersrand-Vereeniging, the southwestern Cape, Durban-Pinetown, and Port Elizabeth-Uitenhage. Covering only 4 percent of the land area, these regions contain 75 percent of all manufacturing enterprises and generate 80 percent of total industrial production. Half the industrial output of the country arises in the first region alone.

In mid-1960 the Permanent Committee for the Location of Industry was formed to coordinate the government's actions, but its weak inducements could not appreciably affect private business location decisions. The Physical Planning and Utilisation of Resources Act of 1967 gave the minister of planning substantial power to regulate the location and expansion of industries. Private industrialists were initially unsettled by the uncertainties arising from the government's new controls over their investment decisions, but the Report of the Interdepartmental Committee on the Decentralisation of Industries (the Riekert Committee) and the accompanying white paper, both appearing in 1971, made clearer the standards and procedures that would be applied. Concessions were spelled out in detail and a number of border industry locations were affirmed or designated.

In 1969 the government decided to permit white investment in the homelands on an agency basis. Additional incentives were given to attract investors, but all contracts provided for the eventual handing over to Africans of the ownership and management of the enterprises. The Industrial Development Corporation had earlier been given primary responsibility for creating the infrastructure, providing housing, and making loans in the border industrial areas. The Bantu Investment Corporation similarly took on these tasks in the homelands and was also to build and lease factory buildings and factory flats. Various Republican and homeland departments would assist the corporations in providing water, power, roads, rail connections, and other services.

In 1975 the government set a target of 6.4 percent annual growth of gross domestic product, a rate that could be attained only by moving African workers into more highly skilled jobs. The continuity of the government's economic thinking was evident: it sought rapid economic growth, sufficient job creation for Africans to reduce black unemployment, and even greater emphasis on establishing poles of development away from present centers and for the most part outside but close to the homelands.

The rationale for the decentralization program is complex, although the main intention remains clearly to stem the movement of black workers to the older white centers. Military safety, pollution, rail and traffic congestion, and water shortages are sometimes advanced as justifications, and cannot be completely dismissed, but the policy of decentralization is primarily a social policy that has economic effects. The restrictions and concessions of the program create incentives designed to induce labor-intensive industry to move away from its existing focal points toward the hinterlands.

Its significance to white society explains why the industrial relocation program remains under the tight control of the Republic's government and why the homeland governments have only the smallest say in their own industrial development. The internal industrial bases and the associated border industries of Bophuthatswana and KwaZulu will thus be planned in accord with the spatial and ethnic group employment designs of the Republic rather than coordinated with their own internal agricultural, mineral, demographic, and infrastructural resources.

Over the past fifteen years approximately fifty small towns and cities near the African homelands have been designated as border industrial areas.

There is no single reason why certain centers have been chosen and others neglected. In the early 1960s border areas were chosen that were merely extensions of the major economic regions. Industrialists received the benefit of the already existing positive external benefits—transport, skilled labor, water, power, housing—of the older urban complexes and, in addition, benefited from the concessions allowed by the government. Both Tswana and Zulu areas were affected by this mild relocation, since Rosslyn, on the northern fringes of Pretoria, and Hammarsdale, between Durban and Pietermaritzburg, and Pietermaritzburg itself, were so designated. Rosslyn and Hammarsdale have impressive industrial parks housing a number of major national and international firms. Rosslyn is a center for automobile assembly, and may have provided 10,000 jobs for Africans, many of whom commute from the GaRankuwa or Mabopane townships. By the late 1960s these areas had filled up and emphasis had shifted to more remote centers: Brits, Rustenburg, Zeerust, and Mafeking in the Tswana region; Empangeni-Richards Bay, Ladysmith Colenso, and Newcastle near the Zulu territories. A 1975 estimate by the minister of planning and statistics claimed 18,058 jobs had been created at Rosslyn, Hammarsdale, and Pietermaritzburg. Over the last eleven years, he said, 68,685 people had been given employment in border industry areas.[24]

With others, Lombard has criticized the results of the first decade of decentralization. He found no evidence of substantial industrial relocation. The first border industry sites were chosen to minimize the short-run direct economic costs to the government of the program. The Tswana and Zulu areas happened to be most affected, but regions with equally underemployed labor in the Transkei and northern Transvaal were ignored. Many non-Tswana and Tswana were encouraged to move as close as possible to Pretoria. Many Zulu were drawn toward the Durban-Pietermaritzburg area. These population movements did not represent departures from the previous situation. The close proximity of the border industrial areas and their satellite African townships to major towns meant that commuters still spent most of their incomes in white shopping areas. More remote industrial development, and the provision of shopping facilities in the African townships, would have reduced the immediate income leakages back to the white areas and stimulated homeland development and employment.[25] The most

24. *Survey of Race Relations, 1975,* 180.
25. J. A. Lombard, "Background to Planning the Development of Bantu Homelands in South Africa," unpub. paper, 1972. Elsewhere, Lombard has said: "I have already stated that this whole matter has a political motivation, that the statecraft should take cognizance of the economically oriented basis of the origin of this problem, and that it will have to condition the economic system of South Africa with its profit motive towards the automatic achievement of its objectives. . . . Insofar as the strategy must rest on industrial decentralization it is becoming more and more

mobile and responsive firms have already moved to the border areas. It is thus becoming more and more difficult to induce white capitalists to move farther and farther away from the historically dominant economic regions.

The concessions to industrialists for moving to border growth areas were numerous and have been further liberalized from time to time. Loans are available at low interest rates (2 to 7 percent) for land, factory buildings, and equipment. Housing for whites is subsidized with loans offered at 2.5 percent below the market mortgage rate. Part of African (or coloured) wages and capital investment can be set against income taxes. There is a cash grant to cover the actual costs of moving from the older regions. Rebates on rail and harbor charges may be allowed. Concessions of up to 10 percent are given on bids for purchases from the government.

It is difficult to estimate the cost of the decentralization scheme or to calculate its effects on black employment and the distribution of industrial activity. Costs that appear high to some are reasonable to others; gains that seem large to proponents of the program are dismissed as inadequate by critics. The various concessions are hard to monetize and overhead costs of power, water, and transport in a region are not easily allocated to the border industrial sites. Some investment would have taken place in these cities anyway, even without incentives, and some black employment would have been generated. It is therefore almost impossible to say with precision what the net costs and net employment changes have been.

According to the Decentralisation Board, a total of at least R637 million was invested in the decentralized areas by the public and private sectors between 1960 and the end of 1973. The Industrial Development Corporation had committed R159 million and corporation-aided industries had invested R349 million. In addition, R500 thousand had been paid for moving industrialists from the older regions, tax and interest concessions totalled R37 million, and rail and harbor rebates amounted to R6 million. Other funds had been spent on townships, water, and power supplies. About 92,000 African jobs had been generated, an average of about 7,000 per year.[26]

Through March 1974 the Industrial Development Corporation had invested R33.3 million in industrial building, loans and share capital, and white housing in Brits, Rosslyn, Rustenburg, and other border areas near

---

clear to me personally that concentration on growth points in border areas alone will not have the desired effect politically. The process will have to penetrate to the heartlands of the homelands, to places such as Butterworth and Umtata in the Transkei, Sithebe, and perhaps other points in . . . Zululand as well, ..." "Political and Administrative Principles of Homeland Development," *Bantu,* XVIII (Feb., 1971), 28.

26. *Survey of Race Relations, 1974,* 274–275. Spending on interior growth points is included. Also see *ibid., 1975,* 180–181.

Bophuthatswana. Private industrialists attracted to these zones added over R76 million of their own capital, R43 million of which went into Rosslyn. A total of 12,208 jobs for Africans were created; there were 1,771 new white jobs. These were presumably directly created work opportunities and did not include secondary multiplier effects. Over 10,000 of the African jobs were in metalworking or machinery and equipment. Approximately 1,000 jobs were added in each of five other classifications: food, beverages, and tobacco; textiles and apparel; wood and wood products (furniture); chemicals, petroleum, coal, rubber, and plastic products; nonmetallic mineral products. In border areas near KwaZulu — Elangeni, Ladysmith, Newcastle, Pietermaritzburg, Richards Bay, and others — the Industrial Development Corporation spent R70.1 million: R28 million on industrial buildings, R33 million on loans and share capital, and R9 million on white housing. Private capital inflows amounted to R163 million and 19,000 African and 2,000 white jobs were created.[27]

There has been sterile debate in South African political and academic circles about the number of jobs decentralization has managed to create and their total, average, and marginal costs. Generally, all have agreed that the additional employment has not been sufficient to absorb the annual increments of the total or homeland African labor force, leaving a fraction to spill over into the historic focal points of the absentee labor system. The incremental cost has been higher than that of merely adding additional workers in established areas. The head of the Bantu Investment Corporation has estimated that 20,000 jobs need to be created in the border areas (or in the homelands) to meet the goals of employment relocation.[28] Bell says that of the 87,500 jobs created between 1960 and 1970 in the border areas, 64,000 would have spontaneously arisen. Therefore, only 2,200 jobs per year can be attributed to the government's efforts. Obviously the cost of creating one of these incremental jobs was far higher than an estimate of the average cost per job using the whole total as the divisor.[29]

One estimate projected an annual increase in the homeland labor force of 66,000 males and 39,000 females in the period from 1974 to 1976; during the same period in the white areas, 60,000 males and 38,000 females were estimated to be added to the labor force yearly.[30] KwaZulu is responsible for the largest additions to the labor force of any homeland. Another source

27. BENBO, *Bophuthatswana, Economic Revue, 1975*, 40; *idem, KwaZulu, Economic Revue, 1975*, 46.

28. *Survey of Race Relations, 1974*, 275.

29. Trevor Bell, "Bantustan Economic Development," *Third World*, II (June, 1973), 30. See also Bell, *Industrial Decentralisation in South Africa* (Cape Town, 1973).

30. University of Pretoria, Department of Economics, *Focus on Key Economic Issues*, 9, *The Homelands* (1974), figure 7.

placed the present annual African male labor force increment at 120,000, of which 60,000 will be in the homelands.[31] Sadie predicted that the total African labor force would expand by 159,200 annually in the 1970s.[32]

BENBO calculates that from 1973 to 1976 the total Tswana labor force will have risen by 72,200: 44,400 in the common area, 27,300 in Bophuthatswana, and 3,000 in other homelands. For the Zulu from 1974 to 1976, 164,000 additional workers would have been seeking employment: 70,100 in the common area, 91,200 in KwaZulu, and 3,300 in other homelands. According to BENBO's planners, all of these figures will be 30 to 40 percent higher in the next three-year period—from 1977 to 1980.[33] Clearly the addition of new labor from the homeland populations puts enormous pressures on capital formation and leaves little leeway for the luxury of high-cost ideological preference for shifting employment from one region to another. If a recent R8,500 estimated average cost per job in the border industries has some validity, the size of the capital formation requirements becomes obvious.[34]

In 1970, Riekert said that adding 44,000 jobs per year in the border areas and the homelands would absorb all new homeland workers; 36,000 jobs would keep the number working in white areas constant (since some would naturally withdraw from the migrant labor force, leaving room for some new workers); and 21,000 jobs would succed in stabilizing the proportion of the African work force in white areas. Allowing for jobs arising in agriculture, services, and other industry, the figures would be reduced to 21,000, 15,000, and 5,000 new industrial employment opportunities.[35] Riekert said that the lowest goal had already been attained, although he did not adduce any evidence in support of his assumption that 16,000 jobs were being created annually in other sectors. These numbers are now too small, but since Riekert was a key figure at the time he spoke, they do indicate that government thinking in the early 1970s was already far removed from any attempt to do more than stabilize or moderately reduce the *proportion* of African

31. Bantu Investment Corporation, *Homelands* (Pretoria, 1973), 1st ed., 125.

32. J. L. Sadie, in an address to the National Labour Conference, Cape Town (April, 1971), quoted in Gavin Maasdorp, "Targets of Development in Relation to Population Trends and Needs," unpub. paper (1972), 6.

33. BENBO, *Bophuthatswana, Economic Revue, 1975,* 20; *idem, KwaZulu Economic Revue, 1975,* 22. The statistical bases are not consistent in these reports. The Bophuthatswana figures are given as 1970 to 1973, 1973 to 1976, and 1976 to 1980; the KwaZulu figures are given as 1971 to 1973, 1974 to 1976 and 1977 to 1980. We assume that inclusive figures, as given for KwaZulu, are correct for Bophuthatswana as well.

34. *Survey of Race Relations, 1975,* 180.

35. P. J. Riekert, "The Economy of the Republic (with Special Reference to Homeland and Border Industrial Development and the Economics of Southern Africa)," Institute of Race Relations (1970), 14, mimeo.

workers who worked in established centers. The number of workers in core areas would at most be held constant, or limited to population increase, while the number and perhaps the proportion of African workers in the Republic would actually rise because of the border industries.

What has emerged from this debate is the conclusion that the border industries program is at best stemming only a fraction of the outflow of absentee labor from the homelands each year. Even if each of the 6,000 to 8,000 jobs arising annually in the border areas generates 2 or 3 more jobs in agriculture, services, or other industries—a very generous assumption— only one-third of the increase in the homeland male labor force can be absorbed. (The Industrial Development Corporation puts the multiplier at only 1.5 additional jobs.)[36] No women are included in the base amount, nor is any provision made for Africans who are now moving out of white agricultural areas, for reductions in unemployment and underemployment, or for the repatriation of urban black workers to the homelands. The numbers are large enough, however, to have an impact on homeland living and working patterns, shifting them somewhat toward commuter communities linked to small- or medium-sized white cities. These satellite townships will be additions to the present distributions of workers and living areas, fed essentially by new population growth, and not offering alternatives to migrancy, employment within the homelands, or permanent work in the core areas.

Developmentally, the border industry scheme provides dubious blessings for the homelands. It does not generate new jobs so much as move employment closer to the homelands. Relocation makes it less necessary than before for African workers to migrate to distant white centers for jobs. Families will rent or own homes in townships built by the homeland governments and white governmental agencies and commute on a daily or perhaps weekly basis to their places of work. Because no one has undertaken a systematic study of its impact on the movements, living conditions, and working habits of black labor, the extent to which this has already happened is unknown. The homelands acquire no property interest in the border enterprises, nor will they have any powers to tax them. Moreover, the new firms are not necessarily linked to the mineral, agricultural, or secondary industrial bases of the homeland economies. The homelands cannot plan or control their economic impacts on their own internal economies. On the contrary, the homelands must constantly face the threat that their own best and most skilled workers, administrators, and technicians will be enticed away by offers of higher earnings in the border areas.

Given the openness of the homeland economies and their lack of policy instruments such as tariffs or currency control, their economic positions are

36. *Survey of Race Relations, 1975,* 180.

highly vulnerable. Workers will spend large fractions of their incomes in the white towns. Funds that the homelands devote to education, urban amenities, and the social welfare of workers will result in direct or indirect benefits for white firms that are under no obligation to pay taxes in return. Unlike the internal growth points, the border industries are merely devices for extracting the cheapest possible labor from African territories with the minimum of inconvenience for the white firms and the white public sector. Self-interest is likely to lead the homeland governments to try to internalize the economic activities now being brought to peripheral growth points, to acquire control over their planning and operation, and vigorously to represent the economic interests of their work forces.

The internal development of industry in Bophuthatswana and KwaZulu has been sluggish, even in contrast to poorer underdeveloped nations. Given the size of their populations and their per capita incomes, the homelands could be expected to have a number of commercial and industrial centers: certainly a large city or two, some rural market towns, and many shops, mills, and backyard workshops distributed throughout small settlements and along country crossroads. Several million persons, each of whom receives an average of over $100 per year in cash, are theoretically capable of supporting a sizeable commercial class and at least a few medium-sized industrial firms. Tea shops, restaurants, laundries, clothing shops, hardware stores, petrol stations, metal workshops, and automobile and farm machinery repair facilities ought to provide visible evidence of economic activity. It is therefore surprising to drive through the homelands without finding many of these signs of commerce or industry. Even the larger settlements lack the common-place business establishments so necessary to satisfy the routine needs of their residents. Isolated general dealerships, selling gasoline, soft drinks, tinned goods, staples and condiments, household hardware and utensils, and ready-made clothes are often the only manifestation of business activity. From their small spaces they fill many needs, but they are poor substitutes for a series of specialized shops. Often expensive, they provide convenience when travel is costly and tiresome. Each is a small-volume monopoly working on the margin between the dealer's wholesale cost of goods and the price of a roundtrip bus ticket to the nearest market town.

It is not hard to explain why there has been so little business development in the homelands. Black South Africans lack the access to capital, credit, technology, and markets that enables the white, and even the politically impotent Asian, community to engage in commerce. There has not been any easy manner in which black South Africans could acquire the managerial, accounting, engineering, and marketing skills needed to prosper in business.

Many white businessmen made their fortunes from the exploitation of mineral rights, land speculation, or sharp business trading. Others made money out of inventions, patents, and foreign collaborations. Most had the support of the government, which provided an infrastructure, erected tariff barriers, and sponsored a legal framework conducive to business enterprise. Africans have never been able to deal in land, mineral rights, capital, and acquire rights to technology on an equal basis with whites. They have been denied acccess to the clubs, bars, and hotels where the social life of business is arranged. They could not easily marry wealth, urge their children to save, or pass on their prosperity to their progeny. Trading rights—the rights to do businesss—have been zealously rationed by white authorities outside the homelands and by chiefs inside. A wealthy professional man, such as a physician, is hard pressed to find a way of conserving or increasing his wealth. The various laws that prevent African land ownership in the cities, and the tenure system of the reserves, mean that Africans cannot readily become housing contractors or real estate agents. Nor can they build a block of flats or shops for rental income. Those redoubtable and notorious entrepreneurs of the townships, the shebeen women, are harassed by police. In the open, they would constitute a successful business class, and it would be surprising if a few did not move their capital into hotels, restaurants, or other service-oriented businesses.

Now that the Republic's developmental agencies have turned their attentions to the homelands, they have realized that, if the homelands are to become more self-reliant, agricultural development must be increasingly supplemented by progress in other spheres. The agencies have thus embarked upon an aggressive program to implant commerce and industry in the townships and rural areas. As with agriculture, however, the making of policy and its administration is all too frequently based on the premise that Africans are noneconomic and nonentrepreneurial.

The Bantu Investment Corporation was established in 1959 as the vehicle for encouraging homeland commercial and industrial development. Given the extremely deficient industrial position of the Tswana and Zulu homelands, the recent history of their business development is virtually identical with the activities of the corporation. When it began operations the corporation had a staff of six whites and one black. Its share capital totaled R1 million. In the first nine months of its existence it considered 246 applications for loans from Africans, conducted 36 complete credit investigations, and made 5 loan commitments totaling less than R40,000. By March 1973, fourteen annual reports later, share capital stood at R40,830,000. Through March 1974, 1,577 loans worth R11 million had been granted, but four-fifths were for commercial undertakings, and only two dozen were for industries. The enlargement of its staff to 1,021 whites and 6,804 Africans and the mounting complexity of its internal organization in the last seventeen years are in accord with the forty-fold growth in its share capital. The corporation has evolved rapidly into a many-branched industrial empire. It reaches into every modern economic activity in the homelands: factories, shops, transportation, farming, construction, housing, banking, insurance, and training. No black has, however, served in an executive or technical advisory capacity.

Under its charter, the Bantu Investment Corporation can stimulate the industrial and commercial growth of the homelands in several ways. It can assist African businessmen by providing them with advice, training, and initial or additional capital. It can purchase existing white or Asian enterprises, such as general dealerships, and transfer them to Africans. The corporation can purchase or construct businesses and operate them for profit (or loss) until such time as it believes an African or Africans can assume ownership and management responsibility. The corporation has the responsibility for encouraging and assisting white businesses to enter the homelands, on an agency basis.

The corporation stands ready to advise any African businessmen seeking management, marketing, or other assistance. It builds and leases shopping centers, garages, factories, and office blocks. Several kinds of training are provided: on-the-job, or "in-the-shop" training in building trades and subcontracting, and training in business skills. The corporation operates fifty-six savings banks. It has lent over R1 million to more affluent Africans for private building and home construction in homeland townships. The new agricultural investments branch finances larger scale projects, including irrigation systems, and engages in the provision of agricultural credit. The corporation channeled R66 million into the homelands during fiscal 1975/76 (over 50 percent more than in fiscal 1974/75) but about R26 million of this amount came from private investment. Eleven bus companies have been started or expanded, and to some of these black directors were appointed for the first time. It is further intended that individual firms can invest directly in the homelands after negotiating directly with the homeland government in question: the Bantu Investment Corporation and the minister of Bantu administration and development would have to be notified, however, and such firms would not qualify for incentives or guarantees.[37]

Under its program to finance African businesses the Bantu Investment Corporation has assisted a disproportionate number of Tswana when compared to the number of Zulu. Through the end of the fiscal 1973/74 accounting period, 423 loans, totaling R3.7 million, had gone to Bophuthatswana, and 417 loans, totaling R3.1 million, to KwaZulu. Since there are roughly

37. Data on the Bantu Investment Corporation are taken from its annual reports and the annual *Survey of Race Relations* summaries of those reports. For most recent data, see *Survey of Race Relations, 1975,* 145–149.

two and one-half times as many Zulu as Tswana in the homelands, Bophutha-tswana has been a more active field than KwaZulu for the corporation. In fact, Tswana received 27 percent of the loans made and these amounted to 32 percent of the total value of all loans (through 1974). The Zulu obtained 26 percent of the loans extended, and 28 percent of the total loan value.

In all of the homelands, the Bantu Investment Corporation had financed 1,300 concerns through the end of the 1974 fiscal year. Of these 1,112 (86 percent) were "commercial," including general dealers (759), cafés (117), butcher shops (66), and liquor outlets (71). "Service industries" numbered 164 (13 percent), the most common types being bus services (47) and garages (19). The 24 (2 percent) manufacturing enterprises started included 5 tailors, 5 brick manufacturers, 4 furniture makers, 3 cabinet makers, and 4 dry cleaners. The mixture of these businesses shows that the corporation has concentrated above all on trying to put general dealerships and other types of family stores into African hands. Yet such single proprietorships are obviously going to generate little employment in relation to the amount of money devoted to the shop, its inventory, and the training and supervision of its operation. Until recently it was corporation policy not to permit African individuals to own and operate more than one business. There remains a "fear of scale" built into the thinking of the corporation that appears to restrain it from encouraging Africans to expand and pyramid businesses. It is difficult to tell whether the corporation and the government do not want to foster large-scale black businesses or whether they actually confuse the attributes of small shopkeeping with those of a large-scale business enterprise.

By the middle of 1974 the corporation owned over 100 large commercial enterprises that it had begun or taken over. These were to be held in trust until such time as an African owner or group of operators was ready to assume control. In general, these enterprises are larger and more complex than the average business or shop. They include, for example, breweries, beer gardens, bus services, arts and crafts centers, furniture factories, garages and petrol stations, holiday resorts, wholesale dealers, savings banks, and movie theaters. There is no explicit timetable for turning over these large concerns, many of which are profitable, to Africans. One major enterprise, the Bophuthatswana Transport Company, is apparently nearly autonomous. It has 221 buses and carries over 1.6 million passengers per month.

At the end of fiscal 1973/74, 552 Africans and 26 whites were working under corporation auspices; the three largest areas of employment were manufacture of food (203), retail and allied services (155), and refreshment and accommodation (100). In KwaZulu the scale of operations was almost exactly double with 1075 Africans and 53 whites in Bantu Investment Corporation enterprises: the three largest areas of employment were building construction (322), wholesale trade (238) and food, beverages, and tobacco

(188).[38] The range of industrial activities is far larger in KwaZulu; it is not clear whether or not this difference is due to variations in policy between the regional offices of the corporation.

The most ambitious undertakings of the corporation are its homeland growth points, which are small industrial parks located inside the homelands. Considerable amounts of money are invested by the corporation in readying the sites of these parks. All transport, water, and power facilities are available and factory sheds may be built or leased, White industrialists are encouraged to locate in these growth points by a number of inducements slightly more attractive than those for the border industries, but they must ultimately turn over the ownership of their operations to Africans. In the growth points African workers are generally freed from the job discrimination restrictions that operate in the white economy. They may theoretically advance to highly skilled jobs and be trained as apprentices in crafts normally closed to them. There are two types of labor cost advantages for the employer. He first obtains immediate access at the lowest market wages to a reservoir of unskilled labor. He also may use trained Africans in positions normally occupied by coloureds, Asians, or whites, and should enjoy substantial wage savings. Firms that require large amounts of labor may thus be drawn to the homeland growth points. The average ratio of white to black workers is said to be 1:30 in the homeland growth points as opposed to 1:3 in the core area.

Three of the six homeland growth points being actively developed by the corporation are in Bophuthatswana and KwaZulu. One of these, Montshiwa, just outside Mafeking, is not yet important, but the other two have become showplaces. Babelegi is about thirty-five miles north of Pretoria and lies adjacent to major rail and road links. An African township, Temba, has been built nearby and is the site of several other corporation projects, including a cane furniture factory, a modern new shopping center, and the corporation's business training school. The development of Babelegi has proceeded rapidly since 1970, when the first ten enterprises were initiated. By March 1974 there were fifty-six agency enterprises in Babelegi, employing 5,559 Africans and 186 whites. About R10.2 million had been spent on infrastructure, buildings, and white housing by the corporation. About one-half the employment had been provided by textile, wearing apparel, and leather firms — traditionally employers of abundant, cheap, mostly female labor. Over 1,000 persons worked in metal fabrication and related firms, making such things as aluminum window frames. All sites are now allocated.[39]

38. BENBO, *Bophuthatswana, Economic Revue, 1975*, 40; *idem, KwaZulu Economic Revue, 1975*, 48.
39. *Idem, Bophuthatswana, Economic Revue, 1975*, 38.

In Isithebe, located about sixty-five miles north of Durban on the Durban-Richards Bay rail line, complete infrastructural facilities are available at forty-nine sites. The nearness of the port of Richards Bay is considered an advantage for export industries. In fiscal 1973/74 sixteen businesses employing 983 black and 42 white workers were located there. At the end of March 1975, employment of 1,558 Africans was reported.[40]

The interior growth point program as it is structured does seem capable of attracting a number of small- to medium-sized firms, such as clothing makers, wig makers, and metalworking and assembly shops. These centers and their associated residential enclaves are an important addition to the homeland economies, but it is unlikely that they will absorb more than a fraction of their burgeoning labor forces. Compared to the border industries, however, the growth points have substantially more linkage effects to the local economies. They provide a potential for recouping public expenditures on infrastructure, housing, health, and education if and when tax reform occurs. Ultimately the growth points may contribute to African business ownership.

It is in many ways premature to judge the efficacy of the corporation's various programs. It has grown so quickly and assumed so many responsibilities that it would be surprising had there been no setbacks. The Tswana are reputed to be dissatisfied with the corporation because of its extremely close supervision of client enterprises. It is said that one or two general dealers may have had their assets disposed of in an arbitrary fashion in order to meet loan obligations. There is the larger problem of the degree to which the homeland governments should be involved in the corporation's loan and investment decisions and in the supervision of its wider activities. Both Mangope and Buthelezi have argued vigorously for independent investment corporations, and in 1976 they had their requests honored. Both would prefer to have themselves, cabinet ministers, and some homeland officials on the boards of their investment banks, but the Bantu Investment Corporation has acceded only in allowing the homelands to name one-half of the board of directors. Political appointments will be discouraged. Yet, strong links still need be built between the public allocative process and the homeland corporations so that greater coordination becomes possible and homeland politics can influence economic decisions.

The homelands are not yet permitted departments of industry and commerce, although Mangope has made a strong plea for one. Control over industrial policy still rests with white authorities, in large measure with the corporation. Except for the control that they exercise over the granting of

40. *Idem, KwaZulu, Economic Revue, 1975*, 46.

"trading rights," which enable Africans to start shops or businesses, the governments of Bophuthatswana and KwaZulu have little influence over any decisions of the corporation.

In 1974 Vorster said that homeland governments would gradually acquire more say over industry and held out the possibility that at least a few white concerns could operate on an ownership, or partial ownership, basis rather than under the agency system. Tomlinson, speaking publicly on homeland policy for the first time in twenty years, lamented that it had taken that much time before the government acceded to a major recommendation of his commission.[41]

As the Republic's primary agency for restraining the outflow of workers from the homelands, the central priority of the corporation is supposed to be employment generation rather than multifaceted development. The activities of the organization have in practice become extremely diffuse; it has been compelled to assume a host of banking, investment, and training responsibilities. In so doing, the corporation has drifted closer toward serving the balanced needs of the homelands than its creators intended. The great tragedy is that time and resources are being devoted to programs to force black development into approved channels rather than allocated in response to community wishes and needs and to build on existing strengths. Hart, who has made one of the few studies of black entrepreneurship in South Africa, found that spontaneous initiative was being quashed in the urban townships while at the same time the corporation and its sister organization, the Xhosa Development Corporation, were trying with mixed success to infuse commercial spirit into single-proprietor dealerships in rural areas.[42]

The firms operating on an agency basis are not always committing substantial capital and new equipment. The corporation owns many of the factory sheds, no one owns the land, and equipment is being depreciated physically and financially. Whatever remains at the termination of the agency will not easily provide the basis for viable businesses. The timing of withdrawal is vague and the terms of transfer are unspecific. On its own account, the corporation is expanding rapidly and shedding enterprises only gradually. The funding of the border industries has been ten times as great as that of the growth points and the business response much stronger. Without genuine black participation at all levels, and the tying of the growth points to the infrastructure, towns, human resources, minerals, agricultural production, and markets of the homelands, they may not readily serve as springboards for more development.

41. *Survey of Race Relations, 1974,* 215.
42. Gillian Hart, *Some Socio-economic Aspects of African Entrepreneurship (With Special Reference to the Transkei)* (Grahamstown, 1972).

Mining

Another potential avenue for development in Bophuthatswana and KwaZulu is mining. Bophuthatswana is known to have reserves of platinum, nickel, vanadium, asbestos, iron, limestone, diamonds, chrome, granite, calcite, manganese, and fluorspar. KwaZulu may have important coal, titanium, and gold resources, but presently only dolerite, sand, kaolin, stone, and coal are being extracted.

The Bantu Mining Corporation was instituted in 1969 to guide greater white and black exploitation of homeland mineral resources. Many of the homelands had not been systematically surveyed for mineral wealth, and mineral rights were held by individual blacks, tribal communities, the Bantu Trust, and sometimes by the state. The Bantu Mining Corporation was to oversee existing operations and act as agent for individual Africans and communities in their negotiations with white companies. Only South African companies were to be permitted into the homelands. In addition, the homeland governments were not empowered to negotiate on behalf of themselves or their citizens. The Bantu Mining Corporation could undertake explorations on its own account and could establish its own enterprises or permit white firms to operate on an agency basis. It was also to encourage black ownership and to train Africans to assume control of at least some mineral firms.

The corporation has acted in its brief history principally to give white mining interests access to homeland mineral deposits. As with industry, mineral development is a vital national interest of the Republic, and the homeland governments have no say regarding mineral leasing or the terms of exploitation. In the underdeveloped world, mining is at best a classic enclave industry, employing local workers at minimal wages held down by the threat of imported or recruited migrant labor. Unless special efforts are taken by an independent government, raw minerals or semiprocessed ores are often shipped away to processing centers outside the country. There are few internal forward linkages into processing and fabrication. The homeland governments are not, however, in a position to regulate the operations of mines, nor can they easily try to develop processing and fabricating industries that would be based on ore production.

In mid-1974 there were sixty-three mines operating in the homelands; of these twenty-five were in Bophuthatswana and nine were in KwaZulu. Approximately 78,000 African workers were employed, earning an aggregate payroll of R31.8 million. Of these 61,000 or 78 percent were working in Bophuthatswana, where they earned R27.0 million.

Through 1974 the Bantu Mining Corporation had granted prospecting and mining rights to 145 applicants. It appears that these numbers do not include firms that had been mining actively prior to the formation of the corporation in 1969. In 1973 only four Africans had prospecting rights, and one African was mining, although what he was mining has not been stated.[43] The corporation is supposed to encourage African mining, but it is apparent from statements in its annual reports that the corporation envisages Africans as small-scale miners using labor-intensive methods on residual holdings that whites are not interested in developing. The assumption is that Africans are satisfied with lower levels of income or profits than whites. Yet the corporation explores on its own account, and, if it chooses, could presumably develop a discovery in a relatively short time for an African takeover.

There are eleven times as many workers in Bophuthatswana's mines as in Babelegi; there are eighty-seven times as many mine workers as persons engaged in commercial farming on Bantu Investment Corporation projects. KwaZulu's mineral resources employed only 307 workers, who earned R128,000 in fiscal 1973/74.[44] The most sought after mineral in Bophuthatswana is platinum, the extraction of which engages 58,349 African miners or 95.6 percent of the mining labor force. Very few Tswana work in the three platinum mines in the homeland, and it is said that this low rate of participation is due to "cultural reasons." The real reason may be that wages in relation to working conditions are superior for most Tswana in the Pretoria-Brits-Rustenburg area. Production of platinum has risen sharply since 1972 to meet the needs of American automobile producers, who use the metal in emission control devices and who have signed contracts worth several hundred million rand with the mine operators. There are very poor linkage effects from these and other mines to the Tswana economy.

At present the Bophuthatswana government receives only indirect and marginal benefits from these ventures, which remain under the control of the Bantu Mining Corporation, an agency of the Republic, and the licensee firms. The terms of the contracts, insofar as they are known, are not favorable to the homeland when contrasted with agreements reached normally between foreign investors and independent nations. The royalties paid are small and go mostly to the Fokeng, and to the Bantu Trust. There are limited employment and income multiplier effects, because few Tswana are employed and the workers do not spend the bulk of their funds in Tswana shops or stores. The power of the white mining unions is such that they have been able to enforce job reservation in the homeland mines despite the government's general policy that discrimination will not be allowed in the homelands.

43. Bantu Investment Corporation, *Homelands*, 2nd ed., 85.
44. *Ibid.*, 85–87.

Developmental Prospects

The development of the homelands by the Republic, acting primarily through its development and mining corporations, must overcome the cumulative disabilities of the homeland economies. Deficient infrastructures, inadequate human resources, ecological collapse, and the competitive attractions of the core area and of the border industrial sites make it exceedingly difficult to create a vigorous commercializing farm sector and profitable industries in the homelands. Further, many programs—indeed the general policy framework itself—are dictated from Pretoria and frequently are based on erroneous suppositions about African responses. Black leaders, civil servants, teachers, extension workers, businessmen, and farmers are imperfectly involved in decision making.

Without case studies it is hard to be certain when projects are yielding spontaneous and sustained results, and when they are merely being kept going by support from one of the developmental agencies. In agriculture, sugar cane growing in KwaZulu and cattle sales in both homelands appear to provide positive signs. Yet irrigation projects at Taung and Tugela have not so far been structured so that land, water, credit, and other inputs can be organized by individuals to yield secure returns in accessible markets. More importantly, widespread gains in garden and grain cropping would seem to be beyond the scope of present extension and support service levels. Too much effort is being devoted to physical planning, which is of transitory usefulness without simultaneous improvements in the extension, technological, and infrastructural spheres.

In industry, the growth points have succeeded in bringing some labor-intensive industries into the homelands, but otherwise industry is very much underdeveloped. Commercial and autonomous craft and service undertakings handled independently by blacks remain rare, and thus gains in industrial employment have limited effects on the local economy. Small shops are important, but a means has not yet been found to put large amounts of capital into African hands. There are few financial institutions to mobilize savings and take advantage of new investment opportunities, although the urbanization of the homelands would appear to offer considerable potential for blacks in construction, housing, and urban services.

In mining, the position of the homelands is peripheral and unsatisfactory. Unless there are substantial institutional changes, Bophuthatswana can only look on as its depletable resources are exhausted to enrich others.

An independent Bophuthatswana could use the extractive sector as the basis for further development, as Zambia, the oil countries of the Middle East, and—not to be forgotten—South Africa itself have done. There is a substantial conflict of interest between Bophuthatswana and the Bantu

Mining Corporation acting as the agent of the Republic and white firms. What is in practice elsewhere essentially an adversary relationship should not be left to a single agency.

The elaborate organizational system created by the Republic over the last decade or so has taken white South Africans, with their own economic interests and developmental models and their ingrained view of African culture and African personal potentials, very deep into the last enclosures of African society and economy. These thrusts in essence complete, although in a different form, a process begun centuries ago. Whether by acting in this manner whites will at long last be able to assist the Africans in the homelands more than harm them, and whether they can successfully dismantle their now burgeoning bureaucracy and disentangle themselves with grace, while ceding their powers to Africans with the necessary alacrity, are prime questions to ask in evaluating the homeland developmental policy in the years ahead. Success would mean, at most, that these small backward economic regions become able to provide more employment, higher incomes, and better living conditions in a manner to be determined by their elected political leaders. There can be no serious hope that an augmented homeland development program will effect a major restructuring of existing South African economic and employment patterns; therefore, success within the context of this policy depends upon a recognition that the economic needs of African residents in urban South Africa will have to be met there and not in the homelands.

9

The Future of
the Homelands

The preceding chapters assert that the homelands have a future both within the context of a gradually changing South Africa and, conceivably, as independent entities. South Africa is increasingly concerned about its relations and image with the black nations of the continent and with the Western powers. It acted pragmatically with respect to the Moçambiquan, Rhodesian, and Namibian situations. Within this context of international insecurity the homelands provide new and potentially beneficial leverage for Africans on the otherwise rigid politics of the dominant power. Such a proposition is controversial for it implies an evolutionary, not a revolutionary, future for South Africa, a radical redistribution of power, and the use of some of that power in favor of Africans. Yet the preceding chapters have demonstrated both the limited nature of the redistribution of power and the many strong constraints on its use.

With the independence of the Transkei, South Africa will have set in motion what it considers to be the final realization of the grand design of separate development. South Africa hopes that the launching of the Transkei will continue the initiatives for the conciliation of the African states that were begun in the late 1960s and that achieved their first major success when Prime Minister Vorster met President Kenneth Kaunda at the Victoria Falls in 1975. However, as a result of South Africa's miscalculation in Angola, and the subsequent intervention of the United States in southern African affairs, the search for détente seems to have foundered much as did the earlier "outward policy."

For the states of black Africa as well as South Africa, the independence of the Transkei, and ultimately the other homelands, is meant to provide a recognizable means of muting, if not resolving, the struggle for power between blacks and whites in South Africa. Granting independence to the Transkei, like South Africa's proposals for important changes in Rhodesia and Namibia, is intended to buy time for the whites of South Africa. South Africa's leaders hope by such purchases to improve relations with black

Africa, and within limits imposed by what Vorster thinks his white electorate will accept, to restructure the internal workings of the South African system.

The independence of the Transkei offers a range of options that have hitherto been available to black and white South Africans only in theory. The concept of a homeland has now been taken to a logical conclusion and, thereby, has given greater credence than most Africans want to white assertions that there are a number of South African peoples, among them whites, with claims to permanency. Ideally, from the Republican government's point of view, each of these peoples will gain a "separate freedom" and discrimination on the grounds of color and race alone will end. In this South African syllogism it follows that Africans in their separate nations will obtain independent spheres in which they can prevail, make policy, and modernize. Further, there is the assumption that an independent Transkei, and other homelands after it, will take their places—the members of the United Nations permitting—alongside the other weak states of the world order. Ultimately—when all of the homelands have achieved independence—a South Africa reduced to its large and prosperous white core would remain, with a legitimacy derived from the contrived process of homeland "decolonization." Thereby, in this white-constructed ideal world of the future, South Africa's relationship with its African peoples would have been transformed from a hierarchical pattern of domination and subordination in one society to a mosaic of juridically equal states, each entitled to allocate rights and responsibilities within its own borders.

Such an ideal consummation will not be easy for South Africa to achieve. It would like all of its homelands to follow the lead of the Transkei and move rapidly toward independence. Yet, independence is an issue among South African blacks, and at the time it made the decision, the Transkei was alone in being willing to accept it. But Bophuthatswana has now chosen to follow the Transkei's lead. It could have been argued a few years ago that independence made some sense for the Transkei because it is largely consolidated whereas the other homelands are fragmented, and because it has had much longer experience of self-government in its South African form than the other homelands. However, the Transkei has poorer economic prospects, especially for industrialization and mining, than either Bophuthatswana or KwaZulu. South African black leaders seem likely to choose, or refuse, independence on far more complex grounds than the simple cataloging of economic resources or length of apprenticeship. Crucial to their decisions will be calculations about whether accepting independence increases their leverage in and on the overall South African system.

The other homelands, except for Bophuthatswana, have resisted the lure of independence. They fear being cut adrift in conditions in which their dependence on South Africa for practically every kind of economic resource—goods, services, jobs, revenue, technology—will remain unchanged, and in which they will have no authoritative say in the allocation of its wealth. Even if the terms of independence were generous and provided continued aid, they would still remain dependent, captive clients. Hence their leaders frequently argue for the maintenance of an undivided South Africa, conceding no more than the possibility of a limited form of autonomy within a South African federation that encompasses the area now constituting the white heartland.

The homelands are still wholly dependent upon South Africa's Parliament for revenue, in the case of Bophthatswana and KwaZulu for over 80 percent of their budgets in the fiscal year 1975/76. Thus, without the South African subvention, the homelands could afford to expend only a small proportion of their current budgets. For KwaZulu and Bophuthatswana, only the ability to tax mining ventures and periurban industry and to receive a significant proportion of the taxes paid by their citizens while absent from the homelands could provide a possible substitute for central funds. Failing the acquisition of a fairer (and from white South Africa's point of view, a radical) distribution of the resources of the Republic, the homelands will find it impossible, even with international assistance, to achieve self-sustaining growth and a rising level of social services for their citizens within the next generation.

The homelands are impoverished, backward, overcrowded, and unhealthy, even by the standards of many parts of preindependent black Africa. Per capita incomes are low by world and especially by South African standards. The greatest proportions of the gross national product of each homeland are derived from remittances from workers in the urban areas and imputed subsistence income. The soils of the homelands, especially those of Bophuthatswana, are poor and hardly conducive to the easy development of cash crops or the raising of stock for income. There is some sugar cane production in KwaZulu, and some limited marketing of cattle in Bophuthatswana. Maize yields per acre in the homelands are only a small fraction of what they are on the farms of the Transvaal. Bophuthatswana has a large and as yet an unrealizable mineral potential. KwaZulu's mineral potential, like those of the other homelands, is much more limited. The homelands are poorly endowed in terms of natural factors and man-built infrastructures.

Although the Republic has attempted in recent years to make the homelands more self-sufficient economically, its efforts have yielded slow and uneven forward movement in agriculture, industry, and education. There has been no generation of cumulative, self-sustaining growth, largely because the deficits of the past have been too great to be overcome even with the grants made available to the homelands by Parliament and the various agencies of the central government. Furthermore, in establishing homeland administration the South African government has placed great stress on administrative capacity. Throughout, South African whites continue to exercise a significant, if not dominant, role within the homeland administrations and as agents there of the branches of the central government that serve the homelands. Moreover, because standards of competence are being set unnecessarily high, because there are few administrative training centers for Africans, and because the black universities are graduating few Africans with the necessary technical skills, the replacement of whites by Africans with the skills and self-confidence to promote rapid development will be slow. This dependence upon South Africa for administrative skills obviously limits the administrative and policy options of the homelands and makes steps toward autonomy that much more dependent upon South African guidance.

The recent land consolidation decisions of the Republic in no way remedy the major limitations on development imposed by the fragmented and dispersed character of the homelands. They perpetuate a division of each homeland into a number of units. As a result, centers of population, government, industry, and education are scattered, making concentration of economic effort difficult. Especially in Bophuthatswana and KwaZulu, economic prospects will continue to be mortgaged by the failure of the Republic to unify and achieve more than a cosmetic consolidation of the two largest homelands and by policies that force the homelands to support ever larger, dependent, unproductive populations.

The legislative competence of a homeland after achieving self-government is limited not merely because its legislation has to be approved by the central government but because of the large number of governmental subjects reserved to the Republic by the Bantu Homelands Constitution Act of 1971. Equally limiting is the Republic's control over homeland financing. It is not merely that 80 percent of homeland revenues come from the Republic, but that they come not by right but by annual parliamentary appropriation. Devolution of functions without devolution of control over the resources to support these functions is a heavily circumscribed transference of power. The homeland legislatures, and their executive councils, spend a great deal of their time ratifying decisions made elsewhere.

Because of the dominance of the Republic, neither Bophuthatswana nor KwaZulu can greatly influence its own agricultural, industrial, mining, or human resource developmental policies. Their limited resources, especially of the revenue under their control, prevents the politicians of the homelands from responding to the expectations of their constituents with the provision of tangible services and benefits. All they can now do, with the help of the media, is to exhort the Republic to take account of their own preferences with regard to the location of industry, rates of pay for black labor, agricultural marketing arrangements, and the exploitation of minerals.

The economies of Bophuthatswana and KwaZulu are totally dependent on that of the Republic and are compelled by the nature of their origins and present arrangements to rely upon the public services of the Republic. Having no trade barriers and belonging to the rand currency zone, they are thus open to external industrial and agricultural competition. Their labor is siphoned off to border growth points, white farms, and the cities. Likewise their commercial, financial, and economic underdevelopment does little to inhibit the flow of earned income to white- and Indian-owned stores and industries. Income earned outside the homelands thus has only a minimal multiplicative effect inside them.

Because of the stubborn facts of underdevelopment and the failure so far to narrow the gap in income between the wealthy core and the impoverished periphery, it is often asserted that the homelands are not "economically viable" and, therefore, that independence would be a sham. Viability, however, has no generally accepted meaning and in most contexts it is not defined. What most people have in mind is probably fiscal independence, adequate employment *at home* for growing populations, the ability to produce sufficient physical and human capital, enough autonomy to exercise tariff, exchange, and investment controls, and, perhaps, the institutionalized capacity for self-sustained growth. Neither Bophuthatswana nor KwaZulu, nor any of the other homelands, now meets, or will meet any of these standards in the immediate future. Many independent nations would also fail to meet all or most of them.

What effect will the Republic's homeland policy have on the various forms of interdependence between these peripheral economies and the core South African economy? As we have argued, the policy has had a measurable influence upon many of the fiscal, employment, investment, and other linkages between the homelands and the Republic. What is striking, however, is that insofar as accelerated development is successful, it will lead to an elaboration and deepening of connections, to an increasing interdependence and a consequent need for machinery to reconcile differences in many areas of policy. Changing economic patterns will compel political responses, but, so far, the policy has had the effect of maintaining economic and administrative dependency. The reluctance on the part of homeland leaders to accept independence — Mangope is a reluctant convert to separate development — shows that they are aware of their continuing dependency.

Mangope and Buthelezi have made clear their skepticism regarding South Africa's ultimate willingness to make available the resources essential to give the independence of a homeland economic and social significance. They are aware that even with independence the homelands are likely to remain clients of a jealous sovereign and that meanwhile it is to the Republic that the homelands must look for periodic infusions of responsibility and the resources with which to accept that responsibility. Homeland leaders have for a long time recognized their ultimate powerlessness beside the South African colossus. As realists they have made no secret of their cynicism about the purpose of the homelands: that their very existence has always served the domestic needs of the Republic and that their recent progress is designed to ward off a growing international challenge to the domestic policies of South Africa.

Despite their origins and clear benefit to whites the homelands have also proven of some use to blacks. Africans in the homelands have for a long time been governed by hierarchical administrations controlled by whites and assisted by traditional authorities whose powers of initiation and opposition were extremely limited. Recent developments have created modern political roles in legislative and executive bodies that make no pretense of being traditional. Limited though the powers and resources of these bodies are, they are not merely part of a hierarchy down which orders can be transmitted. For example, particular steps in constitutional development, including the grant of independence, have to be taken at the request of the assembly concerned. Africans are thus able to influence decisions of importance to their white rulers, and, at the very least, can raise the price of making them.

The partial politicization of this heavily authoritarian system has taken other forms as well. The existence of the homelands has given African leaders a new institutional base and a legitimated platform. Mangope and Buthelezi, especially the latter, have used this platform to articulate the grievances of the African masses, and not merely those of the ethnic groups that they officially represent. The leaders have access not merely to the populations of the homelands, but to their citizens in the cities. It is an access enshrined in official policy and one of which Buthelezi is taking advantage to begin the organization of the urban black populations, ultimately a far greater political resource than the impoverished populations of the homelands. Separate development has, therefore, given African leaders at least the possibility of developing a mass base within which ethnic division will play a lesser part.

In their confrontations with white officials and politicians, homeland leaders are behaving in ways new for Africans since the proscribing of the African National Congress (ANC) and the Pan-Africanist Congress (PAC) in 1960. White politicians are now taking part publicly in discussions with black leaders, and are receiving some candid public criticism, especially from Buthelezi, but also from Mangope. Not only have Buthelezi and Mangope been able to speak out, they and other homeland leaders have constituted a group that cannot be ignored by whites in or out of power. The leaders of the homelands are frequently quoted in the English and the Afrikaans press. They are, therefore, free to criticize, even to embarrass, the government of the Republic, and they address white, black, and multiracial groups of all kinds. This public assertiveness by black leaders may be significant. Considering the deference that most South African whites habitually demand from blacks, this change of tone, limited in itself, may be evidence of the beginning of a move from hierarchical toward political relations. Bargains may ultimately have to be struck, rather than orders transmitted. Changes in manners, however, are relatively cheap; the hard decisions and major concessions have yet to be made.

The leaders of the homelands have developed two important new institutions: meetings of all homeland leaders to plan collective strategies and meetings of those leaders with the prime minister of the Republic and some of his ministers. In meetings of the latter type, a wide range of issues has been discussed, covering both homeland and urban matters. In 1975, after the second summit, important if limited concessions to urban Africans were announced. The minister of Bantu administration and development took care to give credit to the homeland leaders and to point to the fruitful consequences of consultation and dialogue. But these meetings do not as yet constitute negotiations. Grievances are expressed, proposals are considered, and inquiries are initiated, but the institution is still one of a group of subordinate polities pressing for concessions from a dominant one. So far the concessions have been few. Furthermore, homeland leaders do not always act in concert. Mangope and Buthelezi have differences over "black unity" and federation, and Buthelezi voiced a far more radical dissatisfaction with the 1975 summit than did the other leaders. He refused to cooperate in an inquiry into the pass laws and made his exasperation at the slow pace of concession clear.

Self-government in its South African form has given homeland leaders responsibilities for broad areas of policy. Although they have different objectives in view, the homeland governments and the Republic agree on the necessity of rapid development. But the development of the homelands is beset by bureaucratic fragmentation, a lack of interagency coordination, and paternalistic attitudes among officials. Agriculture in the homelands, for example, is now being improved by the Department of Bantu Administration and Development, homeland departments of agriculture, and the Bantu Investment Corporation. The corporation and the Industrial Development Corporation (which concentrates on border areas) compete. Mass education is the responsibility of the Department of Bantu Education and the homeland education departments. Overall, the governments of Bophuthatswana and KwaZulu possess too little power to coordinate developmental projects within their own domains, and, in any event, the key decisions are largely taken by whites beyond their control. Although there has already been a substantial Africanization of homeland administrations, it is largely at the lower levels. Africans are beginning to gain administrative experience and the gap between salaries paid to whites and blacks is being narrowed. But, if present patterns persist, the homelands will for some time lack administrative and technical self-sufficiency.

Although more than half of the *de jure* populations of all but one of the homelands are permanently resident in the urban areas of South Africa, the central government has thus far largely denied any substantial urban roles to the homeland administrations. For the most part this denial has corresponded to the wishes of the urban residents themselves. There has been little enthusiasm, for example, for the linking of urban leasehold rights to the acceptance by urban Africans of homeland citizenship. Nor have the leaders of the homelands attempted to intervene persistently in exclusively urban matters. This hesitancy has stemmed in part from the sheer difficulty of mobilizing urban Africans, subject as they still are to the rigors of influx control and constant police surveillance. It also follows from the central government's ambiguity about the extent to which the homelands should exert leverage on behalf of Africans generally. If the homeland leaders can successfully bring about the amelioration of living conditions, relaxations of petty apartheid, and achieve accretions in political power for all blacks, then—and only then—will urban, student, and radical hostility toward and suspicion about the homelands abate. But it is difficult to see how they will do so, given the government's repeated refusal to share power in the white-dominated core.

The homeland governments that become independent will gain control over political activity in their areas. In particular they will be in a position to permit the now banned African National and Pan-Africanist congresses to organize. The Republic will thus be confronted with an obvious threat to its policies of evolutionary separation. In the homelands, too, these and similar developments could have a destabilizing impact. The homeland governments depend for much of their support on traditional society: if the African populations of the cities demand greater representation in homeland parliaments, on a per capita basis they will naturally threaten the rural power bases and present organizational foci of the homelands. Resistance to such demands could vitiate the legitimacy of the homelands and dramatically limit their future political utility within South Africa. Such a loss of legitimacy would be difficult to overcome even if the homelands—by virtue of large injections of capital and altered South African resource policies—become developmental showpieces.

If South Africa's homeland policy is to continue toward the goal of an independent South Africa and ten independent homelands (possibly linked together in some regional "commonwealth"), the South African government will have to enhance the credibility of separate development. The policy has succeeded so far in bringing forward leaders of distinction and moderation; however much they complain about the slowness of policy change, they have not yet given up hope and refused to participate at all. It is precisely this willingness that has led to their being called "stooges." The preservation of hope—a continued willingness to work within the institutions of the homelands and to accept limited, possibly cumulative, concessions—is a major political challenge facing Vorster's government. How vigorously the homeland leaders put the demands, and what sanctions they threaten to support those demands, may condition how generous a response they receive from the government. If the government's preoccupation with political solutions is to be taken seriously, then it will have to try to persuade African leaders to continue to eschew military ones.

The Portuguese coup probably strengthened South Africa's determination to devolve power to the homelands. Externally, South Africa is now a suppliant power, trying to gain the goodwill of African states, Britain, and the United States. Fearful of the consequences of the development of guerrilla warfare in South Africa, the country's leaders have concentrated upon a policy of diplomatic outreach and selective military withdrawal. They have supported a transfer of power to blacks in Rhodesia and have acknowledged the force of the United Nations' stand on the future of Namibia. Implicitly, South Africa has accepted a need to work constructively with the governments of black Africa. By the chain of events leading from the Portuguese coup to the latest negotiations in Rhodesia, and intervention in Angola, it has demonstrated its willingness to pursue some objectives defined mutually with African states. In the process it has also recognized the interest that leaders of independent African states naturally have in the future of the homelands and the future of urban South Africa. This is an involvement that the leaders of the homelands have themselves furthered by making direct contact with African statesmen. It constitutes the external dimension of their as yet ill-defined political leverage.

A further dimension of this potential leverage results directly from the coming to power in Moçambique of a Marxist, revolutionary-oriented regime and the growth of black power in Rhodesia. Thus far, despite the borders that KwaZulu and Bophuthatswana share with independent states, contact with them has been limited. Botswana, Lesotho, Swaziland, and Moçambique

have done little to involve themselves with the homelands. Yet these governments do possess the capability of providing sanctuaries for guerrillas. In
fact, their capacity for such activity, however limited by fear of South Africa's
armed might, will certainly always be greater than that of the homelands.
The homelands therefore may be threatened both from within and from
neighboring states by groups anxious to compromise the gradualism that
is now the natural posture of the homelands as client states. Confronted by
such added pressures, the leaders of the homelands will have to persuade
their peoples that gradualism is and will continue to be beneficial.

The independence of the Transkei provides the first test. When the
Transkei assumes responsibility for its own internal and, conceivably,
external security, the Republic will have succeeded in shortening its perimeter
of defense at the expense of an increased potential for subversion closer to
home. Of the other homelands, only Lebowa, Gazankulu, Swazi, and
Basotho Qwa Qwa would also be devolved without doing harm to the notion
of a shortened perimeter. The other homelands are as yet too unconsolidated
and too much within and of a piece with white South Africa for the central
government to delegate to them responsibility for security. Bophuthatswana,
KwaZulu, and the Ciskei include major townships that abut important white-
controlled industrial areas. From the point of view of the central government,
removing large African townships from white control has a number of
advantages: doing so has improved the statistics showing the proportion of
blacks resident in the homelands and has conserved white manpower by
transferring responsibility for the townships to black governments and
budgets. But this policy has also given Africans control over areas adjacent
to centers of white population. In terms of industrial action, control over
these townships presents the homelands with political opportunities and,
again, potential leverage.

The intrusion of security issues as an explicit theme in South African white
politics has increased the price that whites seem prepared to pay for the
loyalty of the homelands. The homelands have become integral to South
Africa's battle for the survival of the core as a white-run bastion. South Africa
may soon have to make daring bids for the loyalty of blacks through the
homelands. Major shifts in policy—the ultimate leverage of the homelands—
could thus prove compelling. For example, if the central government were
to permit whites simply to reside permanently in a homeland, the redrawing
of boundaries would prove comparatively easy and consolidation less threat-
ening to whites, and far quicker. In such a manner KwaZulu, the most
fragmented of the homelands, could gain control over the integrated territory
without which independence can have little appeal. As a further concession
of the kind that may be needed to produce results in the homelands for South
Africa, KwaZulu could be given control of and responsibility for most of

northern Natal, including Richards Bay. Similar bold thinking could produce an economically sensible Bophuthatswana. These kinds of moves may before too long appear to constitute relatively inexpensive political, social, and economic options for a South Africa concerned to maximize the security of its white heartland and already appreciative of the advantages of conceding territory if time and maneuverability are gained.

Both from the point of view of the Republic and the homelands, the issue of independence must remain complex, accompanied as any such alteration in status is by considerable risks and opportunities for both sides. In the case of the Transkei, the Republic will want to know whether political control can be maintained from afar. For the Transkei and any successors the test will be whether the acceptance of independence improves bargaining power.

Answers to these questions will obviously influence the decisions of other homelands to follow the first toward independence, although Mangope has said he will follow the Transkei without waiting to see what the Transkei gains. Buthelezi has always said that he can accomplish more for his people by remaining an obvious charge on the Republic's conscience and budget. But the independence of the Transkei, coupled with external events, may demonstrate that more leverage is available outside of the present framework of homeland government. If so, the leaders of the other homelands will not be slow to see and take advantage of such new forms of leverage.

The future of the homelands depends on relations between five major parties—the Republican government, the homeland leaders, the populations of the homelands, the African population of the cities, and what can collectively be called external forces. Two major developments could take place. The first major change could occur in an atmosphere of relative order, with a steady elaboration of institutions in which the correlation of whiteness with privilege and power would steadily if slowly be diminished. Concessions would be made by South Africa's whites at a pace which would give homeland leaders a hold over the legally defined homeland populations sufficient to ensure the preservation of order. By effectively intervening on behalf of urban Tswana and Zulu, Mangope and Buthelezi could enhance the position of Africans belonging to their homelands as well as that of Africans throughout the Republic. Africans could benefit tangibly from a progressive relaxation of petty apartheid, and, intangibly, from the overall raising of black esteem. Consultative institutions could be developed out of the existing "summits" where black and white leaders meet regularly to deal with problems of order and the allocation of resources and benefits. Such a development could itself take two forms: one in which the redistribution of power and resources, though limited and slow, was genuine and progressive, i.e. a state of affairs where observers could disagree over the pace of change, but not over its nature; the other form could be a more corrupt dispensation, with a still dominant South Africa manipulating a system of satellite states with little mitigation of differences in welfare and power.

The second major possible development is an antithesis of the first. The crucial breakdown would occur in the failure, or the refusal, of homeland leaders, or any group of substitutes chosen by the Republic, to maintain their authority over the homeland populations or the African populations in the cities. This again would have two variants: the homeland leaders, in trying to keep up with those whom they were trying to lead, might take the initiative in radicalizing the city populations and in welcoming military help from outside, thus effectively uniting city and countryside; or the cities and the countryside might remain largely isolated from each other, each developing its own leadership, making what deals each could with the Republic, each adopting its own separate strategies of confrontation.

If South Africa is to use the homelands as a mechanism to avoid racial conflict on a large scale, and if it makes major concessions to enhance the credibility of the homelands, it still cannot solve the fundamental problem of urban disparity. That problem may be tackled indirectly as a result of separate development. Although it will be some time before a significant change takes place in the economic development of the homelands, because of the need of South Africa to conciliate black leaders the homelands may soon develop considerable political influence. South Africa's willingness to accelerate the implementation of policy, first from 1959 to 1963, and then again since about 1968, is predominantly a response to a rapidly worsening international position. The failure of South African intervention in Angola, and the development of a new, more interventionist policy by the United States, are not only making southern Africa an arena of great power competition, but are presenting homeland leaders with new options and new potential allies.

The policy of separate development has created a new African leadership that cannot be dismissed cavalierly or replaced easily. These leaders are truly men precariously balanced in a middle role. During the next few years, as the Rhodesian and Namibian disputes approach resolution the already strong pressures on the homeland leaders are bound to increase. They will have to demonstrate that they are not selling out Africans.

Recently those pressures have been increased formidably by the sustained breakdown of order in Soweto, a demonstration of the seriousness of the internal, as well as the external, challenges to the South African order. Separate development has often been spoken of as a policy aimed at externalizing conflict. But such externalization is an effective strategy only if the client states on the periphery have no allies or powerful patrons to whom they can turn, and are willing to abandon claims to the wealthy core. Furthermore, the conflict between dominant whites and the African majority in the core cannot be externalized in the face of the unwillingness of urban populations to regard homeland institutions as adequately representing their interests.

The radicalization of the urban African populations may force the South African government to begin the elaboration of new institutions in the cities parallel to what was done for the homelands from the end of the 1960s. Giving homeland leaders a role in the cities may no longer be an option open to those leaders or to the South African government. Homeland leaders may then find themselves limited to representing the populations in the homelands. If that happens, independence could easily lose whatever attractions it may now have. The city populations are a major political and economic resource far different from the impoverished populations of old men, women, and children normally resident in the homelands.

Whether independence becomes meaningful for the homelands, and whether it can improve prospects for Africans within the remainder of South Africa, depends ultimately upon the price that the homelands and their allies can compel whites in South Africa to pay. Despite the statements of South Africa's rulers that sharing power in the core area is not an available option, a federal sharing of power may become the only way of ensuring that the homelands become allies rather than enemies.

South Africa could conceivably use the present homelands as a nucleus of an arrangement of institutional power-sharing or as the core of some form of partition that is not against the interests of Africans now or in the future. If it does, the homelands may constitute a way station, useful to blacks as well as to whites, on the road to a restructuring of South Africa.

Select Bibliography

There are extensive general bibliographies in Heribert Adam, *South Africa: Sociological Perspectives* (London, 1971), 301-332 covering the period 1960 to 1970, and a complementary one covering the years 1970 to 1974 in Leonard Thompson and Jeffrey Butler (eds.), *Change in Contemporary South Africa* (Berkeley, 1975), 415-431. Included here is material on or directly relevant to the homelands.

Andrews, H. T. *et al.* (eds.), *South Africa in the Sixties: A Socio-Economic Survey* (Cape Town, 1965).

Anon., "A Sorry Story: The History of Decentralisation. . . ." *Financial Mail*, 30 March 1973, 7 ff.

Baldwin, Alan, "Mass Removals and Separate Development," *Journal of Southern African Studies*, I (1974), 215-227.

Bellwood, W. A., *Whither the Transkei: A Vital Experiment in the Development of South Africa* (Cape Town, 1964).

Best, Alan C. G., "South Africa's Border Industries: The Tswana Example," *Annals of the Association of American Geographers,*, LXIC (1971), 329-343.

———, and Bruce S. Young, "Capitals for the Homelands," *Journal for Geography*, III (1972), 1043-1055.

———, and Bruce S. Young, "Homeland Consolidation: The Case of KwaZulu," *South African Geographer*, IV (1972), 63-74.

Biko, B. S. (ed.), *Black Viewpoint* (Durban, 1972).

Blausten, Richard, *Britain and the Bantustans* (London, 1974).

Boshoff, C. W. H. (comp.), *Bantu Outside Their Homelands* (Pretoria, 1972).

Botha, M. C., "Economic Growth in the Bantu Homelands," *Bantu*, XVI (April, 1969), 2-7.

Brownlee, Frank, *The Transkeian Native Territories: Historical Records* (Lovedale, S.A., 1923).

Breytenbach, W. J., "Election in Bophuthatswana," *Bulletin of the Africa Institute of South Africa*, X (1972), 387-388.

Bundy, Colin, "The Emergence and Decline of a South African Peasantry," *African Affairs*, LXXI (1972), 369-388.

Buthelezi, M. Gatsha, "The Past and Future of the Zulu People," *Munger Africana Library Notes*, 10 (1972).

———, "White and Black Nationalism, Ethnicity and the Future of the Homelands," (Johannesburg, 1974).

Carter, Gwendolen M., "Do the 'Homelands' Offer an Acceptable Approach to South Africa's Racial Situation," unpub. paper, 1975, mimeo.

———, Thomas Karis, and Newell M. Stultz, *South Africa's Transkei: The Politics of Domestic Colonialism* (Evanston, 1967).

Comaroff, John L., "Chiefship in a South African Homeland," *Journal of Southern African Studies,* I (1974), 36-51.

Du Toit, André, *Federalism and Political Change in South Africa* (Durban, 1974).

Edginton, M. E., "Disease Patterns in a South African Rural Bantu Population," *South African Medical Journal,* XLVI (1972), 968-976.

Gilson, B. N., "Taking Jobs to Black Workers: A Case History," *Development: Southern Africa,* 3 (1974), 31-33.

Giniewski, Paul, *Bantustans: A Trek Towards the Future* (Cape Town, 1961).

Grice, D. C., "The Approaching Crisis—Land and Population in Transvaal and Natal," *South Africa International,* IV (1974), 195-210.

Grobler, J. H., "The Agricultural Potential of the Bantu Homelands," *Journal of Racial Affairs,* XXIII (1972), 37-43.

Hammond-Tooke, David, "Chieftainship in Transkeian Political Development," *Journal of Modern African Studies,* II (1964), 513-529.

Hart, G. P., *Some Socio-Economic Aspects of African Entrepreneurship, with Particular Reference to the Transkei and Ciskei* (Grahamstown, 1972).

Hatch, John, et al. (eds.), "South Africa's Bantustans," *Third World,* II, 6 (1963), Entire issue of eleven articles.

Hattingh, P. S., *Bophuthatswana: A Select and Annotated Bibliography* (Pretoria, 1973).

Horrell, Muriel, *The African Homelands of South Africa* (Johannesburg, 1973).

Horwitz, Ralph, *The South African Political Economy* (London, 1969), esp. 359-427.

Khoapa, B. A. (ed.), *Black Review* (Durban, 1973), esp. 55-79.

Kotzé, D. A., *African Politics in South Africa, 1964-1974* (London, 1975).

Lipton, Merle, "Independent Bantustans?" *International Affairs,* XLVIII (1972), 1-19.

———, "The South African Census and the Bantustan Policy," *The World Today,* XXVIII (1972), 257-271.

Lombard, J. A., "Political and Administrative Principles of Homeland Development," *Bantu,* XVIII (February, 1971), 24-31.

———, "Problems of Regional Economic Programming in the Development of the Bantu Homelands," *South African Journal of Economics,* XXXIX (1971), 388-401.

McCrystal, L. P., and Catherine M. Moore, "An Economic Survey of Zululand: A Preliminary Report" (Durban, 1967), mimeo.

Maasdorp, Gavin, *Economic Development Strategy in the African Homelands: The Role of Agriculture and Industry* (Johannesburg, 1974).

———, and A. S. B. Humphreys (eds.), *From Shantytown to Township* (Cape Town, 1975).

Malherbe, Paul N., *Multistan: A Way Out of the South African Dilemma* (Cape Town, 1974).

Mangope, Lucas M., "Priorities and Partnership," *Development: Southern Africa,* 4 (1974), 6-8.

———, "The Political Future of the Homelands," unpub. paper, South African Institute of Race Relations, 1974, mimeo.

———, "Will Bophuthatswana Join Botswana?" *Munger Africana Library Notes,* XX (August, 1973).

Marle, J. van, "Farm Prospects for Zulus," *Development: Southern Africa*, 4 (1974), 29.

Mathews, Anthony S., *Law, Order and Liberty in South Africa* (Berkeley, 1972), esp. 240-252.

Mayer, Philip, *Urban Africans and the Bantustans* (Johannesburg, 1972).

——— , "Class, Status and Ethnicity as Perceived by Johannesburg Africans," in Leonard Thompson and Jeffrey Butler (eds.), *Change in Contemporary South Africa* (Berkeley, 1975), 138-167.

Moolman, J. H., "Consolidation," unpub. paper, South African Institute of Race Relations, 1974, mimeo.

——— , and G. M. E. Leistner, *Bophuthatswana: Hulpbronne en Ontwikkeling* (Pretoria, 1975).

Mtshali, B. Vulindlela, "Rough Road to Zulu Independence," *Kroniek van Afrika*, XII (1972), 30-34.

Muller, S. L., "Concessions to Industrialists at Growth Points," *Bantu*, XX (March, 1973), 10-17.

Munger, Edwin S., "Chief Gatsha Buthelezi of the Zulus," *American Universities Field Staff Reports*, XV, 9 (October, 1971), 1-130.

——— , "Problems in the Transkei," *American Universities Field Staff Reports Service*, X, 3 (September, 1962), 1-22.

Paton, Alan, "White South Africa's Only Hope For Survival," *New York Times Magazine* (13 May 1973), 18 ff.

Phillips, J., "Agricultural and Related Progress in Several Bantu Sectors of the Ciskei: Fifty Years in Retrospect," *South African Journal of Science*, LXII, 6 (1966), 173-178.

Quin, P. J., *Foods and Feeding Habits of the Pedi* (Johannesburg, 1959).

Republic of South Africa, Bantu Investment Corporation, *Homelands: the Role of the Corporations* (Pretoria, 1973), 1st ed.

——— , *Homelands: the Role of the Corporations in the Republic of South Africa* (Pretoria, 1975), 2nd ed.

——— , Bureau for Economic Research re Bantu Development (BENBO), *Bophuthatswana: Economic Revue, 1975* (Pretoria, 1976).

——— , *KwaZulu: Economic Revue, 1975* (Pretoria, 1976).

Rhoodie, Nic J. (ed.), *South African Dialogue: Contrasts in South African Thinking on Basic Race Issues* (Johannesburg, 1972), esp. 113-210.

Robertson, T. C., "Future Agricultural Systems in the Bantu Homelands," *South Africa International*, II (1971), 55-60.

Rutman, Gilbert L., "The Transkei: An Experiment in Economic Separation," *South African Journal of Economics*, XXXVI (1968), 24-31.

Sadie, J. L., "An Evaluation of Demographic Data Pertaining to the Non-White Population of South Africa," *South African Journal of Economics*, XXXVIII (1970), 171-191.

Schlemmer, Lawrence, "City or Rural 'Homeland': A Study of Patterns of Identification Among Africans in South Africa's Divided Society," *Social Forces*, LI (1972), 154-164.

——— , "Homeland Development—A Programme for the Seventies," unpub. paper, South African Bureau of Racial Affairs, 1970, mimeo.

——— , and Tim J. Muil. "Social and Political Change in the African Areas: A Case Study of KwaZulu," in Leonard Thompson and Jeffrey Butler (eds.), *Change in*

Contemporary South Africa (Berkeley, 1975), 107-137.

Seiler, John, "Modernizing Racial Domination or Consociational Authoritarianism: The Devolution of Political Power in South Africa," unpub. paper, Association for Sociology in Southern Africa, 1975, mimeo.

Smith, T. W. F., *Retail and Wholesale Trade in Zululand* (Durban, 1973).

Stadler, J. J., "Economic and Demographic Characteristics of the South African Bantu Areas," *Agrekon*, IX (1970), 20-28.

Szeftel, Morris, "The Transkei: Conflict Externalization and Black Exclusivism." in University of London Institute of Commonwealth Studies, *Collected Seminar Papers on the Societies of Southern Africa in the 19th and 20th Centuries*, II (1972), 155-173.

Tatz, Colin M., "Dr. Verwoerd's 'Bantustan' Policy," *Australian Journal of Politics and History*, VIII (1962), 7-26.

Wyk, J. J. van, "Agricultural Development in South African Bantu Areas," *Agrekon*, IX (1970), 64-67.

Young, Bruce, "Development in Zululand," (report of a conference) *Journal of Modern African Studies*, X (1972), 300-304.

Index

By Betsy Pitha